D0072900

The Gathering Biological Warfare Storm

EDITED BY
JIM A. DAVIS AND BARRY R. SCHNEIDER

PRAEGER

Westport, Connecticut
London

Library of Congress Cataloging-in-Publication Data

The gathering biological warfare storm / edited by Jim A. Davis and Barry R. Schneider.
p. cm.
Includes bibliographical references and index.
ISBN 0-275-98314-5 (alk. paper)
1. Biological warfare. 2. War on Terrorism, 2001– I. Schneider, Barry R. II. Davis, Jim A.
UG447.8.G38 2004
363.22—dc22 2003070687

British Library Cataloguing in Publication Data is available.

Library of Congress Catalog Card Number: 2003070687
ISBN: 0-275-98314-5

First published in 2004

Praeger Publishers, 88 Post Road West, Westport, CT 06881
An imprint of Greenwood Publishing Group, Inc.
www.praeger.com

Printed in the United States of America

The paper used in this book complies with the Permanent Paper Standard issued by the National Information Standards Organization (Z39.48–1984).

10 9 8 7 6 5 4 3

Contents

Acknowledgments

We, the editors, wish to thank the authors for their timely responses to our requests for quality work and for meeting deadlines. We also thank the sponsors of the USAF Counterproliferation Center (CPC) who have provided the resources that allow us to support this project, particularly Dr. Tom Hopkins, Director of the Technology Development Division of the Defense Threat Reduction Agency (DTRA/TD), and Colonel Don Minner, then Director of HQ USAF/XONP on the Air Staff. Without their support, this project would never have been undertaken.

Thanks also is extended to Mrs. Jo Ann Eddy who does such an excellent job of coordinating the CPC research, writing, and publication efforts—one of her multiple jobs, all performed so very well. Mrs. Brenda Alexander also was very helpful in typing chapter drafts and assisting in the multiple tasks that need to be done to bring a book to press. We also extend our appreciation to our copy editors, Mr. Armin Reitz, Mrs. Abbey Plant, and Mrs. Lee Costanzo, for their diligence in improving the format, grammar, and clarity of writing in this book. Mrs. Plant was also responsible for developing the index of this book with the author's guidance.

We would be remiss if we did not recognize the contributions of the independent experts who read and commented on earlier drafts of a number of these chapters. Special thanks is extended to reviewers who have provided very valuable expertise, such as Dr. David R. Franz, former Director of the U.S. Army Research Institute on Infectious Diseases (USAMRIID), now Vice President of Southern Research International Inc.; Ms. Tracee Treadwell and Dr. Stephen Morse of the U.S. Centers for Disease Control and Prevention; and LTC (Dr.) John Grabenstein of DOD's Anthrax Vaccine Immunization Program.

Finally, the editors are grateful for the loving support of our wives, Judith Keegan (Schneider) and Brenda Davis. Their encouragement and personal sacrifices were a key ingredient to the successful completion of this work.

Jim A. Davis
Barry R. Schneider

Preface

With the increased specter of asymmetric warfare, biological weapons likely will be seen as attractive tools by leaders of rogue states and terrorist groups. As the later half of the twentieth century was focused on the fear of a nuclear holocaust, the first half of the twenty-first century is likely to be focused on the imminent threat of biological warfare.

This work was originally completed before the events of September 11, 2001, and published at the USAF Counterproliferation Center in April 2002. Because of the timeless nature of this valuable information we are pleased that Praeger Publishers has decided to publish the book to get this important information out to a wider readership. The editors have made modest updates to the original work to enhance its currency.

Jim A. Davis
Barry R. Schneider

Chapter 1

U.S. Biodefense Readiness: Thoughts after September 11th

Barry R. Schneider

The September 11, 2001, hijacking of four U.S. airliners and the subsequent ramming of three of them into the two towers of the World Trade Center and the Pentagon was the worst mass casualty terrorist attack in U.S. history. Approximately 3,000 people from over eighty countries lost their lives at the World Trade Center in New York. Another 179 Americans lost their lives in the Pentagon that same morning.

In the days following the terrorist use of airliners as missiles, the United States was faced with a series of anthrax attacks delivered to victims and target offices through the U.S. mail system. At the time of this writing, there have been five deaths from anthrax, and the offices of ABC News, CBS News, NBC News, The *New York Post*, *The Sun* tabloid offices, Microsoft headquarters, and the offices of Senator Patrick Leahy, Senator Tom Daschle, New York Governor George Pataki, and others have been polluted with anthrax-laced mail.

This late 2001 series of anthrax attacks via the U.S. Postal Service fulfilled the warnings of those who had warned of the inevitability of future bioterrorist events. The anthrax attacks of 2001 in the United States validated the previous warnings by some experts concerning bioterrorism that it was not a question of "if," it was a question of "when." Now such bioterrorism is a historical fact, not just a prediction of the future.

The anthrax attacks of 2001 may be a taste of things to come. They may inspire some inevitable copycat attacks by other high technology terrorists, hate groups, and nihilists much like the April 1995 sarin gas attack in the Tokyo subway by the Aum Shinrikyo cult inspired Japanese copycat attacks using cyanide gas in the year that followed. Inevitably, too, the 2001 anthrax attacks in the United States will inspire a host of additional hoax threats that will keep U.S. biodefenders busy separating the real from the phony of such threats.

It is important that U.S. homeland security and U.S. military officials not learn the wrong lessons from the late 2001 anthrax attacks. One conclusion that might be drawn, a misconception, is that the bioterrorist threat has been overblown since "only" a handful of people have died as a result of these attacks. This would be a serious misunderstanding if it were the conclusion of U.S. officials and the public.

Perhaps the most alarming aspect of the whole series of events leading up to the September 11 attacks and anthrax aftermath was the fact that several of the Al Qaeda terrorists, including Mohammed Atta, had looked into employing a crop duster aircraft prior to settling on the September 11 hijacking of U.S. airliners and subsequent attacks on the World Trade Center towers and the Pentagon.

As of this writing it is not clear whether the anthrax attacks of October and November 2001 were the work of Al Qaeda operations or other terrorists, but if Al Qaeda possessed high quality inhalation anthrax, like the anthrax that was used, and distributed it using a crop duster over a large metropolitan area like Washington, DC, then the losses of September 11, bad as they were, would have been far less serious compared to what might have occurred. If this type of attack had been made, then the fatalities and casualties from such an event might have climbed into the hundreds of thousands, not the handful of biocasualties that actually occurred. Such aerosolized anthrax attacks remain our worst nightmare, whether we are talking about homeland security or the safety of U.S. troops deployed overseas.

One such bioterrorist attack has already been attempted when members of the Aum Shinrikyo terrorist cult in Japan twice attempted to kill U.S. sailors stationed at the Yokohama Naval base in April 1990 using botulinum toxin (BOT). Fortunately, these cultist did not know how to successfully weaponize botulinum toxin, and a tragedy was averted.

Another near miss from a biological warfare (BW) threat was averted in 1991 during the Gulf War when coalition troops led by the United States defeated Saddam Hussein's Iraqi forces and freed Kuwait from Iraq's grasp. What was not known until much later after the cease-fire was that Iraq had cultivated and weaponized anthrax munitions in a lethal aerosolized form. In addition, the Iraqi forces had equipped a Mirage jet with spray tank dispensers and had secured it in a hardened aircraft shelter within range of U.S. and allied troops.

Had Saddam Hussein given the order, this Mirage aircraft, turned into an inhalation anthrax menace, could have flown a mission dispensing lethal anthrax over coalition troop concentrations and killed tens of thousands of them. The Office of the Secretary of Defense (OSD) commissioned a later study of what the potential anthrax threat was to U.S. and coalition forces on the first day of the ground war in Desert Storm. On that day, the coalition had amassed half a million military personnel for its attack; 320,000 of these were in a rectangular area along the coastline southeast of Kuwait City that measured 50 kilometers by 150 kilometers in size. Calculations of OSD analysts show that if one were to assume that none of these had been vaccinated against anthrax, if the Iraqi Mirage were to successfully disperse its anthrax upwind of these allies, and if meteorological conditions were favorable the night of the attack, then an estimated 76,300 of the 320,000 targeted troops would have died of anthrax from the attack.[1]

Contrast this worst case scenario with what really happened. Only 146 U.S. military personnel were killed in Desert Storm altogether, and Saddam Hussein appears to have been deterred from using his anthrax weapons by the veiled U.S. threat of retaliation using nuclear arms.

Nevertheless, the threat of lethal aerosolized anthrax released by a single aircraft upwind poses megathreats to any massed military forces and to urban populations in the fallout pattern. Thus, we should not misread the true lessons of the late 2001 anthrax terrorism in the United States. Bioterrorism has been practiced, and we have yet to see the worst that could be done. Similarly, the past use of biological weapons in warfare against military personnel does not approach the lethal possibilities such biological weapons may pose in the future.

If we do not misread the potential loss of life that biological weapons can pose in the future, then the events following September 11 may serve as a wake-up call to the United States and allied defense communities. For far too long, biological warfare defense has been underfunded and the necessity for a much more aggressive biological defense program has been underappreciated. Years ago, during the Cold War, the United States and its allies seriously neglected biological defenses such as vaccine and antibiotics programs.

Starting with World War II, both the United States and the USSR conducted intensive biological warfare R&D and production programs and continued these into the Cold War. U.S. authorities had every reason to believe the Soviet Union was researching and producing biological weapons during these years, at least until 1972 when both superpowers signed the Biological Weapons Convention (BWC).

However, even after this multilateral treaty banning the research, production, stockpiling, transfer, and use of biological weapons was signed, there was no strong reason to trust in Soviet treaty compliance because the pact had no verification procedures. The U.S. leadership simply stopped the U.S. program and acted as if it trusted that the Soviets would honor their commitment as well.

Hindsight shows this to have been a terrible mistake. The U.S. BW program funding was stopped, and funding was stopped not only for the prohibited offensive BW program, but tragically also was severely reduced for the BW defensive program such as work on vaccines even though the biological weapons convention permitted such activity. There were other reasons for the neglect of U.S. preparations against bioterrorism and biological warfare during the Cold War. The United States and NATO were planning to deter or counter Soviet conventional and chemical and biological warfare threats with nuclear responses. Moreover, the task of equipping U.S./NATO conventional and nuclear forces left little funding for defense against biological or chemical attacks. The U.S. Army Medical Research Institute of Infectious Diseases (USAMRIID) and the U.S. Army Chemical Corps were weak bureaucratic players in the internal competition for defense dollars in the U.S. Department of Defense budget battles. The result was severe underfunding of chemical warfare and BW defense programs.

The result of years of neglect has let the biodefense program fall far behind the biological warfare and bioterrorist threat that has developed since 1972. The Soviet BW program not only did not stop in 1972, the Soviets instead accelerated it. Over the past several decades, Soviet bioweaponeers, some 60,000 strong by 1991, have done experiments on over fifty biological agents and combinations of agents for military applications. Meanwhile, the United States biodefense program proceeded at a snail's pace. We became the unready confronting the unthinkable and now have a long way to go to catch up to the biological weapons threats that have emerged at the beginning of the twenty-first century.

A quick look at the current status of the U.S. vaccine program gives some idea of the ground that needs to be made up in biological defenses. Of the fourteen diseases that experts deem most lethal, effective, and weaponizable, the United States currently has FDA-approved vaccines for only four disease agents (anthrax, smallpox, cholera, and plague). Five are in the investigational new drug (IND) category (Q Fever, tularemia, VEE, viral hemorrhagic fever, and botulinum toxin) and may be years away from final approval. In the case of five other diseases (glanders, brucellosis, SEB, ricin, and T-2 mycotoxins), no vaccines of any kind currently exist. Note, for example, the data from Table 1.1 on "BW Agents—Vaccines, Therapeutics, and Prophylaxis" that itemizes the sorry state of current preparations to immunize U.S. military forces and the public against bioterrorist or biowar attacks.[2] This chart does not even indicate the massive effort needed to produce sufficient stockpiles of vaccines once they are perfected, if they ever are.

The bottom line is that the United States and its allies are far behind the threat posed by bioterrorists and adversaries willing to use biowarfare on the battlefield. Hopefully, the mass casualty terrorist attacks of September 11, followed by the recent anthrax biological attacks, have galvanized U.S. and allied officials to do much more. Needed is investment in vaccines and other biodefense programs to close the threat/response gap that has widened through years of looking the other way and failing to recognize the great menace that biological warfare and bioterrorism pose to our citizens and our armed forces.

Table 1.1
BW Agents—Vaccines, Therapeutics, and Prophylaxis

Disease	Vaccine	Chemotherapy (Rx)	Chemoprophylaxis (Px)	Comments
Anthrax	Bioport vaccine (licensed) 0.5 mL SC @ 0, 2, 4 wk, 6, 12, 18 mo then annual boosters	Ciprofloxacin 400 mg IV q 2h Doxycycline 200 mg IV, then 100 mg IV q 12 h Penicillin 2 million units IV q 4 h	Ciprofloxacin 500 mg PO bid × 4 wk. If unvaccinated, begin initial doses of vaccine Doxycycline 100 mg PO bid × 4 wk plus vaccination	Potential alternates for Rx: gentamicin, erythromycin, and chloramphenicol PCN for sensitive organisms only
Cholera	Wyeth-Ayerst vaccine 2 doses 0.5 mL IM or SC @ 0, 7–30 days, then boosters q 6 months	Oral rehydration therapy during period of high fluid loss Tetracycline 500 mg q 6 h × 3 d Doxycycline 300 mg once, or 100 mg q 12 h × 3 d Ciprofloxacin 500 mg q 12h × 3 d Norfloxacin 400 mg q 12 h × 3 d	NA	Vaccine not recommended for routine protection in endemic areas (50% efficacy, short term) Alternates for Rx: erythromycin, trimethoprim and sulfamethoxazole, and furazolidone Quinolones for tetra/doxy resistant strains
Q Fever	IND 610—inactivated whole cell vaccine given as single 0.5 mL SC injection	Tetracycline 500 mg PO q 6 h × 5-7 d continued at least 2 d after afebrile Doxycycline 100 mg PO q 12 h × 5–7 d continued at least 2 d after afebrile	Tetracycline 500 mg PO qid × 5 d (start 8–12 d post-exposure) Doxycycline 100 mg PO bid × 5 d (start 8–12 d post-exposure)	Currently testing vaccine to determine the necessity of skin testing prior to use.

Glanders	No vaccine available	Antibiotic regimens vary depending on localization and severity of disease—refer to text	Post-exposure prophylaxis may be tried with TMP-SMX	No large therapeutic human trials have been conducted owing to the rarity of naturally occurring disease.
Plague	Greer inactivated vaccine (FDA-licensed) no longer available	Streptomycin 30 mg/kg/d IM in 2 divided doses × 10–14 d or Gentamicin 5 mg/kg or IV once daily × 10–14 d or Ciprofloxacin 400 mg IV q 12 h until clinically improved then 750 mg PO bid for total of 10–14 d	Doxycycline 100 mg PO bid × 7d or duration of exposure Ciprofloxacin 500 mg PO bid × 7d	Chloramphenicol for plague meningitis is required 25 mg/kg IV, then 15 mg/kg qid × 14 d Plague vaccine not protective against aerosol challenge in animal studies
		Doxycycline 200 mg IV then 100 mg IV bid, until clinically improved then 100 mg PO bid for total of 10–14 d Chloramphenicol 1 gm IV qid × 10–14 d	Tetracycline 500 mg PO qid × 7d	Alternate Rx: trimethoprim-sulfamethoxazole
Brucellosis	No human vaccine available	Doxycycline 200 mg/d PO plus rifampin 600–900 mg/d PO × 6 wk Ofloxacin 400/rifampin 600 mg/d PO × 6 wks	Doxycycline 200 mg/d PO plus rifampin 600 mg/d PO × 6 wk	Trimethoprim-sulfamethoxazole may be substituted for rifampin; however, relapse may reach 30%

Source: USAMRIID's *Medical Management of Biological Casualties Handbook*, Fourth Edition, Feb. 2001, U.S. Army Medical Research Institute of Infectious Diseases, Fort Detrick MD. Updated on Internet, see http://www.nbc-med.org/SiteContent/HomePage/WhatsNew/MedManual/Feb01/handbook.htm.

Table 1.1 (Part 2)
BW Agents—Vaccines, Therapeutics, and Prophylaxis

Disease	Vaccine	Chemotherapy (Rx)	Chemoprophylaxis (Px)	Comments
Tularemia	IND—Live attenuated vaccine: single 0.1 mL dose by scarification	Streptomycin 30 mg/kg IM divided bid × 10–14 d Gentamicin 3–5 mg/kg/d IV × 10–14 d	Doxycycline 100 mg PO bid × 14 d Tetracycline 500 mg PO qid × 14 d Ciprofloxacin 500 mg PO q 12 h × 14 d	
Viral encephalitides	VEE DOD TC-83 live attenuated vaccine (IND): 0.5 mL SC × 1 dose VEE DOD C-84 (formalin inactivated TC-83) (IND): 0.5 mL SC for up to 3 doses EEE inactivated (IND): 0.5 mL SC at 0 & 28 d WEE inactivated (IND): 0.5 mL SC at 0, 7, and 28 d	Supportive therapy: analgesics and anticonvulsants prn	NA	TC-83 reactogenic in 20% No seroconversion in 20% Only effective against subtypes 1A, 1B, and 1C C-84 vaccine used for nonresponders to TC-83 EEE and WEE inactivated vaccines are poorly Immunogenic. Multiple immunizations are required
Viral hemorrhagic fevers	AHF Candid #1 vaccine (x-protection for BHF) (IND)	Ribavirin (Arenaviruses) (IND) 30 mg/kg IV initial dose; then 15 mg/kg IV q 6 h × 4 d; then 7.5 mg/kg IV q 8 h × 6 d	NA	Aggressive supportive care and management of hypotension very important
	RVF inactivated vaccine (IND)	Passive antibody for AHF, BHF, Lassa fever, and CCHF		

Smallpox	Wyeth calf lymph vaccinia vaccine (licensed): 1 dose by scarification	No current Rx other than supportive; cidofovir (effective in vitro); animal studies ongoing	Vaccinia immune globulin 0.6 mL/kg IM (within 3 d of exposure, best within 24 h)	Pre- and post-exposure vaccination recommended if > 3 years since last vaccine
Botulism	DOD pentavalent toxoid for serotypes A–E (IND): 0.5 mL deep SC @ 0, 2, & 12 wk, then yearly boosters	DOD heptavalent equine de-speciated antitoxin for serotypes A–G (IND): 1 vial (10 mL) IV	NA	Skin test for hypersensitivity before equine antitoxin administration
		CDC trivalent equine antitoxin for serotypes A, B, E (licensed)	NA	
Staphylococcus enterotoxin B	No vaccine available	Ventilatory support for inhalation exposure	NA	
Ricin	No vaccine available	Inhalation: supportive therapy G–I: gastric lavage, super-activated charcoal, cathartics	NA	
T-2 mycotoxins	No vaccine available		Decontamination of clothing and skin	

Source: USAMRIID's Medical Management of Biological Casualties Handbook, Fourth Edition, Feb 2001, U.S. Army Medical Research Institute of Infectious Diseases, Fort Detrick MD. Updated on Internet, see http://www.nbc-med.org/SiteContent/HomePage/WhatsNew/MedManual/Feb01/handbook.htm.

CHAPTER 2

Agroterrorism and Foot-and-Mouth Disease: Is the United States Prepared?

Michael E. Peterson

INTRODUCTION

Since the September 11, 2001, terrorist attacks on the twin towers of the World Trade Center in New York City and the Pentagon building, the United States has gone on full alert to the possibilities of mass casualty terrorist threats. Already, the economic costs of those attacks have exceeded $100 billion if one factors in the expenses of cleaning up the sites, replacing the structures, compensating the families, and rebuilding the businesses lost. The attack also had negative impacts on the stock market and consumer confidence and had devastating effects on the airline and related travel industries.

Moreover, the costs of the war on terrorism at home and abroad could run into the hundreds of billions over time. The United States has prosecuted a war in Afghanistan against the Taliban/Al Qaeda and other terrorist operatives and has begun a major new homeland security effort.

The anthrax attacks that followed the September 11 attacks confirmed the previous warnings of some experts that, in the cases of biowarfare or bioterrorism, it was not going to be a question of "if," but rather of "when" such attacks would take place. When has already occurred, and the U.S. executive branch, Congress, the media, and the public are now much more alert to the danger of biological agents being used in the continental United States as well as elsewhere in the world.

The United States and other nations lost approximately 3,200 lives within an hour at the World Trade Center and Pentagon. Additional victims were claimed by the subsequent anthrax attacks and war in Afghanistan. This has led to a heightened sense of risk, since over-run laboratories maintained by Al Qaeda and Taliban operatives indicated their interest and work toward acquiring nuclear, radiological, biological, and chemical weapons for future use.

This heightened sense of risk has made U.S. homeland defense officials more sensitive to other key targets that might be attacked in the continental United States. One such target might be the cattle and pig herds and other meat industries that could be subject to attack by highly contagious biological agents such as foot-and-mouth disease (FMD). This disease has already devastated the herds of the United Kingdom in a recent naturally occurring epidemic. The fear now is that the next chapters in our war with terrorism may see agroterrorist attacks using foot-and-mouth disease as a weapon.

Across the English countryside in 2001, workers faced the grim task of dousing thousands of pig and cattle carcasses in oil and placing them on pyres of coal, straw, and rail ties for incineration. Markets were running out of domestic beef and tens of thousands of livestock-related jobs were lost. In an attempt to lessen the spread of the disease and keep the movement of people and animals to a minimum, government officials closed national parks and canceled horseracing, rugby, and soccer matches. In Ireland, government leaders canceled Dublin's St. Patrick's Day celebration while Scotland disinfected all vehicles entering from Britain. In 2001, across the English Channel, Belgian farmers clashed with police outside the European Union headquarters amid growing fears that foot-and-mouth disease would spread to continental Europe. Teams wearing protective clothing disinfected British aircraft arriving in Germany, and agricultural workers in Spain, France, Holland, Belgium, and Germany began the preventative slaughter of over 55,000 animals. For the first time since 1967, foot-and-mouth disease re-emerged in the United Kingdom and was a threat to spread throughout Europe.[1]

All indications up to this point reveal that the February 19, 2001, outbreak of foot-and-mouth disease at a small pig farm in Northumberland, Great Britain, was caused by a natural introduction of the virus.[2] But what if a terrorist had caused this biological disaster, and what if this catastrophe were to take place on U.S. soil? Throughout the past decade and particularly after September 11, 2001, the U.S. government has become much more concerned with the proliferation of weapons of mass destruction (WMD) and how the United States might respond to a terrorist WMD attack on a major city. Until September 11 and subsequent anthrax attacks, however, the government had virtually ignored the threat of a possible terrorist attack on U.S. farms and feedlots. "Agroterrorism," a threat unknown to the average man, is an economic disaster still waiting to happen. According to Dr. Corrie Brown from the College of Veterinary Medicine at the University of Georgia, "[a] terrorist wishing to cause severe reverberating financial consequences could simply introduce a foreign disease into American livestock, which would set off a chain reaction touching virtually every citizen's pocketbook."[3] Foot-and-mouth disease, the most contagious livestock disease known, is a likely pathogen a terrorist might choose to conduct an attack.[4] An outbreak of foot-and-mouth disease could cripple the U.S. livestock industry, devastate consumer confidence, and cause untold billions of dollars in losses. Moreover, the United States and its allies have faced a worldwide terrorist network whose active aim is to inflict great harm on the United States. Consequently, the United States must act now. An agroterrorist incident involving foot-and-mouth disease is a serious threat to U.S. national security. Federal, state, and local governments and agencies must accelerate their efforts to prepare for a possible attack.

THE VIRUS

Foot-and-mouth disease is the world's most important and contagious animal pathogen. The World Organization for Animal Health defines it as a "List A" disease. List A diseases are "transmissible diseases that have the potential for very serious and rapid spread, irrespective of national borders, that are of serious socioeconomic or public health consequence and that are of major importance in the international trade of animals and animal products."[5] Foot-and-mouth disease is a virus that has the remarkable ability to survive in carcasses, animal byproducts, water, straw bedding, and pastures. It can withstand freezing temperatures and cling to clothing, vehicles, and farm implements. While it is a viral disease of cattle and swine, foot-and-mouth disease also affects sheep, goats, deer, and other cloven-hoofed animals. There are seven separate types and as many as seventy subtypes of the foot-and-mouth virus. Infected animals develop large, painful blisters in the oral cavity and on the feet and exhibit signs of depression, anorexia, lameness, and salivation. With an incubation period of two to twenty-one days (three to eight days is the average), foot-and-mouth disease can spread up to sixty kilometers overland and three hundred kilometers by sea as an aerosol on the wind. Found in thirty-one countries throughout South America, Africa, Asia, and Europe, foot-and-mouth disease is the virus that causes the greatest concern among farmers and agricultural regulators.[6]

Foot-and-mouth disease is not a new phenomenon, nor are the antilivestock programs that have focused on this particular disease. Examples of antilivestock weapons programs were evident throughout the twentieth century and continue today. During World War I, the allies found "incontrovertible" evidence that German agents inoculated horses and cattle leaving U.S. ports for shipment to Europe with disease-producing bacteria.[7] During World War II, the Germans took an active interest in countering the foot-and-mouth disease threat to their own cattle while they explored possible foot-and-mouth disease uses as an offensive weapon. Defensive vaccine production began in 1940, and by 1943, the Germans experimented with foot-and-mouth disease distribution by dropping little bunches of infected grass or hay at specific heights in order to create an "inconspicuous dispersal."[8]

Early in the Cold War, the Soviet Union's Ministry of Agriculture created its own successful biological weapons program. Under a special antilivestock weapons division known as the "Main Directorate for Scientific and Production Enterprises," the Soviets created a biological warfare (BW) program code-named "Ecology."[9] Here scientists developed different variants of foot-and-mouth disease and explored ways to spray the viral agent from tanks attached to Ilyushin bombers flown low over a target area along a straight line for hundreds of miles.[10]

Today, biological weapons research continues around the world. At least twenty nations are suspected of pursuing offensive biological warfare capabilities with eight high-profile nations topping the list: Iran, Iraq, Israel, North Korea, China, Libya, Syria, and Taiwan.[11] While these countries might not carry out an agroterrorist act against another nation, they could conceivably sponsor a terrorist organization and supply it with the foot-and-mouth disease pathogen.

Obtaining the foot-and-mouth disease virus from a state with an active antilivestock biological weapons program is but one of three basic ways a terrorist can acquire an animal pathogen. A terrorist can also isolate the organism from the environment on his own, or he can attempt to order it from a biological collection or a laboratory. Of the three methods, obtaining a foot-and-mouth disease sample from the environment is probably the easiest.[12] While a terrorist might be able to find a state sponsor, he might also encounter states reluctant to lend their support for fear of U.S. retaliation after an agroterrorist event and especially since the United States declared war on terrorists and their supporters in late 2001. A terrorist will struggle even more to obtain the foot-and-mouth disease virus from a U.S. biological laboratory. The virus is not held in state veterinary laboratory collections in the United States. The Plum Island Animal Disease Center in New York is the only laboratory in the country that studies foot-and-mouth disease, and it keeps this highly contagious virus under very close control in its "Foot-and-Mouth Disease Unit."[13] Therefore, a terrorist will probably turn down the path of least resistance and look to the environment for his virus sample.

Unlike deadly human pathogens like those causing Ebola and other hemorrhagic fevers that are difficult to isolate from the environment, animal diseases are far easier to obtain and cultivate. A terrorist could travel to any one of the thirty-one countries in which foot-and-mouth disease is endemic, purchase an infected animal, and with a "rudimentary knowledge" of microbiology, obtain a sample of the pathogen for intentional introduction into our herds.[14]

Following the acquisition of the virus, no special process is required to weaponize the agent. The animal pathogen only has to come in contact with the target host to cause infection. Thus, once a terrorist has the foot-and-mouth disease virus in hand, his next concern will be to find a way to spread the disease and carry out his attack.

There are several ways the highly contagious and survivable foot-and-mouth disease virus is transmitted during an outbreak. The virus can be transmitted via direct or indirect contact (droplets), animate vectors (humans or animals), inanimate vectors (vehicles or implements), or through the air in a fine particle aerosol form.[15] Although a terrorist could conceivably use any of these means to spread the disease, he is likely to use either direct/indirect contact in the form of droplets or cell material, or he might use an aerosol for rapid dispersal over a larger area. He would probably avoid close human or vehicle contact with a target area to decrease his risk of being detected and instead rely on natural means of transmission to help spread the disease following the initial outbreak.

Because foot-and-mouth disease is capable of virtually uncontrollable spread on its own, a terrorist would not need any special dispersal devices to execute his attack. With something as simple as a "VIP" (vial in pocket), a terrorist could set off an epidemic with relative ease.[16] In an attack on the swine industry, for example, a terrorist could take a sample of tongue epithelium from an animal infected with foot-and-mouth disease and place it in the air intake of a large hog operation.[17] Or, in an assault against the dairy and beef industry, imagine the following chilling scenario:

> A terrorist arrives in the nation's capital armed with a weapon obtained by scraping off lesions from the blistered tongue of an African cow with hoof-in-mouth disease (foot-and-mouth disease).
>
> With several million particles of virus stored in a lunch cooler, he rents a car at Dulles International Airport outside Washington and drives south into the Virginia countryside. At several farms, he stops where cows or horses stand near fences and, using wads of cotton, calmly rubs some of the virus into their nostrils.
>
> By the time he reaches Richmond, an epidemic is virtually assured.[18]

Perhaps the most frightening scenario, though, where the greatest number of animals could be infected takes place at the cattle feedlot. With some of the largest feedlots today holding between three hundred thousand and eight hundred thousand cattle, an intentional introduction of foot-and-mouth disease would be catastrophic. Not only would hundreds of thousands of animals be lost at the feedlot, but countless thousands of other animals would also be infected and destroyed across the country. Considering that a single feedlot ships up to ten thousand cattle a day to slaughterhouses and other production facilities where infected animals would get the opportunity to mingle with other animals, it would not take long for a terrorist to make a huge dent in the U.S. livestock industry.[19]

POSSIBLE TERRORISTS

Any number of nations around the world might have an incentive to carry out a vicious agroterrorist attack against the United States. A nation like Iraq, for example, might send an agent to spread foot-and-mouth disease throughout the United States in an act of revenge after ten years of economically crippling sanctions. Or a nation like China might execute a clandestine act of economic sabotage against the United States in an attempt to bolster their markets and economy. By smuggling some foot-and-mouth disease infected pigs into California, China could cause the U.S. swine export trade to come to a halt and then step in to fill the market gap. Many Taiwanese suspect that the mainland Chinese regime conducted this type of attack against their nation in 1997 when Taiwan lost eight million hogs to this disease and over $15 billion in export trade. Whether this was a true act of sabotage or a natural disease outbreak is still open for debate.[20]

In addition to the threat from various nations hostile to the United States, criminal or terrorist groups also pose a danger to the U.S. agricultural sector. An organized crime syndicate, anxious to control commodity and futures markets, might turn to agroterrorism, or a Colombian drug cartel might carry out foot-and-mouth disease attack to "retaliate in kind" after U.S. operations against their narcotic-producing crops.[21]

Since the mass casualty terrorist events in New York and Washington, DC, led by Al Qaeda terrorists and financed and directed by Osama bin Laden, the U.S. government has been on a heightened alert status against terrorist acts of all kinds.

Because U.S. farms and farm animals are such key assets and potentially so very vulnerable to agroterrorist attacks, U.S. homeland security officials and programs should be especially active in providing a biodefense of such rural assets against the Al Qaeda bioterrorism threat.

Nor are these the only possible set of terrorist threats to U.S. agricultural assets. Militia groups in the Pacific Northwest might also turn to bioterrorism against agriculture to fulfill the teachings of the *Turner Diaries*, while millennial groups might unleash a foot-and-mouth disease attack as their contribution to societal collapse.[22] Perhaps future agroterrorist attacks will come from those organizations that already have experience striking U.S. agricultural facilities. Extremist environmental protection and animal rights groups conduct hundreds of types of attacks a year in the United States, Canada, and Britain to make a statement against the use of genetically engineered crops and animals.[23] An attack using a virus like foot-and-mouth disease would give one of these groups plenty of media attention without having to kill a single human being.

The final type of terrorist who might intentionally infect U.S. livestock with foot-and-mouth disease is the individual perpetrator. This category might include fanatics devoted to a particular issue or people seeking revenge or economic gain. In an age where politically motivated terrorism appears to be on the decline and terrorism carried out in the name of a particular religion is on the rise, it would not be unusual to see a religious zealot strike out against the United States in the form of an agroterror attack.[24]

Individuals like Ted Kaczinski, the schizophrenic "Unabomber," might surface as well. Instead of holding a grudge against the industrial system, the next "Kaczinski" might be anxious to inflict pain, for whatever reason, on the agricultural system. Disgruntled employees from the agricultural sector or speculators on the commodities market could also capitalize on an agroterrorist incident.[25] Regardless of their reasons, each of these individuals will find U.S. livestock an extremely vulnerable and attractive target.

FOOT-AND-MOUTH DISEASE'S APPEAL AS A WEAPON OF CHOICE

The U.S. livestock industry might represent the ideal target for future terrorist attack using a biological agent. Agroterrorism, using the foot-and-mouth disease virus, for example, has tremendous appeal because it is non-threatening to the terrorist and relatively easy to accomplish, and can produce a devastating effect on the target. The use of foot-and-mouth disease in an agroterrorist act is nonthreatening to the terrorist for several reasons.

First, unlike lethal human pathogens, foot-and-mouth disease is harmless to human beings. A terrorist can obtain a sample, hand-carry it to a target farm or feedlot, and distribute it without having to worry about infection.[26]

Second, after introducing the foot-and-mouth disease virus, a terrorist would not have to worry very much about being apprehended. The risk of detection after an agroterrorist attack is low because health authorities will undoubtedly find it extremely difficult to differentiate between an intentional act from a natural outbreak.[27] Even if the U.S. government can somehow determine that a terrorist caused the foot-and-mouth disease outbreak, the average three- to eight-day incubation period will give a terrorist plenty of time to leave the country before the first signs of the disease appear.

On the off chance that U.S. authorities can track down the terrorist and apprehend him and if he or she is a U.S. citizen, the terrorist is likely to face a light penalty. Under section 43 of title 18 of the U.S. code, anyone who causes economic damage in excess of $10,000 to an animal enterprise can only be jailed for up to one year and forced to pay the appropriate agricultural damages.[28] Whether he is caught or not, the agroterrorist currently has little to fear when he carries out his attack, if it were an isolated act. On the other hand, if he or she is implicated in a larger terrorist operation like Al Qaeda's, then it would be a different and more serious outcome. Those caught would then be subject to a military tribunal, and, if an American citizen, charged with treason. That could lead to a far more severe penalty.

If relatively risk-free to the terrorist, a foot-and-mouth disease attack might be also quite easy to accomplish. Because the highly contagious and hearty foot-and-mouth disease virus can be found throughout the world, it is easy to obtain and ultimately quite simple to dispense the pathogen. A terrorist would only need enough microbiological expertise to recognize the symptoms of the disease in an infected animal, obtain a sample, and maintain the material in an infectious state during transport. Infectious material can come in the form of fluid from a blister, fecal material, or a tissue sample from the deceased animal.[29]

Once the terrorist has the foot-and-mouth disease virus in his possession, he can travel to any number of sites to distribute the biological weapon with ease. After all, agricultural facilities are "soft targets" with little or no security protecting them.[30] Farms, feedlots, slaughterhouses, and auction houses have very low security, while pastures and fields have essentially no security at all.

If, for some reason, those tempting objectives seem too risky, a terrorist can even attempt an attack from outside the target nation. Many countries today import agricultural materials like straw and animal feed. If a terrorist were to infect these items with foot-and-mouth disease before they were exported, he could potentially cause multiple outbreaks once these materials were distributed to their various destinations.[31]

Last, while a foot-and-mouth disease attack might be physically easy for a terrorist to execute, it is psychologically "palatable" as well. Infecting animals with a disease presents fewer "ethical quandaries" for a terrorist than infecting human beings.[32] The Aum Shinrikyo cult in Japan had to deal with this dilemma after one of its members developed "cold feet" while carrying out a biological attack. Apparently, the individual failed to arm a biological weapon because he suddenly realized that attacking innocent people was wrong.[33] It is much less likely that an agroterrorist would suffer from a similar bout of morality when he unleashes the foot-and-mouth disease virus.

Safer and relatively easier to attempt, agroterrorism is also appealing because it could inflict such devastating effects on the target nation. To make matters worse, a terrorist armed with the foot-and-mouth disease virus can produce these disastrous physical and psychological effects with minimal effort.[34] One small outbreak can cripple an economy and destroy consumer confidence virtually overnight. Witness the recent epidemic in the United Kingdom. What started out as a natural outbreak of foot-and-mouth disease at a small pig farm quickly spread to over nine hundred locations throughout England, Scotland, and Ireland.[35] In the meantime, life in the United Kingdom came to a standstill, while the beef industry, already shaken by "mad cow" disease, had to somehow recover from yet another staggering blow.

A terrorist could achieve similar results by intentionally infecting just a small number of farms or feedlots with foot-and-mouth disease. A limited outbreak would decimate a nation's livestock industry with trade embargoes, lost revenues, the wholesale loss of herds, and carcass removal and disinfection costs. In addition, consumers would likely turn away from a product considered tainted with disease and not resume buying it for weeks or months.[36]

If a limited outbreak of foot-and-mouth disease were to occur in the United States—one that affected only about ten farms and was quickly diagnosed and eliminated—the estimated overall loss would still be in excess of $2 billion.[37] Unfortunately, the United States is highly susceptible to both small outbreaks and full-scale epidemics.

THE UNITED STATES AS A TARGET

The Al Qaeda kamikaze attacks with hijacked airliners against two skyscrapers in New York City, the similar attack on the Pentagon building, the aborted airliner attack downed in Pennsylvania, the subsequent anthrax attacks on targets using the U.S. mail system, and the revelations about Al Qaeda attempts to secure weapons of mass destruction (i.e., nuclear explosives, radiological bombs, chemical arms, and biological weapons) all have sounded the alarm. The United States is no longer a sanctuary, and some of its key assets are at risk in its war with terrorism.

To the terrorist, the United States must appear to be a target-rich environment. At risk might be our major urban centers, our political leaders, our power grids and communications centers, key dams and nuclear power plants, military bases, and symbols of U.S. power like Wall Street, the White House, the U.S. Congress, the Pentagon, and the Department of State. Of equal importance is the United States agricultural sector, and agroterrorism could pose a major threat to it.

When and if a major agroterrorist attack does occur somewhere in the world, there is good reason to believe that it will take place on U.S. soil. The United States is extremely vulnerable and a "high risk" nation for several reasons. To begin with, the U.S. government and the general public are just becoming familiar with the concept of agroterrorism, and funding for defensive preparations is limited. Consequently, the threat of an antilivestock "Pearl Harbor" is very real.

According to Randall Murch, the FBI's deputy assistant laboratory director for investigative technologies, "[t]he public understands a terrorist attack on the Olympics, but not on someone's farm."[38] Most Americans have enjoyed safe, abundant food supplies their entire lives and are largely unaware of any internal or external threats.

An examination of congressional appropriations for agricultural counterterrorism programs in the fiscal year 2001 budget reflects a lack of appreciation for the growing threat. For fiscal year 2001, before September 11, Congress appropriated $10 billion to fight terrorism, but only $6.5 million of that total went to U.S. Department of Agriculture (USDA) counterterrorism programs.[39] Congress devoted less than one-tenth of 1 percent of the counterterrorism funds to combat what many experts believe is a disaster waiting to happen.

Since the U.S.-led war on terrorism was declared, after the September 11 attacks, the U.S. Congress appropriated an emergency counterterrorism budget of $40 billion in the fall of 2001. It remains to be seen how much of that amount will be used to prepare biodefenses of the agricultural community. Several negative trends need to reversed.

Budget woes in fiscal year 2001 had taken their toll on the team of experts needed to respond to a foot-and-mouth disease outbreak. The Animal and Plant Health Inspection Service (APHIS), the key agency responsible for protecting U.S. livestock against foot-and-mouth disease, has seen its funding recently diminished. As a result, it has been forced to curtail its cadre of field veterinarians and animal pathologists who would respond to a crisis. According to Dr. Ty Vannieuwenhoven, a senior staff veterinarian with USDA-APHIS Veterinary Services, Emergency Programs, fewer veterinarians are in the field now than in 1984.[40]

Ironically, another vulnerability that makes the United States a likely target for foot-and-mouth disease agroterrorism can be attributed to the improved health and protection of American livestock. For example, because foot-and-mouth disease has been absent from the United States since 1929, animals have not developed an immunity to it nor have they been vaccinated against it.[41] Therefore, any outbreak could result in the rapid spread of the disease throughout all sections of the country. In addition, American veterinary students get little to no education on the subject of foot-and-mouth disease due to the fact that it has been absent from the United States for over seven decades. Few students get the opportunity to train at the Plum Island foot-and-mouth disease laboratory, and few get the chance to travel to countries experiencing a foot-and-mouth disease outbreak. As a matter of fact, it is likely that most practicing veterinarians in North America would not be able to recognize a foot-and-mouth disease outbreak until large numbers of animals were infected and the disease was firmly established.[42]

New and improved methods of livestock production and processing have also created weak points in America's ability to defend its agriculture industry. Today, the United States utilizes "factory farming," which makes it extremely susceptible to a foot-and-mouth disease attack.[43] Factory farming concentrates large numbers of animals in a few vulnerable locations. Swine farms and cattle feedlots routinely hold tens if not hundreds of thousands of animals each. This trend to consolidate herds to reduce overhead costs will only increase in the coming years. By the year 2010, agricultural experts predict that approximately 80 percent of U.S. livestock will pass through only 2 percent of the nation's feedlots, while only four meatpacking plants will process 80 percent of all animals slaughtered.[44] With such large concentrations of animals in just a few low-security locations, a highly contagious foot-and-mouth disease attack would clearly have devastating effects. The tremendous movement of livestock across the United States would also greatly facilitate the spread of foot-and-mouth disease. Today's food animals are extremely mobile and travel to numerous farms, feedlots, and ranches during a very short time span. Cattle reared in the South, for example, might be fed or grazed in several states across the country before they are shipped to slaughter. In addition to animal transfers, the movement of people and vehicles and the sharing of equipment can contribute to a foot-and-mouth disease epidemic as well.[45]

Perhaps the most critical U.S. vulnerability to an agroterrorist attack is the sheer economic value of agriculture to the nation. The U.S. agriculture industry generates over $1 trillion dollars of economic activity per year and over $140 billion in export trade. According to Dr. Floyd Horn of the U.S. Department of Agriculture, if a terrorist introduced foot-and-mouth disease into cow-calf operations or feedlots, it would "disrupt the exports of beef almost immediately, like the day after."[46] Such a disruption would cause ripples throughout the United States and world economies. With 30 percent of the world's population fed by U.S. agriculture and twenty-two million American jobs directly or indirectly tied to the agriculture industry, people around the world would suffer from an agroterrorist attack in the United States.[47] The "domino effect" would extend beyond farms and slaughter-houses and severely impact restaurants, grocery stores, shipping companies, sporting events, tourism, and simple day-to-day outdoor activities. As Peter Probst from the Office of Special Operations and Low-Intensity Conflict in the Pentagon so aptly stated, an agroterrorist attack in the U.S. is an "irresistible temptation to those who wish to do us harm."[48]

The American people would likely feel the consequences of a major foot-and-mouth disease attack for several years. Dr. Corrie Brown testified before the Senate that if a terrorist introduced foot-and-mouth disease into the United States, the loss in export trade alone would be $27 billion. This figure does not include the extensive costs associated with disease diagnosis and surveillance, the depopulation, cleaning, disinfecting and quarantining of animals, or the direct, indirect, and induced losses in the domestic economy.

Considering the fact that a foot-and-mouth disease outbreak in the United States could potentially impact one hundred million cattle, seventy million swine, ten million sheep, and many of the nation's forty million cloven-hoofed wild animals, Americans could certainly expect an immediate and sustained increase in the price of food. Americans currently spend about nine cents out of every dollar for food, perhaps the lowest amount in the world. After an agroterrorist incident, that amount might jump to twenty to twenty-five cents out of every dollar.[49] The corresponding loss of disposable income would cut into the average person's ability to spend money in stores, restaurants, or on vacations.

Undoubtedly, the U.S. stock market and overall economy would decline in response to this cut in spending. Public confidence in the U.S. government and the agriculture industry might also decline after a foot-and-mouth disease attack. As a matter of fact, it is not inconceivable that widespread panic might temporarily erupt. Senator Pat Roberts of Kansas feels this is a definite possibility and states, "At the hint of a snow storm or hurricane, grocery store shelves are emptied. Now, stop and think a minute about what a food scare would do to that [*sic*] all over the country, and think of the chaos that would occur."[50] After a foot-and-mouth disease attack, people would not go hungry in America, but they would definitely experience some physical and psychological effects for quite some time.

Government and private sector estimates paint a bleak picture of the aftermath of a foot-and-mouth disease attack in America. As valuable as estimates are, however, they still do not provide the "wake-up" call that most Americans need regarding agricultural vulnerabilities and agroterrorist or agrowar threats. Hopefully the events of September 11 and the subsequent bioterrorist events in the United States will focus more attention and resources on this problem. Nevertheless, since most U.S. citizens have never experienced a foot-and-mouth disease outbreak during their lifetimes, they would be wise to learn from the unfortunate experiences of three other industrialized nations.

In 1983, for example, Italy experienced a small outbreak of foot-and-mouth disease. While internally it only cost the Italians eight thousand head of cattle at a value of $11 million, externally they lost over $120 million in export trade.[51]

The 2001 outbreak of foot-and-mouth disease in the United Kingdom was a disaster. In February 2001, the UK food industry alone was losing over $72 million a week, and the National Farmers' Union estimated that if the disease was not brought under control within three months, the costs to the food and farming industries would easily exceed $1.2 billion. Many people in the British Isles compared this foot-and-mouth disease outbreak to the one that devastated their economy in 1967–1968. That crisis took eight months to control and resulted in the slaughter of almost half a million animals. Despite its best efforts to control the 2001 foot-and-mouth disease outbreak, Britain quickly earned the reputation as the "agricultural pariah of Europe."[52]

Finally, the most economically devastating outbreak of foot-and-mouth disease in recent years took place in Taiwan in 1996–1997. Taiwan, a major supplier of pork to Japan, saw its lucrative export market literally disappear overnight following the diagnosis of foot-and-mouth disease. After four years, Taiwan had slaughtered eight million hogs and experienced losses in excess of $15 billion. Taiwanese officials also estimate that their hog trade will not recover for at least a decade. Americans should pay close attention to the Taiwanese disaster. While the United States is famous for its safe food supplies and reliable agriculture industry, Americans would be wise to note that Taiwan had the best veterinary services in Asia when they suffered a devastating foot-and-mouth disease outbreak.[53]

TODAY'S RESPONSE

If a terrorist were to strike a U.S. farm today with the foot-and-mouth disease virus, federal, state, and local response plans do exist to deal with the crisis. During any foot-and-mouth disease agroterrorist attack, time would be one of the most critical factors. In a 1999 California risk assessment that examined the cost of delay in dealing with an outbreak of foot-and-mouth disease, estimates revealed that each day of delay would cost about $1 billion dollars.[54] Therefore, quickly identifying the presence of disease and accurately diagnosing the virus would be an absolute imperative. The following list outlines the basic priorities farmers, veterinarians, and emergency response teams would follow after an attack:

1. Identify attack and confirm the agent.
2. Develop a case definition.
3. Identify exposed or potentially exposed herds.
4. Control movement of animals and vehicles out of affected area.
5. Isolate, slaughter and dispose of (or vaccinate) exposed herds.
6. Vaccinate around the outbreak, if possible.
7. Throughout the crisis, inform and educate the public.[55]

The local farmers, feedlot operators, and veterinarians are the all-important first line of defense in this time-critical process. Quick recognition could contain and control an outbreak and prevent an economic disaster. Once the private practitioners determine they are dealing with an abnormal or foreign animal disease (FAD), they would call on the U.S. Agriculture Department's APHIS Veterinary Services (VS) unit and its Emergency Program's (EP) staff for assistance.

The APHIS is the lead agency responsible for the diagnosis and management of all suspicious agricultural disease outbreaks. It has a memorandum of understanding with every state and the Department of Defense to cooperate in disease emergencies, and it has the authority to seize property and eliminate all animal hosts within certain concentric quarantine zones. In the event of an foot-and-mouth disease agroterrorist attack, the APHIS-VS division would coordinate the entire emergency response plan with state veterinary officials, veterinary colleges, industry officials, the Department of Defense, the Federal Emergency Management Agency, the American Veterinary Medical Association, private veterinarians, and livestock producers. Part of the APHIS's rapid response strategy would be to respond to the local veterinarian's call for help with a foreign animal disease diagnostician (FADD). Approximately 350 FADDs, specially trained federal, state, military, university, and private veterinarians, are strategically located throughout the United States and available to respond within twenty-four hours of a suspected outbreak. The FADD takes the samples and works with the

APHIS lab to get a diagnosis as quickly as possible. If the lab confirms the foot-and-mouth disease virus, APHIS-VS works with local and state authorities to contain, control, and hopefully eradicate the disease.[56]

If state and local authorities do not have the resources to contain and control the foot-and-mouth disease outbreak, APHIS can call on the Regional Emergency Animal Disease Eradication Organization (READEO) for additional help. The United States currently has two thirty-eight-person READEO teams, an eastern and a western team, and they are each composed of APHIS-VS employees, state veterinarians, military support personnel, industry liaisons, and representatives from other units with Veterinary Services, Animal and Plant Health Inspection Service, and the U.S. Department of Agriculture. The teams are available for immediate call-up and train regularly with field and tabletop exercises. Their last full-scale exercise took place in November 1998 when both READEO teams mobilized for one week together, with local and regional veterinary personnel, and the FBI in response to a simulated terrorist release of an foot-and-mouth disease-similar virus.[57] The only drawback to the READEO system is the small number of teams available. In a time when the number of READEO teams should be increasing, they have actually been decreasing. Down to just two teams in 2001, READEO boasted four teams in 1993 and as many as six in the 1980s.[58] Clearly this trend must stop. While most experts agree that the current APHIS/READEO system could respond adequately to a single point agroterrorist attack, a large scale or multipoint attack would overwhelm the current system.[59]

A new idea from the Oregon Department of Agriculture might relieve some of the pressure on the underfunded APHIS-VS division and the reduced number of READEO teams in the event of an agroterrorist incident. State veterinarian Andrew Clark recently developed the "V.E.T.T.," the Veterinary Emergency Team Trailer. When an emergency animal disease call comes in, the V.E.T.T. can respond anywhere in the state of Oregon in a matter of hours. Fully stocked with personal protective gear, personnel disinfection items, animal movement control items, premises decontamination items, and office supplies, the V.E.T.T. is a pioneering effort to be proactive when it comes to rapid response. While other states have yet to develop their own version of the V.E.T.T., they are watching Dr. Clark's program closely to see how well it performs.[60] This current initiative is definitely a step in the right direction, but more work must be done soon at the federal, state, and local levels. Hopefully the September 11 terrorism attacks and the aftermath anthrax mail assaults will spur some added impetus to corrective measures.

WORK REMAINS IN COUNTERING AGROTERRORIST THREATS

With little doubt, the United States needs a total unified effort to successfully counter the future foot-and-mouth disease agroterrorist threat. The responsibility for prevention, protection, and response stretches from Congress down to the farmers of America. The federal government, however, must lead the charge.

United States lawmakers must first change the basic definition of "weapons of mass destruction" in title 50, chapter 40 of the U.S. Code, Defense Against Weapons of Mass Destruction Act. Currently, biological agents that do not cause illness or death to people are not included in this definition. Once Congress amends the definition and includes a foot-and-mouth disease attack as WMD terrorism, then it can stiffen the penalties for future agroterrorists.

Next, the president and Congress must seriously address agroterrorism in their domestic preparedness and homeland security initiatives. The creation of the new U.S. Office of Homeland Security under former Governor Tom Ridge should direct steps to improve biodefenses against potential agroterrorist attacks. In October 1997, the President's Commission on Critical Infrastructure Protection failed to even mention agriculture in its discussion of domestic terrorism threats. During this same time frame, Senators Nunn, Lugar, and Domenici, in their Domestic Preparedness Program, also neglected to address agroterrorism and consequently failed to provide any assistance to the agricultural community. Most recently, the Gilmore Commission conducted a "domestic response to terrorism" study for the Secretary of Defense in December 2000 and mentioned agroterrorism, but deferred exploring current efforts to counter this threat until 2001.[61] Especially in light of the Al Qaeda attacks in late 2001, future government programs and panels would be wise to move this agroterrorist concern topic to the top of their respective agendas.

In future budget plans, Congress must also appropriate more funds to national and international programs in the battle against foot-and-mouth disease agroterrorism. For example, the Cooperative Threat Reduction (CTR) program, an interagency effort sponsored by the Department of Defense to reduce the Soviet WMD proliferation threat, needs continued support. Approximately ten thousand scientists worked on agricultural biological agents in the former Soviet Union. After the economic implosion in Russia in the early 1990s, the concern here in the United States is about "brain drain" to potentially proliferant nations. To reduce the likelihood of their turning to nations like Iraq, Iran, and Libya for jobs, the United States developed programs affiliated with the International Science and Technology Center to increase transparency through funding scientist-to-scientist collaborations. The USDA's Freedom Support Act and the Special American Business Internship Training initiative are designed to put these scientists to work in the civilian sector.[62]

Domestically, the executive branch and Congress must also provide improved assistance to the USDA's APHIS. Receiving less than one-tenth of 1 percent of the counterterrorism funds in fiscal year 2001, the USDA's lead organization responsible for protecting U.S. livestock against foot-and-mouth disease is in dire need of dollars. Thomas Frazier, the president of GenCon, a company that tracks international disease outbreaks and related genetic-research issues, has called on the U.S. government to spend $350 million over the next four years to help the USDA and state agricultural agencies build up their infrastructure defense systems.[63] If approved, such a substantial funding increase would have an immediate, sweeping effect on training and agricultural defense programs at the federal, state, and local levels.

With more money, the APHIS could bolster its cadre of field veterinarians, USDA inspectors, diagnosticians, and rapid response teams. In the event of a foot-and-mouth disease agroterror event, early detection, diagnosis, and response will be absolutely critical. To improve its current capabilities, APHIS is actively recruiting veterinarians from around the country to act as a "ready reserve" in the event of a foot-and-mouth disease outbreak.

In an emergency, APHIS would bring these private practitioners onto the personnel rolls of the federal government where they would supplement the agency's existing employees for up to sixty days.[64] In addition to a reserve network of veterinarians, APHIS also needs to hire more USDA inspectors to guard U.S. ports of entry against foreign disease agents. With only 126 inspectors handling the import of 16.7 million animals annually, and only fifty-eight dog-detector teams patrolling U.S. international airports for illegally imported meats, the sheer volume of people and material overwhelms the current system.[65] Finally, APHIS needs more money to create additional rapid response teams. The current APHIS-VS system that relies on only two Regional Emergency Animal Disease Eradication Organization teams would be entirely insufficient to react to a multipoint foot-and-mouth disease attack. In addition to creating more regional emergency response teams, APHIS should consider forming small teams to patrol U.S. farms and feedlots on a regular basis.[66] Helping the local farmers detect a foot-and-mouth disease outbreak in its early stages would likely contain the virus and prevent a nationwide epidemic.

Improved federal funding will also allow APHIS to accelerate its current foot-and-mouth disease vaccine and diagnostics research at the Plum Island facility in New York. In the past, foot-and-mouth disease vaccines have been problematic for several reasons. Traditionally, scientists have had difficulty developing foot-and-mouth disease vaccines because the pathogen mutates and changes its surface from year to year. In addition, foot-and-mouth disease exists as a virus with seven serotypes and seventy subtypes, and a vaccination against one type does not guarantee protection against another. Furthermore, veterinarians cannot easily distinguish a vaccinated animal from an infected animal, although a test is now available to do so.

Therefore, to completely eliminate the disease, farmers would ultimately have to destroy both infected and vaccinated animals. Today, the Plum Island

Animal Disease Center is working on chimeric vaccines that have components of two foot-and-mouth disease virus serotypes and on a drug that can prevent foot-and-mouth disease virus replication. Its scientists are also conducting research on vaccination with parts of the foot-and-mouth disease virus that may lead to vaccines that do not cause the disease. Until researchers at the Plum Island facility make further progress, however, the APHIS will maintain a relatively small vaccine stockpile for emergency use only. In the event of a widespread outbreak or epidemic, so long as the supply holds out, the foot-and-mouth disease vaccine would enable the APHIS to set up a buffer zone and limit the spread of the disease.[67]

In addition to vaccines, diagnostic tests are becoming better, faster, and can now be conducted on the farm. Continued improvement in test sensitivity and ease will greatly facilitate the rapid identification of infected herds, thereby, allowing them to be destroyed before they can infect neighboring herds. Maintaining a strong research tech base is critical to dealing with the unknown. We must continue to build our research programs at Plum Island, the other U.S. Department of Agriculture labs within the country, and at agricultural universities. Such research is dual-use in that it will prepare us to deal with a naturally occurring outbreak or a terrorist event.

Together with increased congressional funding, the APHIS needs to receive more help from the Defense Department in its preparations to limit the effects of any future foot-and-mouth disease agroterrorism. The Department of Defense has had a long-standing relationship with the Department of Agriculture, but most of that interaction has involved training at the veterinarian level. The APHIS has trained more than seventy-five military veterinarians on the recognition and treatment of foreign animal diseases and continues to train more on an annual basis. The two departments also have a Memorandum of Understanding (MOU) dating back to 1964 in which the Defense Department agrees to assist the Agriculture Department in the event of biological contamination to the U.S. agricultural base. The last major test of this MOU occurred in 1983 when the Pentagon supplied manpower and equipment to help clean up an avian influenza outbreak in Pennsylvania.[68]

Today, with the growing threat of agroterrorism, the Defense Department, and in particular, the National Guard, should play a more prominent role in responding to a biological attack against agriculture. Although the National Guard has attempted to form and train Weapons of Mass Destruction Civil Support Teams for a chemical/biological attack against humans, the Guard has yet to form a similar team to offer support in the event of agricultural attacks. Some members of the U.S. Senate believe that with the proper training, these initial response teams could "cross over" and help out the APHIS with rapid diagnosis, containment, and eradication during a foot-and-mouth disease attack. After three years and $143 million, however, the

National Guard has yet to produce a team ready to respond to a chemical/ biological attack against humans, let alone train a team to help out with an agroterrorist event.[69]

While increased assistance from the Department of Defense or Homeland Security Office to fight agroterrorism would certainly be helpful, increased awareness and stronger biosecurity measures among farmers and private industry are absolutely essential. Most farmers and members of the agriculture industry have never seen an animal suffering from foot-and-mouth disease and would be hard-pressed to identify a case if they saw one. Dr. Corrie Brown, College of Veterinary Medicine at the University of Georgia, recommends that the U.S. Agriculture Department distribute pamphlets to agricultural field personnel, which describe various types of foreign animal diseases. Dr. Brown would also like to see the APHIS develop a "1-800 Hotline" for reporting suspicious diseases and more mobile response units like Dr. Clark's V.E.T.T. program in Oregon.[70]

As for local biosecurity measures, agricultural personnel need to employ better safeguards and security at farms, feedlots, and warehouses. Locks, perimeter fencing, and surveillance equipment might not prevent an agroterrorist attack, but they might make one more difficult to accomplish. Farmers would also be wise to quarantine all newly arriving animals to check for possible foot-and-mouth disease infection. Many ranches or feedlots utilize a quarantine system today. Without such a system, all new arrivals would immediately be mixed with thousands of other animals greatly facilitating the chance for disease transmission.[71] Heightened awareness of the threat and some basic security measures are state and local responsibilities that might deter or at least control a terrorist foot-and-mouth disease assault.

In summary, in the past decade the United States has increasingly been a target of terrorists, particularly the target of Islamic radicals such as the Al Qaeda terrorist organization led by Osama bin Laden. They have inflicted damage on U.S. embassies in Kenya and Tanzania. They have aided terrorist attacks on the USS *Cole* anchored off Yemen's coastline. They have initiated two separate attacks on the World Trade Center—one in 1993 and a most disastrous mass casualty strike on September 11, 2001, the same day a hijacked airliner was used to ram the Pentagon. Subsequent to September 11, a spate of anthrax-laced letters were sent through the mail to U.S. senators, to the U.S. Department of State, to the governor of New York, and to certain media offices. In the subsequent U.S. war on terrorism that reached into Afghanistan, much information has been documented that showed Al Qaeda interest in acquiring weapons of mass destruction. A bioterrorist attack using foot-and-mouth disease on U.S. livestock could be devastating and acute biodefense measures are needed to protect the

U.S. livestock food supply that is so vital to the United States. The agroterrorism threat posed by a foot-and-mouth disease attack could inflict such catastrophic costs unless negated by timely U.S. biodefensive programs. It is time to take urgently needed remedial measures to protect these vital assets.

CONCLUSIONS

Biological warfare against animals is not a new concept, but the topic of foot-and-mouth disease agroterrorism is a recent development. Foot-and-mouth disease research took place in World War I and II and was the focus of ten thousand Soviet scientists during the Cold War. Today, terrorists might be conducting their own foot-and-mouth disease research, and this possibility should cause tremendous concern within the United States. Unfortunately, though, very few people are familiar with the foot-and-mouth disease threat.

According to Dr. Floyd Horn of the U.S. Agriculture Department, "[a]griculture simply has not been the focus of our national attention in biological weapons preparedness, even though it is the foundation of our national security, the repository of our national wealth, the basis of our preeminence in the global marketplace, and the sustenance of our rural economy and ideological psyche."[72] Foot-and-mouth disease is one of the most highly contagious viruses known to man and is capable of almost uncontrollable spread. In the hands of a terrorist, this biological weapon could severely damage the U.S. economy. Sadly enough, there are people in the world today who have the desire to harm the United States, and the foot-and-mouth disease virus is an easy agent to obtain and disseminate. To make matters worse, the United States, a free society, is an extremely vulnerable target making it more a question of "when" rather than "if" a foot-and-mouth disease attack will occur.

To counter this increasing threat, federal, state, and local agriculture personnel have developed some solid agroterrorism prevention and response initiatives. Congressional funding, however, has been lacking in coping with possible agroterrorism. While the current APHIS infrastructure might be sufficient to counter a single point attack on one location, a multipoint attack could easily overwhelm its current system. Congress must appropriate monies and federal, state, and local agencies must team their resources and minds to prepare for an inevitable and perhaps imminent foot-and-mouth disease terrorist attack. Without immediate action, the United States may be setting itself up for an economic catastrophe. In the words of Dr. John Wefald, Kansas State University president, "[t]he vision of National Guard troops having to machine-gun tens of thousands of diseased cattle in Kansas' feedlots doesn't present a pretty picture."[73]

Oftentimes in history it takes a disaster or tragedy of epic proportions to trigger a change in an organization, a town, or a nation. After witnessing the past foot-and-mouth disease crisis in the United Kingdom, Taiwan, and Italy, the United States should take heed and learn a valuable lesson from their problems. As we become more aware of the various threats to the U.S. and its allies in the post–September 11 world, we need to get out in front of the major biological warfare or bioterrorist threats that may be posed and should not leave ourselves vulnerable to the huge threat posed by a possible foot-and-mouth disease on U.S. livestock.

CHAPTER 3

Surveillance and Detection: A Public Health Response to Bioterrorism

Barbara F. Bullock

INTRODUCTION

Perhaps the most frightening apparition of our times is the possibility that a biological agent (bacterium, virus, or toxin) will be used to attack our unprotected civilian population and inflict mass casualties. Until the fall 2001 anthrax attacks, delivered through the mail to various U.S. senators, the governor of New York, and various media offices, the previously expected use of a weapon of mass destruction against the United States had been a nuclear device that exploded or a chemical cloud that was set adrift. However, today, of all the weapons of mass destruction (nuclear, chemical, and biological), biological weapons are the most feared by many defense experts but these are the ones that our country is least prepared to deal with.[1] Like the concept of a "nuclear winter," the potential destructiveness of a biological attack can come in many forms and is presently very hard to detect and control, and its results could be catastrophic. The unleashing of biological agents against an unprotected civilian population also, in some cases, constitutes the ultimate medical disaster with the capability to completely overwhelm the present healthcare system. Patients might go to health facilities in unprecedented numbers, and demands for intensive care could well exceed available medical resources. Discerning the threat of bioweapons and appropriate responses to them are critical if we are to prevent the devastating effects of bioterrorism.

In the last century not a single American is known to have died as a result of bioterrorism.[2] Yet, even before the anthrax attacks of late 2001, in previous years, the threat of bioterrorism used against our civilian population had attracted the attention and the resources of U.S. leaders through congressional hearings, government warnings, funding, research studies, and commentaries.[3] For example, during the first National Symposium on

Medical and Public Health Response to Bioterrorism held in 1999, Donna Shalala, former secretary of Health and Human Services, identified four challenges that our government cannot meet alone in combating this emerging threat: (1) awareness, (2) preparedness, (3) public health and medical communities taking the lead in this fight, and (4) cooperation between all levels of government and the medical community.[4]

Awareness, our first challenge, centers on recognizing that an act of bioterrorism in the United States has already happened. In late 2001, someone mailed anthrax-laced envelopes to various U.S. senators, the governor of New York, media leaders, and others in the wake of the September 11 terrorist events sponsored by Osama bin Laden's Al Qaeda organization. Because of America's unrivaled military preparedness, potential enemies (rogue states, international terrorists, and national terrorists) are more likely to resort to asymmetrical biological attacks rather than conventional military confrontations. Jonathan B. Tucker, noted expert at the Monterey Institute of International Studies, states that "a biological arsenal might serve as the basis of an 'asymmetric strategy' in which, instead of confronting a superior conventional military power head-on, the weaker state employs biological weapons to inflict high casualties, spread terror, and undermine the enemy's will to fight."[5]

Biological weapons share seven characteristics that make them ideal weapons for rogue nations and terrorists: (1) ease and low cost of production; (2) ease of dissemination as aerosols; (3) efficient exposure of great numbers of people through inhalation; (4) delayed effect; (5) high potency; (6) high subsequent mortality and morbidity; and, (7) their ability to wreak psychological havoc.[6]

Biological attacks could create mass casualties if properly manufactured, if appropriate delivery systems are provided, and if meteorological conditions are right. For example, Secretary of Defense William Cohen has stated that a bioterrorism attack of one hundred kilograms of anthrax, properly dispersed, would have the impact of two to six times the fatality consequence of a single megaton nuclear bomb.[7] Initially, discussions about the implications of bioterrorism were largely restricted to the Department of Defense, Department of State, Federal Bureau of Investigation (FBI), and the intelligence communities. Only recently have the civilian medical and public health communities begun to engage the practical challenges posed by this threat. Professional societies have begun to incorporate discussions of bioterrorism in national meetings, and in 1998, the World Health Organization established an expert group to review and revise its 1970 landmark document, "Health Aspects of Chemical and Biological Weapons."[8]

Once aware of the threat, preparing a credible national medical response to any such attack is the second challenge. In May 1998, President Clinton signed Presidential Decision Directive 62 to define the administration's policies on preparedness against weapons of mass destruction and other unconventional threats and to designate the first national coordinator to bring together various federal programs on unconventional threats.[9] The Department of Health and Human Services spent $158 million and $230 million in fiscal years 1999 and 2000, respectively, to fund its ongoing "Anti-Bioterrorism Initiative," devised to significantly raise our level of preparedness to include public health surveillance, epidemiological capacity, medical response, building a stockpile of pharmaceuticals, and research and development.[10] Public health surveillance, the ongoing systematic collection, analysis, interpretation, and dissemination of health data, plays a major role in our preparedness by enabling epidemiologists to use the collected data to detect biological outbreaks and characterize disease transmission patterns by time, place, and person.

With a bioterrorism attack, the public health and medical communities are our frontline response. They are the ones who must first detect that the incident has actually occurred, identify the biological agent, decontaminate the area (if needed), determine the likelihood of secondary transmission, identify the exposed population, and provide preventive measures and treatments.[11] First responders are emergency department physicians and nurses, infectious disease physicians, infection control practitioners, epidemiologists, laboratory experts, public health officials, and hospital administrators. Rapid detection, accurate diagnosis, and speedy treatment by the first responders can save many lives. Hence, our third challenge is to ensure that first responders are capable of performing this mission.

Successfully combating biological warfare requires unprecedented cooperation between the federal government, state and local agencies, and the medical community, and is our fourth challenge. The federal government [Health and Human Services (HHS), the Federal Bureau of Investigation (FBI), Federal Emergency Management Agency (FEMA), and others] plays a key leadership role by supporting state and local planning efforts with funding, expertise, training, and developing an infrastructure for detecting biological attacks and delivering mass medical care. Hence, medical response plans for managing the consequences of bioterrorism must be well integrated and coordinated with other emergency response systems.

Of the four challenges cited by Secretary Shalala, ensuring that first responders are capable of performing this mission (the third challenge) is the most critical because the efficiency of the first responders determines the casualty count. Our medical response to a biological attack is vested in the local public health systems being able to detect that a biological attack has occurred, identify the biological agent, provide an accurate diagnosis, and effectively treat an uncommon disease. Because we do not have extensive experience with a biological attack, our public health systems would be challenged to undertake emergency management of bioterrorism. Special measures would be needed for patient care and hospitalization, obtaining laboratory confirmation regarding the identity of the biological agent, providing vaccine or antibiotics to a large population, and identifying and possibly quarantining patients. Rapid and accurate surveillance detection and epidemiological investigation by the first responders would be a key factor in minimizing suffering and loss of life. The limitations of our public health departments in conducting disease detection and surveillance and epidemiological investigations have caused many public health experts to raise concerns about the adequacy of the country's infectious diseases surveillance network and its ability to function in the midst of a biological attack.[12]

LOCAL DISEASE SURVEILLANCE AND DETECTION BY PHYSICIANS

The current system of medical response to a bioterrorism attack in the United States emphasizes the critical role of the first responders, the local emergency care systems, in the initial period of a biological attack. Knowing that a biological attack has occurred (detection) is the first challenge faced by first responders, since biological agents lend themselves to clandestine dissemination in the air, food, or water supply.[13] The release would most likely be unannounced by the attacker and would most certainly be undetected. For example, an airborne or aerosol release would produce a cloud that would be invisible, odorless, and tasteless. Depending on the biological agent used, no one would know until days or weeks later that anyone had been infected. This knowledge would come long after a considerable amount of damage had been done. It is highly probable that most victims of an unannounced biological attack will delay seeking medical care because most of the biological agents used in such attacks will manifest flulike symptoms in the early stages of infection.[14] Because of this delayed reaction, even the possibility of a bioterrorist attack causes trepidation in the medical community. It is not surprising that first responders from twenty-two cities who attended federal bioterrorism preparedness planning, training, and equipment programs provided an average self-assessment rating of 4.1 out of a possible 10 points for their municipality's medical bioterrorism response capability.[15] These poor ratings are indicative of just how far emergency officials in these cities receiving federal aid to combat bioterrorism believe they have to go before they could truly handle a major infectious disease outbreak.

Regardless of the trepidation of the first responders, eventually patients would begin appearing in emergency rooms and physician offices with possibly flulike symptoms and physicians would return most of them home without having ordered any diagnostic testing.[16] A tide of patients would return to their care facilities and only then would physicians begin extracting cultures such as throat swabs, urine, stool, and blood samples. The severely ill would be admitted to intensive care units and medical wards. Due to the harried pace of the medical personnel, it is doubtful that anyone would notice that the influx of patients currently being treated in multiple emergency facilities came from the same geographic area.[17] The patients would be treated by another set of physicians who are even less likely than their emergency department colleagues to recognize the symptoms that manifest from exposure to biological attacks, since few physicians have seen a case of anthrax, smallpox, or the plague.[18]

A physician in Pennsylvania's Allegheny County tested how alert his on-duty colleagues were to the signs of smallpox, a disease that has not been seen in the United States for decades.[19] Of seventeen physicians quizzed, only one of the two infectious disease specialists correctly connected the symptoms to smallpox. In another example, a Maryland emergency room physician who had completed the domestic preparedness training program, estimated that numerous people would have to be coughing up black blood, others on ventilators, and dozens dead before he and his colleagues would connect the symptoms to anthrax.[20] A 1998 survey of seventy-six physicians (53 percent reported that their emergency medicine residency programs included formal training in biological warfare agents) heightens the concern that most physicians would miss the clinical signs of a bioterrorist attack. Of those surveyed, over 70 percent rated their ability to detect the clinical signs of bioterrorism as very poor or less than adequate.[21] Because bioterrorism is seen as a low probability event, active participation by critical private sector players may be minimal. This is evidenced by the "Train the Trainers" sessions on bioterrorism held in Baltimore in 1999 where only five emergency room physicians and no hospital representatives attended.[22] If clinicians seeing a host of cases with similar symptoms considered factors such as the normal patterns of a disease, or a disease not endemic to a particular geography worthy of further investigation, they would get a head start on discerning a terrorist attack from a natural occurring disease (see Table 3.1).[23]

Despite the emphasis on emergency room physicians as the early response team, the medical community may not identify the reason people are falling ill until days or even weeks later, after hospitalization and when laboratory results are available.[24] By this time, many lives would have been lost. A 1972 outbreak of smallpox in Yugoslavia clearly illustrates this point.[25] The last smallpox outbreak in Yugoslavia occurred in 1927, but Yugoslavia continued population-wide vaccinations to protect against imported cases. A pilgrim returning home from Mecca became ill with an undiagnosed febrile disease and was hospitalized. He received visitors from a number of different localities; eleven of the visitors became ill within two weeks with high fever and rash. The patients were unaware of each other's illness, and their physicians, few of whom had ever seen a case of smallpox, failed to make a correct diagnosis. The first cases were correctly diagnosed two days after one of the visitors died and four weeks after the first patient became ill. By then, 150 persons were already infected. Nine weeks after the first patient became

Table 3.1
Epidemiological Clues to a Possible Bioterrorist Attack

- Distribution of cases that is inconsistent with normal disease patterns (geographically and/or temporally), with greater than anticipated numbers of patients, especially in a distinct population.
- More severe illness than is typical for a given pathogen, as well as unusual routes of exposure (e.g., inhalation anthrax as opposed to cutaneous or gastrointestinal cases).
- Disease that is not endemic to a given geographic area, unusual for the time of year, or impossible to transmit naturally, since the disease carrier (e.g., mosquito, rodent) is not present in the area.
- Simultaneous upswings of different diseases.
- Disease outbreak affecting both animal and human populations.
- Unusual strain of a disease or atypical antibiotic resistance patterns.
- Higher rates of disease among those who were located in certain areas at a certain point in time (e.g., inside a building where agent was released, outside if the attack was outdoors).
- Intelligence data that a country or terrorist group possessed a certain biological warfare agent or agents.
- Claims by a terrorist group to have released a biological agent.
- Direct evidence (e.g., environment samples, delivery system) that an agent was released.

Source: Julie A. Pavlin, "Epidemiology of Bioterrorism," in *Emerging Infectious Diseases 5, no. 4* (July/August 1999), 529.

ill, 175 persons had contracted smallpox and 35 had died. High casualty numbers were averted due to mass vaccination clinics held throughout the country.

LOCAL LABORATORY SURVEILLANCE AND CAPACITY

The next impediment to detection that hinders a rapid response by the first responders occurs in the laboratory. When a clinical specimen reaches the laboratory, diagnosis may be hindered for several reasons.[26] First, microbes that grow rapaciously in the lungs or intestines can be difficult to grow in a petri dish. Second, microbiologists have an even harder time growing cultures when samples are not taken with precision and properly prepared and stored. Prior to being received in the laboratory, cultures are handled by clinicians and delivery service personnel who may not be trained in the appropriate procedures for taking, preparing and storing cultures. It is not difficult to imagine this happening among harried medical personnel working with a large influx of patients. Before the late 2001 terrorist anthrax attacks against U.S. senators, the governor of New York, and selected mass media leaders, it is likely that if microbiologists were to receive an unexpected test result like anthrax, they previously might have been likely to consider it a fluke caused by mishandling and disregard the result. Hopefully, that is no longer the case. Third, microbiologists routinely run a series of time-consuming tests for ordinary diseases before they start testing for exotic ones. Fourth, if a disease is presented to them that they have only seen in text-books, technicians are likely to restart the test, often requesting that a new culture be drawn from the patient. At some point, the cultures that are difficult to identify go into the stack of unknowns to be scrutinized by a pathologist, who may request additional diagnostic assays such as those shown in Table 3.2.[27] Fifth, some microbiologists may be unfamiliar with how to plate and test for biological warfare agents; for example, a special medium has to be used to test for anthrax.[28] Sixth, until September 11, 2001, and its aftermath, the vast majority of hospital, public health, and private laboratory technicians were not attuned to the possibility of a bioterrorist attack because they had not been targeted for awareness or other technical training.[29] That may be changing but there is still a long way to go to train this group sufficiently to handle the level of threat we may face. A difficult, unknown culture still may be referred up the laboratory chain, with the hospital or private laboratory sending the culture to the local public health laboratory, which could pass the culture on to its state counterpart, which may pass it on to the CDC or the U.S. Army Medical Research Institute of Infectious Diseases.[30] With delays for retests, several weeks may pass before laboratories unravel the mystery. Delays in determining the scope and magnitude of a biological attack may result in illness and deaths that may have been avoided if a rapid response, based on accurate and timely surveillance data, were made.[31]

PROBLEMS WITH CURRENT EPIDEMIOLOGICAL INVESTIGATION

A major mission of public health departments is prompt identification and suppression of infectious diseases. Our national concept of operations for an early bioterrorism response relies heavily on local, state, and federal health organizations being able to detect a biological attack through surveillance by first responders and their reporting of a possibly uncommon disease. Surveillance systems for collecting, analyzing, and interpreting reports of such cases and trained staffs to monitor for disease outbreak are the foundation of public health epidemiology.[32] They are also the core of the problems with our current epidemiological investigation capabilities.

Surveillance systems that rely on voluntary disease reporting from health-care providers are called passive surveillance systems and are notorious for their poor sensitivity, lack of timeliness, and minimal coverage.[33] Because the passive system is inexpensive to implement, it comprises the majority of surveillance systems in place at local, state, and federal levels. Generally, the

Table 3.2
Diagnostic Samples, Assays, and Isolation Precautions for Biological Warfare Agents

Agent	Diagnostic Sample	Diagnostic Assay	Patient Isolation Precautions
Anthrax	• Blood (Level 2)	• Gram stain • Antigen—ELISA* Serology—ELISA	• Standard precautions
Smallpox	• Pharyngeal swab • Scab material (Level 4)	• ELISA • Polymerase chain reaction • Virus isolation	• Airborne precautions
Plague	• Blood • Sputum • Lymph node • Aspirate (Level 2/3)	• Gram or Wright-Giemsa stain • Antigen—ELISA • Culture Serology • ELISA immunofluorescence assay	• Pneumonic: droplet • Precautions until patient treated for 3 days
Viral hemorrhagic fevers	• Serum • Blood (Level 3 for Rift Valley, Yellow, and Korean hemorrhagic fevers; Level 4 for others)	• Virus isolation • Antigen—ELISA • Reverse transcriptase polymerase chain reaction • Serology—antibody ELISA	• Contact precautions • Consider additional precautions if massive hemorrhage
Botulinum	• Nasal swab (Level 2)	• Antigen—ELISA • Mouse neutral	• Standard precautions

*ELISA: enzyme-linked immunosorbent assay

Source: David R. Franz et al., "Clinical Recognition and Management of Patients Exposed to Biological Warfare Agent," *Journal of the American Medical Association 278,* no. 5 (6 Aug 1997), 400–401.

quality of information in passive surveillance systems is greatly limited, making them not well suited to the needs of bioterrorism surveillance. The CDC oversees a large number of passive disease surveillance systems. They are based on collaboration with state and local health departments, which in turn depend on physician-initiated reports of specific diseases or information from state health laboratories; the National Notifiable Disease Surveillance System is probably the best known. The CDC and state epidemiologists compile and periodically review a national list of fifty diseases; this list currently includes anthrax, smallpox, plague, hemorrhagic fevers, and botulism. By state laws, clinicians, hospitals, and laboratories are required to report cases involving any of these fifty diseases.[34] Although many states have legal penalties against a healthcare provider that does not report, the penalties are seldom imposed. Hence, the reliability of passive surveillance systems is often low because physicians or hospitals often fail to make the initial report or do not report in a timely manner. Because little if any federal funding is provided to support surveillance, local and state health departments have little incentive to actively support it.

Active surveillance, which requires a staff to actively search for and identify new cases, provides more timely and accurate information than the passive systems but must have sufficient numbers of adequately trained epidemiologists to collect, compile, analyze, and interpret the data to determine the source of the biological agent; an example of an active system is the Sentinel Surveillance Networks.[35] Detecting and characterizing an outbreak caused by a covert release of a biological agent can be difficult, but it may also be startlingly obvious. A reported case of anthrax in an area of the country where anthrax is never reported or in an individual with no obvious risk factors for the disease would raise the suspicions of the public health epidemiologist. Although intentional infection would not necessarily be the first explanation investigated, a process of elimination or additional case reports would eventually lead to a serious consideration of this possibility. The time it takes to reach this point can determine if there is a small casualty count or mass casualties. In the case of a biological attack, lost time may quickly translate into lost lives. Therefore, it is a critical infrastructure resource and expertise problem of national importance that we have a sufficient number of adequately trained epidemiologists at both the local and state levels. The CDC trains a cadre of Epidemic Intelligence Service (EIS) officers who are available to assist state and local epidemiological response. Surprisingly, the EIS was created during the Korean war in response to fears about biological weapons and the perception that state and local public health resources were inadequate to deal with disease outbreaks.[36] Now, nearly fifty years later, facing a threat from these same biological weapons, our country finds itself understaffed and underprepared.

Former Minnesota state epidemiologist Dr. Michael Osterholm surveyed the policies and scientific capabilities of all fifty state health departments. He discovered that the tremendous variations in disease reporting reflected enormous discrepancies in the policies and capabilities of the health departments.[37] In the United States, all disease surveillance begins at the local level and then is transmitted to the state level and finally to the CDC. Because the United States has a very mobile population, a weak link in the local to federal chain severely compromises the entire system and could lead to unnecessary deaths when dealing with a biological attack.

In a General Accounting Office (GAO) report on state surveillance systems, which also found that disease surveillance is not comprehensive in all states, many state laboratory directors and epidemiologists blamed inadequate staffing, information-sharing problems, and the CDC as culprits in hindering their ability to generate and use laboratory data to conduct infectious diseases surveillance.[38] First, the state laboratory directors and epidemiologists asserted that the number of laboratory staff to perform tests and the number of epidemiology staff who can analyze data, translate surveillance information into disease prevention, and control activities are insufficient. The number of epidemiologists who are prepared for fieldwork is limited because the public health sector competes poorly with academia and industry for new epidemiology graduates.[39] Second, they reported that participants in the surveillance network (especially at the local level) often lack basic computer systems needed to allow them to rapidly share information. Third, they cited a requirement for training to ensure that their staffs have the skills to take advantage of the technological advances in laboratory methods and information-sharing systems. These three assertions reinforced a prior study by Dr. Osterholm, which discovered that nearly two decades of government belt tightening, coupled with decreased local and state revenues, had limited the ability of public health departments to hire the quantity of trained personnel needed and to purchase new equipment and training.[40] Advances in information technology, in large part, have not reached local and some state health agencies. The capacity of state and local health departments to communicate electronically with each other is limited, with fewer than 50 percent of local health departments having any capacity for Internet connectivity. Fourth, they expressed concerns about CDC's many separate data reporting systems rather than an integration of its many systems. This results in duplication of effort and further drains limited resources. Fifth, they wanted CDC to help the states build systems that link them with local and private surveillance partners. Large medical practices and managed care facilities often have patient medical records in electronic form that may identify a case of a potential biological terrorism–related illness. Sixth, the states wanted CDC to provide more hands-on training experience. They placed high value on CDC's testing and consulting services, but they also stated that CDC needed to improve its on-site expertise. Last, state officials pointed out that obtaining assistance with problems that cut across programmatic boundaries could be improved if CDC's departments communicated better with one another. The many separate departments often failed to share information within CDC.

EFFORTS TO ENHANCE SURVEILLANCE AND DETECTION

Detection and identification of biological agents, either in the environment or in victims' bodies, is currently a piecemeal operation that, in the absence of other information, is as much art as science.[41] Local health officials and emergency planners, state public health officials, and the CDC are striving to find more expedient ways to detect and respond to a biological attack.

At the local level, several surveillance concepts are being implemented to achieve early detection of suspicious disease outbreaks by auditing fluctuations in the number of patients admitted to hospitals; the numbers are derived from the activity levels of the emergency management systems (EMS).[42] In some cities like Boston, Cleveland, and Denver, doctor supervision of the EMS personnel provides valuable information about community health problems, enabling the doctors to identify a disease outbreak early. Some cities are operating Web sites to monitor the number of incoming patients, the diversion status of hospitals, and the number of incoming patients with similar symptoms. Additionally, they are requiring the EMS crews and hospital emergency departments to inform the attending emergency doctor or charge nurse when they see a rapid or developing rise in patients with similar symptoms.

State public health departments are also becoming more diligent about active surveillance. A few states have instituted a statewide system to recognize an elevation in hospital admissions by requiring a designated area hospital to notify the state public health department if two or more of the hospitals in the network are experiencing an increase in same-symptom cases.[43] State health officials then determine if something out of the ordinary is taking place and, if so, send a high priority facsimile to hospitals and EMS services throughout the state.

Some states are also employing the syndrome surveillance approach in a rather unique manner: rather than waiting for laboratory identification of a culture, data about disease types and rates are collated from various sources, allowing the geographic and temporal evolution of a disease in a given area to be mapped.[44] This information can assist public health officials in differentiating between disease patterns, in determining if the disease is contagious, and in deducing whether the disease outbreak was natural. This surveillance approach uses sources such as over-the-counter medication sales, private practice physicians, and primary care clinics to detect a covert bioterrorist attack. In New Mexico, the state health department and some hospitals are testing a syndrome-based surveillance system designed to differentiate normal cycles of disease from a possible bioterrorist attack by documenting patient admissions for five different causes (flulike illness, mental status change with fever, fever and skin rash, hepatitis/acute jaundice, and diarrhea with fever). The data is transmitted in real-time and tabulated in a central database, which is used to provide the doctor information on whether the patient being treated is an isolated case or part of a more widespread pattern of illness. Additionally, this system will help the state healthcare authorities to manage a budding healthcare crisis by increasing shipment of medicines and controlling access into and out of an affected area.

In 1994, the CDC identified three complementary programs to help rebuild the U.S. public health infrastructure for surveillance and response to infectious diseases that will prove useful in a bioterrorism incident: the Epidemiology and Laboratory Capacity (ELC) program, the Emerging Infections Programs (EIP), and provider-based sentinel networks.[45] The goal of the ELC program is to help large health departments develop the core capacity to meet the infectious disease threats of the future by providing technical tools, training, and financial resources. ELC activities include developing innovative systems for early detection and investigation of disease outbreaks and ensuring electronic reporting of surveillance data. Between September 1995 and September 1998, the CDC entered into ELC agreements with thirty states and localities and plans to involve all fifty states by 2002. The goal of the EIP is to conduct population-based surveillance and research to address new problems in infectious diseases and public health and to enhance laboratory and epidemiological capacity. The EIP also evaluates certain disease syndromes of unknown origin. The CDC 1994 plan established provider-based sentinel networks to study conditions that are not covered by health department surveillance and that are likely to be seen by specific kinds of health providers. Since 1997, three networks have been established. The first is the Emergency Department Sentinel Network for Emerging Infections (EMERGEncy ID NET). This is a network of academically affiliated emergency medicine centers that operate emergency departments at eleven hospitals in large cities and monitors syndromes such as bloody diarrhea, illnesses that follow exposure to animals, illness in immigrants and travelers, and first-time seizures not associated with head trauma. The second is the Infectious Diseases Society of America Emerging Infections Network (IDSA EIN), which is a network of over five hundred infectious disease practitioners whose purpose is to enhance communications and health education among its members, collaborate on research projects, and provide assistance in case-finding during outbreak investigations. The third is the Sentinel Network of Travel Medicine Clinics (GeoSentinel), which is composed of twenty-two travel medicine clinics located in the United States and other countries that monitor temporal and geographic trends of infectious diseases among travelers, immigrants, and refugees.

With the cooperation of healthcare personnel in Atlanta, Seattle, Philadelphia, and Los Angeles, the CDC has also begun to test its own variation of an active syndrome surveillance system. During the Centennial Olympic Games held in Atlanta in the summer of 1996, the CDC worked with forty federal, state, and local agencies to develop an operational concept for response to a chemical or biological terrorism incident.[46] Subsequent tests occurred in Seattle during the World Trade Center Convention in December 1999, in Philadelphia during the Republican National Convention in July 2000, and in Los Angeles during the Democratic National Convention in August 2000.[47] In Philadelphia, the template included surveillance at first aid stations, hospital census data (number of admissions in the emergency department, ICU, regular admissions, and the number of deaths), and sentinel emergency department surveillance data.[48] These data were used to track patients with the following disease syndromes: (1) respiratory tract infection with fever; (2) diarrhea/gastroenteritis; (3) rash and fever; (4) sepsis and/or acute shock; (5) meningitis/encephalitis; (6) botulism-like syndrome; and (7) unexplained death with history of fever. Syndrome surveillance promises to be a powerful disease detection tool.

An important laboratory development is the ability to sequence different parts of microbial genomes.[49] By identifying distinct features of different genes, it is possible to identify not only microbes of interest but specific strains and, thus, more precisely track infectious disease outbreaks. This fingerprinting technique is useful as a sentinel indicator that a new strain has entered a community and in distinguishing natural occurrences from intentional releases by identifying microbial or viral strains that are foreign to the normal community or by matching new outbreak pathogens with pathogen strains from suspected terrorist groups. An example of a sentinel system utilizing fingerprinting technology is the PulseNet system, a national network of state health laboratories initiated in 1998. These systems allow seemingly disparate infectious disease outbreaks, a likely objective in a bioterrorist attack, to be potentially linked. Through their computerized databases, these systems can possibly detect attacks of bioterrorism and minimize their aftermaths by allowing outbreaks to be more rapidly recognized, investigated, and information to be more rapidly shared.[50]

RECOMMENDATIONS

Efforts to improve disease surveillance and to continue research and development of better diagnostic capabilities, therapeutic agents, and effective response plans capable of mitigating the effects of a biological attack remain paramount.[51] Although authorities are to be commended for the improvements already initiated by them, much work is still needed. Hence, the following recommendations for improvements in local, state, and CDC surveillance and epidemiology infrastructure are provided.

TRAINING

Availability of Training

Training is cheaper if it is available locally; therefore, federal grants should be sent directly to the cities to avoid siphoning funds by state governments.[52] Additionally, the CDC and other such national organizations should develop or sponsor Internet-based training, videos, and other information exchange technology aimed at the education of local and state health departments. Because training would be conducted locally, scarce funding previously allocated to training could be used in other areas.

Institutionalization

If preparedness—our ability to survey, detect, and identify biological agents—is to take hold nationally on the frontlines and be sustained, then it belongs in the local and state training academies and in the nursing and medical schools.[53] Responsibility for institutionalizing training belongs to the federal government, with the CDC as the agency responsible for its implementation. The CDC should be tasked to develop a standardized syllabus to be used in all local and state training and medical facilities.

Certification/Recertification

First responders should be tested at least annually on their knowledge of biological agents, their surveillance and detection skills, and should receive annual refresher/update training in epidemiological improvements.[54]

Standards

Standards are the backbone of accountability and should be established nationally for surveillance and detection of biological agents so they do not differ from state to state.[55]

Public Awareness

Because a bioterrorism attack would likely be directed toward the civilian population, public awareness of the threat must occur. If nothing else positive flows from the anthrax attacks in CONUS that occurred after the Al Qaeda attacks of September 11, at least the public, media, and Congress are all aware of the potential for future bioterrorist attacks and, perhaps, how they could have been much more serious. In much the same way as the public prepared for a nuclear holocaust during the Cold War era, today's citizens must be better educated on this biological threat. Public service announcements using television and radio are good beginnings. All levels of government and large corporations should institute an annual training awareness program on how to react and deal with this threat. The time devoted to this could pay huge dividends in the event of an actual attack by avoiding unnecessary panic and casualties.

EPIDEMIOLOGY AND LABORATORY CAPACITY

Regional Laboratory Network

The establishment of a network of regional laboratories capable of rapid diagnostic testing is essential to mitigate the number of fatalities caused by inadequate laboratory capabilities. Because biological warfare is a low-occurring event, many of our laboratories may not be capable of performing the required assays, and even the "experts" (to include some at the CDC) may miss the identification.[56] This forwarding of cultures will more than likely be of limited benefit to the initial victims but will facilitate rapid diagnosis of delayed or secondarily infected patients.

Symptom-Based Diagnostic Aids

An interactive diagnostic decision-making system to assist clinicians in considering a biological exposure (and possibly provide an early warning) would be of great value.[57] This type of system would necessitate a complex, multiple search mechanism that includes early signs and symptoms of atypical disorders caused by biological agents. An integrated system that utilizes natural disease rates, clinical probabilities based upon signs and symptoms, and laboratory findings could further enhance an early warning system.

COMMUNICATION

Electronic Communication

Advances in information technology must be used to enhance the capacity of local and state health departments to communicate electronically with one another. Few public health epidemiologists have sophisticated knowledge about biological warfare, but through information technology, many could have access to some of the best minds in this field. The Federation of American Scientists established the system, Program for Monitoring Emerging Diseases (ProMED) (approximately one hundred thousand scientists participate in it), to provide communication among sentinel stations around the world capable of reporting unusual disease outbreaks, including those resulting from a biological attack.[58] ProMED could serve to improve the response capabilities of public health departments by electronically bringing together experienced scientists to discuss the situation.[59]

Laboratory Reporting System

A national electronic laboratory reporting system would assist immensely in getting important laboratory information quickly to the epidemiologists, enabling the country to improve its public health response to a biological attack.[60] A national reporting system could provide epidemiologists with nearly real-time notification of a suspected biological agent. The linchpin in our ability to respond is early detection.

FUNDING

Political Coalitions

Government programs for responding to bioterrorism should be designed to be multipurpose rather than highly specialized, so that they are considered worthwhile regardless of how the threat is assessed.[61] The measures needed to impede the threat of bioterrorism are similar to those needed to control and prevent emerging infections. Improving capabilities and capacities to respond to one issue will almost certainly benefit the other. For example, developing rapid diagnostic techniques that would make it possible to quickly detect bioterrorist attacks involving anthrax or plague would have considerable usefulness in the routine clinical diagnosis of pneumonia.[62] Policies that provide social benefit as well as reduce the country's vulnerability to bioterrorism make it easier to build political coalitions that support funding responses to bioterrorism.

CONCLUSION

Biological terrorism, aimed at our unprotected civilian population, is more likely than ever before and far more threatening than nuclear or chemical attacks. Our population is vulnerable and the terrorists are motivated and capable. Because of the accessibility to knowledge about the manufacturing of biological agents and the inexpensive cost of doing so, preventing bioterrorism is nearly impossible. Because biological agents lend themselves to clandestine dissemination, detecting their release will almost always be delayed with the first evidence of such use being in our medical emergency departments, clinics, and physician offices. Thus, the medical community will constitute our frontline of defense. The rapidity with which the medical community reaches a proper diagnosis will determine the speed with which preventive and therapeutic measures can be applied. It will be the difference between a small casualty count and mass casualties. However, few of our physicians have ever seen a case of, or would recall the characteristics of, anthrax, smallpox, plague, hemorrhagic fever, or botulism, the most likely candidates to be used in a biological attack. Few diagnostic laboratories are prepared to promptly confirm such diagnoses.

Our medical community must be prepared to detect, to diagnose, and to characterize epidemiologically outbreaks of disease resulting from the intentional release of a biological weapon. We need at all levels of government (local, state, and national) a greater capacity for surveillance and detection, an improved network of laboratories, better diagnostic instruments, and a more adequate cadre of trained epidemiologists, clinicians, and researchers. The federal government, specifically the CDC, would be prudent to refine syndrome surveillance and evaluate its effectiveness for recognizing unusual disease patterns in order to direct more intensive laboratory analysis, epidemiological investigation, and medical intervention as early as possible in a disease outbreak.

The medical community plays an integral role in detecting biological warfare because it participates in the network of disease surveillance and reporting that may be the first indication of a biological attack. From a public health perspective, timely surveillance, clinician awareness of syndromes potentially from bioterrorism, epidemiological investigation capacity, laboratory diagnostic capacity, continued research and development of improved diagnostic capabilities, and the ability to rapidly communicate critical information remain paramount. Recognition of the need for preparedness at all levels of government provides an opportunity to strengthen the public health system and its linkages with current and new partners.[63] As former President Bill Clinton said in his address at the National Academy of Sciences in January 1998, "[t]hese cutting edge efforts will address not only the threat of weapons of mass destruction, but also the equally serious danger of emerging infectious diseases. So we will benefit even if we are successful in avoiding these attacks."[64]

CHAPTER 4

The Anthrax Terror: DOD's Number-One Biological Threat*

Jim A. Davis and Anna Johnson-Winegar

Today the U.S. military faces a variety of threats around the world, ranging from nuclear ballistic missiles to information warfare. The ability to conduct biological warfare (BW)—to employ biological agents like anthrax as weapons—lies within our adversaries' threat arsenals. This increasingly discussed threat is not as readily appreciated and understood as kinetic-energy threats but presents a no less, and perhaps an even more, daunting challenge to the Department of Defense (DOD) and the nation. The sobering reality is that this threat impacts our national security, and its effects could dramatically change our society.

The relative ease with which biological weapons can be obtained, along with other changes in the world, sets the stage for a different type of warfare in the twenty-first century. BW may reshape the way nations fight wars. If used on a massive scale against the civilian populace, BW could redraw the patterns of our society as people become increasingly concerned about being victims of this silent and deadly mode of warfare. Scientists predict the next several decades will pose challenges as current BW technology evolves into futurist biological weapons such as binary BW agents, stealth viruses, and malicious designer genes. In fact, biological warfare capabilities today are probably where nuclear weapons were in the 1940s.[1]

Underscoring how seriously the U.S. military views biological weapons in general and anthrax in particular, the Joint Chiefs of Staff in 1996 declared anthrax the number-one biological-weapon threat to our military forces.[2] Why is DOD so concerned about biological warfare and particularly anthrax? What can be done to mitigate this threat? Knowing that all vaccines have potential risks, is DOD justified in having a goal of vaccinating 100

*Reprinted from *Aerospace Power Journal*, Winter 2000, 15–29.

percent of the military against anthrax, or should alternative solutions be adopted?

WHY THE CONCERN ABOUT BIOLOGICAL WARFARE?

Millions of defense dollars are currently funding projects to protect our military forces and nation against potential BW attacks. During the last seventy-five years, several international treaties and arms control agreements have been put into place, yet the number of nations with BW programs has not seemed to wane.[3] Based on the incidence of past use of BW in the twentieth century, globalization, technology transfers, and an increasing interest in BW, our military forces should expect and be prepared to encounter and cope with BW use during the twenty-first century. The world is changing, and these changes are escalating the BW risk. Today, rogue states and some terrorist groups are able to overcome technological barriers more easily due to the increased flow of information and access to technologies that were heretofore unavailable. Along with nuclear and chemical arms, biological weapons are part of an unholy trinity of weapons of mass destruction (WMD).

Although chemical warfare (CW) and BW programs require different equipment and expertise, they do have several common features. Both are considered inexpensive weapons that can inflict massive casualties, and both are usually most effective when inhaled. If given advance warning, military personnel can don protective masks and suits that will protect them from both chemical and biological weapons. Neither type of threat destroys property like conventional or nuclear weapons. As a result of these and other factors, countries that have CW programs usually have BW programs. Similarly, countries with BW programs are likely to have CW programs. Since chemicals have been used more widely as weapons, the past use of BW has often been overlooked. Yet the historical incidence of BW (including anthrax) and the emergence of several other factors make it an increasing threat for our near and distant future.

BW USE IN THE PAST

During the U.S. Revolutionary War, General George Washington received reports that the British were spreading smallpox among colonial troops. At first Washington gave little credence to these reports until his troops began to come down with the dreaded disease.[4] At a time when smallpox was killing 16 percent of the people it infected, Washington had to make some tough decisions if he was to preserve the colonial army. His only apparent option was to order mandatory inoculation of his forces,[5] which he knew at the time would cause a mortality rate of 0.33 percent (one per three hundred inoculated would die). On January 6, 1777, Washington gave the order for the colonial army to be variolated. Variolation involved the intentional inoculation of smallpox organisms into the body, a more dangerous procedure than vaccination with cowpox virus (smallpox vaccination), which developed a few years later in 1796.[6] Although data is not available on the number of deaths caused by inoculation, most of the people who underwent variolation survived and were protected from smallpox.

Biological warfare was used in World War I by the German military, who recognized the mule and the horse as important to the Allies for moving equipment. Accordingly, the Germans embarked on an antianimal BW campaign. They achieved their most notable success when they infected 4,500 mules and horses belonging to the Allies in Mesopotamia with glanders.[7] Additionally, the Germans are known to have set up a laboratory in a private house in Chevy Chase, Maryland, where large quantities of anthrax and glanders organisms were grown. A German agent, Captain Frederick Hinsch, used these to inoculate horses in Baltimore, Maryland. An extensive network of German agents in the United States injected horses, mules, and cattle with glanders and anthrax at the stockyards just before the animals' departure to the European theater.[8] The Germans were also accused of covert BW attacks on humans, allegedly using cholera in Italy and plague in Saint Petersburg, Russia.[9]

The Japanese Imperial Army experimented with over sixteen biological agents as tools of warfare between 1932 and 1945. This took place in numerous locations in Asia, where the Japanese experimented with and employed multiple types of biological-weapon delivery systems. It is estimated that some ten thousand Chinese prisoners, U.S. prisoners of war, and British detainees were killed by some of the most gruesome human experimentation in history.[10] The Japanese used BW agents such as anthrax, plague, tularemia, and smallpox to gauge effects and to help them understand how to weaponize such diseases.[11]

Dr. Ken Alibek, the former deputy director of Biopreparat and chief scientist of the Soviet offensive biological warfare program, defected to the United States in 1992.[12] Alibek has alleged that the Soviets employed biological warfare during World War II. In his book *Biohazard*, he states that there is evidence tularemia was used by the Soviet troops to help stop the German panzer troops in the Battle of Stalingrad. The resulting tularemia outbreak may have halted the Nazi advance, but the Soviet troops also developed the disease because of what Alibek suspects was a sudden change in wind direction. Over one hundred thousand cases of tularemia were reported in the Soviet Union in 1942, a tenfold increase in incidence experienced in 1941 and 1943. Seventy percent of the cases were the respiratory form of the disease, which is the form that would have been expected from a biological weapon rather than a natural outbreak of the disease.[13]

From 1974 to 1981, the USSR was actively using chemical/biological warfare (CBW). *The Textbook for Military Medicine*, published in 1997, states that there were 10,923 deaths from CBW use by the Soviets from aircraft spray, rockets, bombs, and other methods. Those were the result of 497 CBW attacks in Afghanistan, Laos, and Kampuchea (Cambodia).[14]

The Soviet Union developed a huge offensive BW program during the 1970s and 1980s. "Secret" cities were built as part of a communist strategy to keep a massive, clandestine program. While the U.S. offensive BW program (1942–1969) focused on BW agents that were curable, the Soviets were constantly striving to develop agents that were difficult to treat. Not wanting to repeat the incident at Stalingrad, where Soviets were infected by their own weapons, they began to formulate a strategic focus—targeting deep strikes into the United States. As recently as 1988, BW agents such as anthrax, plague, smallpox, and an Ebola-like virus were earmarked for placement in SS-18 missiles pointed at major U.S. cities. An SS-18 could carry enough anthrax to wipe out New York City.[15]

Not only are states willing to deploy such unconventional weapons, but now terrorist groups have gained an interest in them. The Aum Shinrikyo cult is best known for its nerve (sarin) gas attack in the Tokyo subway on March 20, 1995. Fortunately, the lack of sarin purity and the Aum Shinrikyo's poor delivery mechanisms limited the effects to twelve deaths and 55,000 casualties. What is not generally well known is that the group also had manufactured biological weapons and attempted to use them. They tried to deploy anthrax on four occasions and botulinum toxin at least four other times.[16] One planned target of a botulinum toxin attack was the U.S. naval base in Yokosuka in April 1990.[17] Fortunately, none of these attacks was successful; otherwise, the casualties could have been in the tens or even hundreds of thousands.

WORLD ENVIRONMENT

The Department of State has identified seven states as sponsors of international terrorism. These state sponsors include Iran, Iraq, Syria, Libya, Cuba, Sudan, and North Korea.[18] Even more alarming, several of these states are also believed to have biological warfare capacity.[19] The 1980s and 1990s brought an escalation in the number of nations deciding to develop their own biological weapons program. Most conspicuous among other states often mentioned as possessing an offensive BW program are China, Russia, and Israel.[20] Russia's declining economy has also caused other international concerns as Russian scientists and workers who were previously employed in the BW program may decide to work for other countries.

The actual and potential movement of highly skilled professionals (the so-called brain drain) from the previous Russian and South African offensive BW programs is alarming.[21] At its height, the Soviet BW effort had as many as sixty thousand people working on different aspects of the program.[22] A good number of those individuals have marketable skills that could be used by countries eager to develop their own program. Many of the former Soviet BW scientists are either unpaid or receive only minimal pay (about $100 per month), making relocation to another country appear lucrative.[23] Likewise, the South Africa BW program began receiving scrutiny under President F. W. de Klerk in the early 1990s, which led to the firing of numerous scientists working the program. This kind of activity only adds fuel to rogue states seeking South African scientists to assist with their countries' development of programs.[24] South Africa recently declared it no longer has an offensive BW program and that all its BW activities are related to defense.

The Internet is another source of ready information for those bent on obtaining a biological weapons capability. Heretofore, one of the greatest barriers to a full understanding of the acquisition, production, and deployment of BW has been a lack of technical knowledge. The Internet now provides a massive repository of information on BW from hundreds of sources. BW exercise scenarios used by governmental agencies on the Internet supply ideas to terrorists on how to effectively deploy BW. Books are available that describe how to obtain, grow, and deploy BW agents such as anthrax, ricin, and botulinum toxin. Other unclassified information goes into great detail discussing the benefits or shortfalls of particular BW agents.

Along with the change from a bipolar to a multipolar world and the proliferation of information through the Internet, terrorists' increased interest in biological weapons has DOD concerned.[25] The trend of terrorism might be captured in two words—*massive lethality*.[26] Although the number of terrorist events was down in 1999, such events are involving larger numbers of people and more fatalities per event. Examples of this trend include the murder of 270 people aboard Pan Am Flight 103 in 1988 and the U.S. embassy bombings in Kenya and Tanzania where 224 people were blown up in 1998.[27] Additionally disturbing in the terrorism trends is the evolution toward transnational groups.[28] Osama bin Laden or the Aum Shinrikyo organizations serve as operative examples. They have or have had a massive international network capable of exporting terrorists around the globe in pursuit of their political objectives.

WHAT IS ANTHRAX?

Anthrax is one of the oldest recorded diseases known to man. The disease is endemic to wild and domestic animals, primarily herbivores such as cattle, horses, and sheep, but it also infects other animals including cats, monkeys, and humans. Naturally occurring anthrax in humans is a disease acquired by contact with infected animals or contaminated animal products, such as hides, and it generally manifests itself as cutaneous lesions. It is thought that the fifth and sixth plagues the Egyptians suffered in approximately 2000 B.C. were due to an anthrax infection. During the Middle Ages, the disease, called Black Bane, ravaged the European countryside, killing scores of cattle and sheep.[29] Inhalational anthrax is a new form of the disease that emerged in the industrial age due to aerosolized particles in wool mills.

In 1876, Robert Koch definitively proved that *Bacillus anthracis* was the causative agent for disease. His development of "Koch's postulates" through experimentation with anthrax provided medical practitioners and scientists with a method to prove that a specific bacterium caused a specific disease.[30] *Bacillus anthracis* was not only the first bacteria to be proven to cause a disease, it was also the first bacteria (as opposed to a virus) against which a vaccine was developed.[31] In 1796, Edward Jenner created the first vaccine for a virus, smallpox, but it was nearly one hundred years later before the first vaccine against a bacterium was developed.[32] In 1881, Louis Pasteur created the first bacterial vaccine against *Bacillus anthracis.*[33]

Although the United States experienced approximately 130 cases of anthrax each year in the early 1900s, this has been reduced to about one case per decade since the 1970s.[34] While rare cases of cutaneous anthrax are reported in the United States, no case of inhalational anthrax has been reported in the United States since 1978.[35] Much of the decrease is probably due to vigorous livestock vaccination programs in endemic areas and human vaccination of high-risk individuals.[36] The largest human epidemic occurred in Zimbabwe in 1978–1980, resulting in more than six thousand cases, of which almost all were the cutaneous form.[37]

Anthrax infection in humans comes in three forms: cutaneous, gastrointestinal, and inhalational.[38] These forms of the disease also describe how a person is exposed to the *Bacillus anthracis* spore. Hemorrhagic meningitis can be a secondary condition in any of these forms of the disease if the disease progresses to bacteriemia.[39] The cutaneous form of the disease is the most common form, making up 95 percent of all occurrences.[40] Without treatment, one in five people would die from cutaneous anthrax. With treatment, virtually 100 percent survive.[41] The gastrointestinal form of the disease is much more severe and may result in a fatality rate of 50 to 100 percent of untreated persons.

Inhalational anthrax is the form most likely to be seen in a BW attack, and it approaches a 100 percent fatality rate if treatment is not administered almost immediately.[42] If treatment begins forty-eight hours after symptoms from inhalational anthrax, the mortality rate can still be as high as 95 percent.[43]

An incubation period (without symptoms) would range from one to six days.[44] Individuals would initially manifest nondiscrete flulike symptoms (e.g., fever, headache, muscle aches). This period may last twenty-four to seventy-two hours, followed by a few hours of "improvement." The terminal stage is an almost precipitous decline resulting in death within hours.[45] None of the available treatments can slow the incidence of mortality significantly once the initial symptoms appear.

Bacillus anthracis is a large, gram-positive bacterium found in many soils around the world and can survive in spore form for decades. There have been cases where the spores have been found still alive after two hundred years.[46] Although some strains have a greater virulence than others, they all must have certain characteristics to cause disease.

In its vegetative (growing) form, the bacillus has a protective capsule that keeps a human's immune system from killing it.[47] Disease-causing strains of anthrax bacteria are characterized by three protein components that they produce.[48] These three components (protective antigen, lethal factor, and edema factor) combine to produce the two deadly toxins (edema toxin and lethal toxin) that cause damage to the human body.[49] In experimental animal studies, once toxin levels reach a critical threshold, death occurs even if antibiotics are used to eliminate the bacteria.

Thirty-three different strains of disease-producing *Bacillus anthracis* have been tested in guinea pigs, seven strains in rabbits, and four strains in rhesus monkeys; all testing in these animals confirms that the same toxins produce disease in animals as well as man.[50] In laboratories, *Bacillus anthracis* can be grown in such a way that the protective antigen can be isolated. This technique has helped scientists to develop the current Food and Drug Administration (FDA)-approved vaccine that utilizes this key disease-mediating protein (protective antigen) to develop antibodies to prevent the disease.

IS DOD JUSTIFIED IN LABELING ANTHRAX AS THE NUMBER-ONE BIOLOGICAL THREAT?

Millions of dollars from the DOD budget are currently being spent to mitigate the potential effects of biological weapons. Because anthrax is number one on the list, it receives a large share of the counter-BW budget dollars. If DOD is focusing on the number-two threat, rather than on what is the most likely BW agent threat to our nation and military, we could be extremely vulnerable. Several factors support DOD's decision to focus on anthrax, including the intermittent use of anthrax in the twentieth century, the unique benefits of *Bacillus anthracis* as a BW agent, and the proliferation of BW programs worldwide with anthrax as the core biological agent.

ANTHRAX: THE BIOLOGICAL WEAPON OF THE TWENTIETH CENTURY

During the first half of the twentieth century, there have been a number of attempts at using anthrax as a weapon. Besides the previously mentioned uses of anthrax by the Germans in World War I and by the Japanese from 1932 to 1945, other countries saw value in having anthrax as an offensive weapon. During World War II, the United States and Britain started their offensive biological warfare programs, and both came to recognize *Bacillus anthracis* as one of several primary biological agents for possible warfare use. There is no record of any U.S. or British use of biological weapons, but work was done to attempt to weaponize a variety of BW agents.

In 1969, President Richard M. Nixon made an international announcement that the United States would unilaterally disband its offensive BW programs and destroy all its BW weapons.[51] Additionally, in 1972 other nations joined with the United States and the USSR in signing the Biological Weapons Convention (BWC), which prohibited the research, production, or use of BW. All was well until the Sverdlovsk anthrax incident.

On April 2, 1979, an accident involving *Bacillus anthracis* occurred at a secret biological weapons facility in the town of Sverdlovsk (now Yekaterinburg) in the USSR.[52] Unlike the Chernobyl nuclear meltdown, where the accident could be seen and heard for miles, this accident happened silently in the early hours of the morning when an employee did not properly replace a filter on an exhaust vent. As a result, between 64 and 104 people died from anthrax infection.[53] The cover story was that these people died from infected meat. The USSR denied it was a BW accident until thirteen years later when Boris Yeltsin admitted the infection came from the escape of anthrax from a BW production facility, confirming the fact that the USSR had been in direct violation of the BWC. The Communist official in charge of the cover-up in 1979 was none other than President Yeltsin. The U.S. biological program had only two recorded cases of accidental anthrax infections (1951 and 1958), and both were fatal.[54]

Although Saddam Hussein was ready to use anthrax in the 1991 Gulf War,[55] his lack of use might lead some to believe the anthrax threat was exaggerated. One study done by the Office of the Secretary of Defense (OSD) modeled the scenario of Iraq's using its weaponized anthrax by spraying it from one of Saddam's dedicated F-1 Mirage aircraft equipped with spray tanks. In ideal weather conditions, an estimated 76,300 deaths would have been suffered by U.S. forces within the first few days of the Desert Storm ground campaign. This would have devastated our forces by killing 24 percent of the 320,000 U.S. soldiers in the region. However, if they had all been vaccinated, only 122 deaths might have resulted.[56]

After the nerve gas attack in Tokyo in 1995, extensive investigations revealed that Aum Shinrikyo had acquired, produced, and weaponized *Bacillus anthracis.* On four repeated occasions (1990–1995), the cult tried to spray the bacterial agent over Tokyo.[57] Fortunately, they were not successful in inflicting mass casualties. A few deaths could have been caused by their anthrax release and would probably have never been discovered due to the large number of unexplained deaths that routinely occur in large cities. These attacks failed due to the cult's lack of technological understanding of anthrax as a BW agent. If Aum Shinrikyo had developed and disseminated an anthrax spore similar to the one released at the Sverdlovsk accident, there could have been many thousands of deaths. In other words, Tokyo escaped a BW catastrophe.

THE BENEFITS OF EMPLOYING MOST BIOLOGICAL AGENTS

Biological weapons offer an opportunity for the less powerful nation to "level the playing field" against the world's military superpower or for a terrorist group to incite a public reaction of enormous magnitude. How can this be? Five key attributes underlie the attractiveness of all biological weapons.

First, biological weapons are inexpensive to produce compared with other weapons of mass destruction.[58] These weapons are often referred to as the "poor man's nuke." With only a few hundred dollars to purchase fermentation equipment for "home brewing," many people could grow large amounts of viable bacteria in a few days. With a few thousand dollars, one would have sufficient funds to acquire, produce, and deploy bacterial agents that could kill thousands of people. It has been calculated that to get the same lethal effect from a nuclear weapon, you would have to invest $800 for every dollar invested in a BW program.[59]

Second, dual-use equipment gives a BW perpetrator the ability to produce either legal vaccines/pharmaceuticals or BW agents.[60] Since the same equipment is required for legal uses, the perpetrator can easily deny that the equipment was used for production of biological weapons.[61] This also helps to lower the overall cost of the biological weapon production if the facility also can be involved in a legal activity that produces consumer products. Dual-use capability also means a staff of trained personnel is always available for production.

Third, bullets are fast, bombs are loud, and their effects often dramatically evident, but BW silently inflicts its damage. The victim would likely be unaware an attack was taking place. Imagine being able to deliver a tasteless, odorless, and colorless weapon that could kill your enemy.[62] These attributes allow an adversary to disseminate these infectious agents without being noticed. The victim might have to take only one good breath of this invisible cloud, and his fate would be sealed.[63]

This leads to the fourth attribute, plausible deniability. A state or a terrorist group can deny that it delivered a BW attack. Short of DNA sequencing of the agent used in the attack and matching it with an agent in the perpetrator's possession, proof of the attack may be speculative at best and, even then, sequencing may not provide conclusive evidence of culpability.

Finally, most military weapons act immediately to get the desired effect, but the delayed effect (incubation period) from BW could work to an enemy's advantage. Various BW agents have incubation periods that range from one to sixty days. Imagine an adversary who knew he could not mass troops on a border because satellites would pick up his movements and U.S. forces might respond to the threat. In the case of anthrax, the adversary could wait to move troops until seventy-two hours later when most people were either dead or starting to show symptoms. The U.S. forces would be in a "survival mode" trying to save every soldier, which could impede the U.S. ability to respond with an appropriate military response.

SPECIFIC BENEFITS OF USING ANTHRAX AS A BW AGENT

Although most of the attributes of *Bacillus anthracis* discussed below are not unique to anthrax, it is the only biological agent that has *every* attribute. While some attributes, such as lethality, are seen as positive for *Bacillus anthracis,* it may actually be negative to a perpetrator that prefers a nonlethal agent. Nevertheless, the following is a list of the agent's attributes that contribute to DOD's decision to designate anthrax as the number-one biological threat to the military.

- *Highly lethal*—Virtually 100 percent of exposed personnel will die from one breath of air with a lethal concentration of anthrax spores.[64] A lethal concentration has been estimated to be 8,000 spores to 50,000 spores.[65]
- *Noncontagious*[66]—This allows a military to use it against another military without concern of secondary spread from person to person. It also allows anthrax to be targeted at specific populations. Both of these features are particularly attractive to certain tactical, operational, or strategic applications. Smallpox and pneumonic plague (*Yersinia pestis*) are often high on the list of BW agents, yet these are both communicable and thus much more difficult for operational or tactical applications and also more dangerous to work with.
- *Easy to protect with advance preparation*[67]—An enemy could vaccinate its troops prior to an attack and know they were protected. Likewise antibiotics can be given in advance to mitigate the effects. This would add an enormous advantage physically and psychologically for invading forces to know that they were protected when entering a contaminated zone.
- *Stores well for long periods*—Anthrax spores can remain viable for years.[68] Climate control is not as critical as with other microbes because the spores have been known to live for decades in arduous environments. Anthrax was tested in the 1940s on Gruinard Island off the coast of Scotland, and viable spores could still be found until it was decontaminated in 1986.[69]
- *Stable in multiple weapon systems*—Many biological agents cannot withstand the turbulence experienced from being sprayed or detonated over a target. Yet the hardiness of anthrax allows enough of it to survive to retain its lethality. This versatility lowers the complexity for a BW perpetrator because one agent can be used in a missile warhead, artillery or mortar shell, or can be disseminated by a sprayer.

- *UV resistant*[70]—Sunlight (ultraviolet rays) will cause all potential BW agents to degrade. BW agents like tularemia die rapidly when exposed to sunlight. Only two agents, *Bacillus anthracis* and *Coxiella burnetii*, are considered resistant to degradation from sunlight.
- *Short incubation period*—If a weapon were to be used against military forces, being able to predict its time of effect is important. Since the incubation period (lag time between the attack and the first symptoms) of anthrax is one to six days, prediction of the timing of the effect would be much easier than for an agent such as brucellosis that has an incubation period ranging from five to sixty days.
- *Easily available*—Because anthrax is an animal disease that occurs around the world, soil samples from many different locations make anthrax readily available at numerous locations around the globe. Additionally, there are approximately 1,500 microbiologic repositories internationally that sell cultures worldwide to laboratories, vaccine companies, and other entities presumably for diagnostic and treatment purposes. These distribution centers serve as a potential source for anthrax procurement.[71]
- *Easy to produce*—Unlike viral agents that require more complicated production equipment, Bacillus anthracis can be produced in equipment common to almost any biologic production. It is easier to produce than almost any other BW agent.[72]
- *Naturally occurs at one to five microns*[73]—This is the optimal size for a BW agent because it is the right particle size to be breathed in and to get to the bottom sacs (alveoli) in the lungs. One of the more difficult aspects of developing a BW agent is to get it small enough so that it can get into the alveoli but large enough to stick to the wall of the alveoli and not be blown back out the airways. *Bacillus anthracis* is no exception. Although the spores naturally occur at the proper size, special milling is required to keep the spores from clumping into larger particles.
- *Can be used as a powder or liquid*—This flexibility allows anthrax to be used in various delivery systems, thereby enhancing a perpetrator's options.[74]
- *Requires a small amount for a mass effect*—The Office of Technology Assessment for the U.S. Congress estimated that 220 pounds of anthrax delivered from an aircraft as an aerosol line in an area like Washington, DC, would result in up to three million casualties with ideal weather conditions.[75] Another assessment by Oak Ridge National Laboratories showed that to produce the same lethal effect on a square-mile area, a perpetrator would need 1,763 pounds of nerve gas (sarin), 0.2 pounds of botulinum toxin (Type A), or only 0.02 pounds of anthrax spores.[76]

WHO HAS AN ANTHRAX BW OFFENSIVE PROGRAM?

The open literature is filled with charts and reports indicating who has BW programs and who has suspected programs.[77] It is very difficult to judge how extensive the BW threat might be since such capability could well be within range of most countries and biotech/pharmaceutical corporations and groups. Intuitively, one would think that any country that has an offensive BW program would probably have anthrax as a key component of its program. Consider the former Soviet Union, the United States, the Aum Shinrikyo, Iraq, and others.[78] Anthrax was one of the agents at the top of their list for production and weaponization. Likewise, many countries currently have weaponized anthrax, and many others are trying to acquire it.[79] Table 4.1, compiled by renowned biological terrorism expert Dr. Seth Carus, provides an idea of reported BW programs from different sources.

Any country listed on the table that has even a suspected BW program has probably thought about anthrax as a biological weapon. The DOD recently responded in an unclassified document that "more than seven countries including Iraq, Iran, Syria, and Russia have or are suspected of developing this biological warfare capability."[81] Israel, Taiwan, and Libya are also suspected of having the infrastructure prepared to grow and weaponize anthrax.

Secretary of the Air Force F. Whitten Peters told the Senate Armed Services Committee on July 21, 1999, that "[anthrax] has been weaponized and we know it is deployed in about ten countries around the world."[82] Others have stated that there are at least seventeen nations with BW programs. Three countries—the USSR, Iraq, and South Africa—had BW programs of which anthrax was an important part during the last twenty years. Their large, covert

Table 4.1
BW Programs by Country and Sources of Information[80]

Country	ACDA* 1995–97	DOD* 1996–98	FIS* 1993	DOD 1988–90	Open Sources Pre-1993
Bulgaria					×
China	×	×		×	×
Cuba		×			×
Egypt	×		×		×
India			×		
Iran	×	×	×	×	×
Iraq	×	×	×	×	×
Israel			×		×
Laos					×
Libya	×	×	×	×	×
North Korea		×	×	×	×
Russia/Soviet Union	×	×		×	×
South Africa					×
Syria	×	×		×	×
Taiwan	×			×	×
Vietnam					×

*ACDA = Arms Control and Disarmament Agency
*DOD = Department of Defense
*FIS = Foreign Intelligence Service of the Russian Federation
Source: W. Seth Carus, "Biological Warfare Threats in Perspective," *Critical Issues in Microbiology* 24, no. 3 (1998), 154.

BW programs sent a strong signal to the international community.[83] The message is that a state can have an active BW program, sometimes of gargantuan size, which can be relatively hidden from the intelligence community.

Ken Alibek reports that the USSR's intricate BW enterprise produced tons of BW agents including anthrax, plague, tularemia, smallpox, and the Marburg virus. During the 1980s, some of the Soviet Union's intercontinental ballistic missiles (ICBM) reportedly were loaded with "cocktails" of these agents and targeted at major U.S. cities such as New York, Chicago, Los Angeles, and Washington, DC. Alibek states that one ICBM could carry enough anthrax to wipe out the population of New York City. Many of his revelations about the magnitude of the Soviet BW program have been corroborated by other credible sources such as Jonathan B. Tucker, director of the Chemical and Biological Weapons Nonproliferation Project at the Center for Non-Proliferation Studies in Monterey, California.[84]

Likewise, Saddam Hussein's BW program seemed to slip by the awareness of U.S. intelligence.[85] Everyone was aware that Iraq had CW because of its documented use of nerve/mustard agents in the Iran-Iraq War and Iraq's use of cyanide/nerve agents on its own citizens, the Kurds. The United States and others also suspected that Iraq previously had a BW program, which was confirmed in 1991/92 by the UN Special Commission (UNSCOM) inspections. It wasn't until the 1995 defection of Lt. Gen. Hussein Kamal, Saddam's son-in-law and the former head of the Iraqi BW program, that the real magnitude of its program came to light. The information he shared with Rolf Ekéus, executive chairman of UNSCOM, revealed that the Iraqis had a much larger program than UNSCOM realized and that it was organized around anthrax and botulinum toxin. Iraq indeed had large stores of weaponizable anthrax and many weapons loaded with anthrax (bombs, Scuds, Al Hussayn warheads, 122 mm rockets, artillery shells, spray tanks for fighters and remotely piloted aircraft).[86] Iraq had been able to hide much of its BW program in spite of the intrusive UNSCOM inspections.[87]

South Africa's previous BW program still seems to be a bit obscure. Investigation into alleged atrocities was initiated in the early 1990s. There are claims that Rhodesian troops were provided anthrax in the late 1970s to be used against guerilla rebels trying to overthrow the white minority rule.[88] Dr. Wouter Basson, a former special forces army general and physician to former president P. W. Botha, headed the South Africa BW program.[89]

IS VACCINATION THE RIGHT DECISION?

Again, an aerosol exposure to anthrax spores causes respiratory anthrax, which is rapidly fatal in nearly 100 percent of cases if untreated. Given the rarity of the disease and its quick progression, a diagnosis of inhalational anthrax is difficult to make. Treatment consists of massive doses of antibiotics and supportive care. However, there are no human studies available on postexposure treatment. Limited studies in monkeys have shown that postexposure treatment with antibiotic (ciprofloxacin or doxycycline) plus administration of vaccine is effective in preventing death.[90] Given the potential for an unrecognized weapon release, it makes sense to provide protection to our military personnel with an effective vaccine before exposure.

The U.S. vaccine known as Anthrax Vaccine Adsorbed (AVA) is an inactivated cell-free product and has been licensed by the Food and Drug Administration since 1970. The bacteria's toxin components are the primary factors in disease. Because the toxin plays such a critical role in the pathogenesis of anthrax, it was a logical step to develop a vaccine based on toxin components. The protective antigen, a constituent of lethal and edema toxin, is the primary component of the currently licensed anthrax vaccine. The filtrate of the cultures of an attenuated strain is adsorbed to aluminum hydroxide to increase antibody responses, and preservatives are added for stability. The Michigan Department of Public Health (MDPH) held the license and produced modest quantities of vaccine as needed between 1970 and 1990. Primary customers included at-risk veterinarians, wool-mill workers, and laboratory workers who handled anthrax cultures or potentially contaminated materials.

At the time of Operation Desert Shield/Desert Storm, the MDPH had a limited production capacity. Due to DOD's critical need for large quantities of vaccine, the MDPH immediately began to produce as much vaccine as possible in the existing facility. Because specialized equipment (such as 100-liter fermenter tanks) was essential, DOD authorized purchase of additional tanks to set up three identical production lines. The MDPH produced all the AVA that was used for U.S. forces in Desert Shield/Desert Storm. A total of approximately 150,000 individuals received one or more doses of anthrax vaccine, approximately 250,000 doses in all.

The vaccine is licensed to be given in a six-dose series, with the first three doses given at two-week intervals. Doses four, five, and six are given at five- or six-month intervals. The perfectly administered series is referred to as zero, two, and four weeks, six, twelve, and eighteen months. Thereafter, annual booster doses are required to maintain immunity. The vaccine was licensed on the basis of a study conducted in wool-mill workers showing that AVA was effective in reducing the number of cases—the cutaneous and inhalational forms jointly—of anthrax infection.[91]

Because it is unethical to expose humans to biological warfare agents, most of the information available on the efficacy of the vaccine against inhalational anthrax is derived from animal data. Studies have been conducted in mice, guinea pigs, rabbits, and nonhuman primates using the aerosol route of exposure.[92] Rabbits and rhesus monkeys have been found to be the animal model most like humans in terms of disease pathology and antibody response. In one series of experiments using experimental monkeys, inoculation with two doses of this vaccine completely protected all the animals against an aerosol challenge given at eight or thirty-eight weeks after vaccination.[93] In all, 62 of 65 vaccinated monkeys and 114 of 117 vaccinated rabbits survived lethal challenge, whereas all unvaccinated control animals died.[94]

When the state of Michigan decided to divest its vaccine production capability, BioPort Corporation bought the MDPH facilities in September 1998. BioPort has renovated the facilities and has submitted a Biological License Application supplement in meeting the standards set by the FDA. All doses administered to U.S. forces have passed potency tests and tests for sterility, purity, and safety.

In two different studies, the incidence of significant local and systemic reactions to the vaccine in the placebo-controlled field trial was 2.4 to 2.8 percent and 0.2 to 1.3 percent.[95] Local reactions consist of induration, erythema, edema, warmth, and tenderness at the injection site. These reactions peak at one to two days and usually disappear within several days. Systemic reactions may include myalgia, headache, and moderate malaise that may last for a few days. These types of reactions have been seen with many other routinely administered vaccines and present no cause for concern.

The Secretary of Defense announced in December 1997 a plan to immunize all active and reserve military personnel with the AVA. The secretary stipulated that immunizations would not begin until DOD (1) established a means of testing the vaccine over and above tests required by the FDA, (2) developed a system for tracking vaccinations, (3) approved operational and communication plans for the vaccination program, and (4) had an outside expert review the health and medical aspects of the program. In May 1998, the secretary announced that all these conditions had been met, and in August 1998, DOD began the Anthrax Vaccine Immunization Program. To date, over 1.8 million doses of vaccine have been administered to more than 488,000 people.

CONCLUSION

The anthrax threat to the U.S. armed forces is real. Evidence continues to mount that more states and nongovernmental organizations unfriendly to the United States either have or are building BW programs. The lethality, hardiness, and ease of production of the anthrax bacteria have made it a mainstay of known BW programs. These same qualities make producing and weaponizing anthrax a top priority for many developing countries and nonstate actors trying to boost their influence on the global stage. The chance of U.S. forces encountering anthrax is greatly enhanced by multiple deployments to high-risk regions of the world. These factors, combined with a near 100 percent postinfection mortality rate, make it strategically and morally necessary for DOD to do whatever it can to defend its forces against this potentially devastating weapon.

The only defense against an anthrax attack, other than destroying the weapons before an attack and making use of personal protection during an attack, is to vaccinate service members. The vaccine currently being administered to the U.S. armed forces has been used safely for thirty years and has passed extensive testing by the FDA. As with most commonly used vaccines, uncomfortable reactions to anthrax vaccinations do occur in a small percentage of cases. These reactions present little cause for concern and pale compared to the effectiveness of the vaccine against a virtually untreatable and fatal disease. The data is convincing and clear that the protection provided by the anthrax vaccine makes it the appropriate choice for protection of U.S. forces against this biological warfare agent.

CHAPTER 5

Efficacy and Safety of the Anthrax Vaccine

Richard A. Hersack

INTRODUCTION

The ongoing debate over the safety and efficacy of the anthrax vaccine is extremely complex. It is possible, however, to categorize the issues and concerns with the Anthrax Vaccine Immunization Program as either clinically related or administrative policy related, then address the two categories separately.[1] An important aspect of the clinically related issues is to determine if the anthrax vaccine, Anthrax Vaccine Adsorbed (AVA), hereafter to be referred to as "the vaccine," is safe and provides effective protection against the effects of exposure to anthrax spores. This review is intended as a clinical assessment based on data in the published, peer-reviewed medical literature and medical textbooks.[2]

If medical personnel determine the vaccine is clinically safe and effective, then senior level policymakers can make a policy decision to vaccinate the Defense Department personnel based on intelligence estimates and relative risk assessments related to the potential use of anthrax spores as a biological weapon. Clinicians and service medical corps officers do not set policy, nor do they have the authority to order vaccination of all personnel.

Military commanders and supervisors should have pertinent clinical facts and information about anthrax and the vaccine, written in lay terms, to serve as a working reference for use to educate those within their chain of command. This includes having an analysis of the major objections opponents to vaccination raise. The research methods employed for this chapter include a review of the peer-reviewed medical literature, medical textbooks, press releases, and Internet World Wide Web sites presenting information and opinions both for and against vaccination.[3] Due to time and space limitations, this chapter is not intended to be an exhaustive review on the use of anthrax as a biological weapon.[4] More detailed reviews and discussions of the evidence related to the risk of the use of anthrax as a biological weapon and the policy decision to vaccinate Defense Department personnel are presented in the chapter by Davis and Johnson-Winegar in this book and several other sources.[5]

PATHOPHYSIOLOGY OF HUMAN ANTHRAX INFECTIONS

The organism *Bacillus anthracis* exists in the soil in dormant spores and can be found throughout the world.[6] The spores are able to exist in the soil for years under the right conditions, such as cool, dry climates with adequate protection from sunlight.[7] Grazing animals consume the spores, which germinate and multiply inside the animal, causing disease, eventually leading to death. After the animal's body decomposes, the anthrax bacteria is exposed to the air. Oxygen in the air stimulates the bacteria to sporulate and the new spores are then released into the environment, either being deposited into the soil or spread by birds and insects.[8]

The word "anthrax" comes from the Greek word *anthrakis,* meaning "coal," and refers to the coal-black skin lesions caused when anthrax bacilli infect the skin.[9] Incidents of anthrax infections of both humans and beasts have occurred throughout history. The fifth plague against Egypt, recorded in the Book of Exodus may have been an outbreak of anthrax.[10] Ancient Greeks, Romans, and Hindus also describe diseases associated with anthrax infection of humans.[11]

Certain groups of people such as veterinarians and workers in the goat-hair or wool industries have been identified as having a higher risk of contracting anthrax. During the 1800s, anthrax was a significant agricultural and industrial problem.[12] Indeed, another name for inhalation anthrax is "woolsorters' disease."[13] Exposure to anthrax spores in the work place is effectively controlled through animal vaccination programs, good animal husbandry, vaccination of workers at risk for exposure, and improvement of working conditions. Such efforts have virtually eliminated anthrax as an occupational hazard in the United Kingdom since 1940.[14] In the United States, human anthrax is extremely rare with only 224 cases reported over fifty years.[15] There has never been a case of human-to-human transmission of anthrax reported, leading most to conclude that anthrax is not contagious.[16]

In humans, the anthrax bacillus causes three types of infections: cutaneous, inhalation, and gastrointestinal. Ninety-five percent of human anthrax infections are cutaneous. Spores enter through a break in the skin and germinate to form anthrax bacilli, leading to a localized infection. A vesicle then forms and ruptures to produce the characteristic coal-black lesion. Cutaneous anthrax is easily treated with antibiotics and the lesions heal without scarring. Most patients survive and develop an immunity against anthrax.[17] If left untreated, the mortality rate is between 10 and 20 percent.[18]

Inhalation anthrax occurs in 5 percent of human anthrax infections and is caused when spores enter through the lungs, lodging in the alveoli, the microscopic air sacs where oxygen exchange with the blood occurs. The anthrax spores may reside in the lung alveoli for several weeks before germinating.[19] Macrophages, cells designed to consume foreign bacteria as part of the body's immune system, engulf the spores and then migrate from the lungs to lymph nodes in the chest. Inside the macrophages, the spores germinate, growing into mature anthrax bacilli. The bacilli multiply and eventually erupt from the macrophages, spreading throughout the blood stream.

The initial symptoms of inhalation anthrax signal germination of the spores into mature bacilli and are similar to any common upper respiratory tract infection. Because the symptoms are so nonspecific, diagnosis at this point is not possible unless there is reason clinically to suspect anthrax exposure. After a few days, the symptoms subside for a brief period, typically twelve to twenty-four hours. This latent period is followed by an explosive period of severe symptoms, shock, and cardiovascular collapse, leading rapidly to death. During this final phase, massive numbers of anthrax bacilli circulate in the blood throughout the body releasing deadly toxins.

Once initial symptoms develop, nearly 100 percent of all cases of inhalation anthrax are fatal (usually within three days), even with aggressive treatment using antibiotics and supportive intensive medical care. Therefore, if a potential exposure to inhalation anthrax is suspected, treatment must be initiated immediately before any symptoms occur. Treatment should be continued either until the possibility of anthrax exposure is excluded or no more dormant spores are left in the lungs (believed to be approximately sixty days).[20]

To develop inhalation anthrax, the subject must inhale a minimum number of spores. The number of spores required to kill at least 50 percent of subjects has been reported to be 8,000 to 10,000 but may range from as few as 2,500 to 55,000.[21] The late 2001 anthrax attacks in the United States, using the United States Postal Service, and the subsequent analysis of what causes a lethal dose shows that the lethal dose varies from person to person and that original estimates may have been based on insufficient data. Occupational studies of unvaccinated goat-hair and wool workers demonstrated they inhaled over five hundred anthrax spores each day, but they did not develop inhalation anthrax.[22] Prior to September 11, 2001, there had been no cases of inhalation anthrax reported in the United States since 1978, and only eighteen cases in the previous eighty years.[23] Between September 11 and January 2002, there were five reported deaths, and twenty-two total cases of persons harmed by the mail-delivered anthrax attacks.[24]

Without deliberate aerosolization (such as during attack with a biological weapon), it is extremely rare for there to be a sufficient concentration of spores in the inhaled air to cause disease, even if there are large amounts of spores deposited on surfaces or in the soil. Studies indicate that secondary aerosolization typically will not stir up enough spores from contaminated soil or surfaces to achieve sufficient concentrations in inhaled air to cause disease. Therefore, decontamination of large areas and soil is usually not indicated, and the presence of residual anthrax spores may not necessarily hinder military operations, as some imply.[25]

Gastrointestinal anthrax results from consuming animal products or meat contaminated with anthrax spores. The initial infection occurs either in the mouth and throat or in the intestines. As in inhalation anthrax, macrophages engulf the spores, which germinate, forming bacteria that enter the blood stream. The bacteria multiply and release toxins, leading to death in 50 percent of cases. Gastrointestinal anthrax is the rarest form of anthrax infection and has not been reported in the United States.[26]

Rarely, anthrax may also infect the central nervous system, causing hemorrhagic meningitis.[27] This form of anthrax infection does not represent a separate way for anthrax to infect humans. It is actually a complication of cutaneous anthrax, caused by anthrax bacilli spreading through the blood or lymphatic systems to infect the brain and spinal cord.[28] This complication is not frequently seen with inhalation or gastrointestinal anthrax, probably because patients die before meningeal infection by anthrax bacilli occurs. Meningeal anthrax is almost always fatal.

ANTHRAX VACCINE ADSORBED

The human body normally fights infection two ways: by producing antibodies that circulate in the blood that recognize and attach to foreign proteins, called antigens, and by special cells (such as macrophages) that engulf (called phagocytosis) the bacteria to kill and digest them. Usually these two processes work together. Antibodies bind to antigens on invading bacteria to mark the bacteria. This attracts macrophages to the bacteria so the macrophages may phagocytize them. Antibodies also bind to circulating antigens, produced and released by bacteria into the blood stream, to neutralize their effect.

Anthrax bacilli that are able to cause disease inhibit both parts of the immune process. First, the protective capsule formed by anthrax bacilli in the blood inhibits phagocytosis. Then, they produce protective antigen and two toxins called edema factor and lethal factor. The toxins couple with protective antigen and penetrate into the patient's cells where antibodies in the blood cannot get to them to neutralize their toxic effect. As a result, the body's defenses are rendered ineffective. Understanding these basic concepts are important in order to understand the strategy of treatment regimens and vaccination programs.

Anthrax Vaccine Adsorbed is the Food and Drug Administration (FDA) approved and licensed vaccine for use to immunize humans against anthrax infection. The strain of anthrax bacteria used to make the vaccine lacks the ability to make the protective capsule (cannot prevent the body's defensive macrophages from phagocytizing the bacteria) and is unable to produce disease in humans. There are no live bacteria and no intact cells in the vaccine, so it is impossible to get infected with anthrax bacteria from the vaccine. The vaccine consists of protective antigen isolated from these attenuated (unable to produce disease) anthrax bacteria.[29] Protective antigen has been shown to be the essential antigen for provoking the immune response against anthrax in both animals and humans. Every type of anthrax vaccine developed that has been demonstrated as effective in immunizing test subjects against anthrax involves the use of protective antigen as the primary agent to trigger the immune response.[30]

After injection, the vaccine stimulates the individual's immune system to produce antibodies against protective antigen, which protect the individual from future infections by anthrax bacilli. After vaccination, it takes the individual some time to develop enough immunity to confer protection, and one dose may or may not be fully protective.[31] Therefore, a nonimmunized person exposed to aerosolized anthrax spores, in addition to immediate vaccination with the anthrax vaccine, requires treatment with antibiotics to prevent disease.

Formaldehyde (up to 0.02 percent) is used as a stabilizer in the vaccine and benzethonium chloride (0.0025 percent) as a preservative.[32] The FDA has approved the use of formaldehyde in these trace amounts as a preservative.[33] The use of formaldehyde as a preservative is actually quite common and has been used for the past forty years. For example, tetanus toxoid, given to all schoolchildren in the United States, contains trace amounts of formaldehyde, yet it has been used safely for decades to induce immunity in millions of people by stimulating the production of antibodies against tetanus.[34]

The anthrax vaccine, does not contain, nor has it ever contained, squalene as an additive. Squalene is a substance sometimes used to increase the potency of certain vaccines.[35] Squalene occurs naturally in humans and is a precursor in the synthesis of cholesterol.[36] Squalene is also found in large amounts in deep-sea shark liver. There are currently several health food supplemental products on the market containing squalene. Proponents claim squalene improves the delivery of oxygen to cells and facilitates the clearance of metabolic toxins.[37]

Recent reports have stated that newly developed tests have detected trace amounts of squalene in AVA and other commonly used vaccines.[38] Previous tests were only able to detect the presence of squalene in parts per million, but the newer, more sensitive tests are able to measure the presence of squalene down to the parts per billion. The concentration of squalene detected in the anthrax vaccine, diphtheria vaccine, and tetanus toxoid, using the newer tests, is about ten parts per billion. The normal concentration of squalene circulating in human blood is many times higher, about 250 parts per billion, suggesting the presence of trace amounts of squalene in the anthrax vaccine is not clinically significant. The presence of trace amounts of squalene in the anthrax vaccine and in the other vaccines may be a normal by-product of the production process.[39]

There have been articles in the press attempting to draw a connection between the use of the vaccine and Gulf War Syndrome, claiming the agent causing Gulf War Syndrome is squalene. These press reports claim veterans suffering from Gulf War Syndrome have antibodies to squalene in their blood, which they got from the anthrax vaccine.[40] Others have gone so far as to charge the Defense Department may have secretly added squalene to lots of the vaccine used for inoculating troops to increase its efficacy. They claim, without presenting any evidence, that anthrax vaccine vial labels may have been altered and that lack of documentation in personal shot records suggest a cover-up.[41]

HISTORY OF PRODUCTION

Merck, Sharp & Dohme developed the first anthrax vaccine for use in humans during the 1950s to protect workers routinely exposed to anthrax spores.[42] Clinical trials performed in the late 1950s and published in 1962 demonstrated that the vaccine was effective in preventing cutaneous anthrax.[43] Later, the Department of Defense (DOD) approached the state of Michigan to manufacture anthrax vaccine for military personnel. DOD chose the state of Michigan because there was little profit potential to motivate private industry to manufacture a vaccine that would not be used in the general public, and Michigan had extensive experience manufacturing other vaccines such as rabies vaccine.

Therefore in 1970, Michigan Biological Products Institute (hereafter called "The Institute") began to produce AVA for DOD. This is essentially the same vaccine as initially produced by Merck, Sharp & Dohme, except that the current anthrax vaccine is more potent and more pure, due to some minor differences in production technique.[44] In 1970, the National Institute of Health's Division of Biologics Standards licensed the vaccine and then in 1972 transferred the license, along with oversight and regulatory authority, to the FDA.[45]

Licensing was based on data collected during studies using both the older anthrax vaccine and AVA to protect workers at risk from infection. A 1962 study based on the older, less potent vaccine measured its effectiveness in protecting wool-mill workers at risk for both cutaneous and inhalation anthrax. A later Centers for Disease Control and Prevention (CDC) study of the current vaccine, conducted for over a decade, showed how effectively it prevented cutaneous anthrax in workers at risk from infection. Of note, it was demonstrated that there was a low risk of serious side effects.[46]

As tensions in the Persian Gulf mounted in early 1990, the U.S. Defense Department asked Michigan Biological Products Institute to dramatically increase the production rate of the vaccine.[47] The Institute informed DOD it would not be able to meet production expectations with the facilities it possessed at that time. The Institute then worked out a plan to upgrade its production facilities with DOD funding and presented the plan to the FDA in 1995, and the FDA approved the facility upgrade plans.

Between 1995 and 1997, the FDA performed several inspections of the Institute's facilities used to produce rabies vaccine and plasma derivative products. During these inspections, the FDA found numerous discrepancies with policies and procedures, recordkeeping, analytical laboratories, quality control practices, raw materials handling, filling and packaging, and storage, warehousing, and distribution.[48] It must be noted that none of these production facilities, nor any of the FDA's findings, involved the production, safety, or quality of vaccine. In March 1997, the FDA sent the Institute a letter indicating the FDA would begin procedures to revoke the Institute's license due to lack of adequate progress to address the discrepancies noted during the inspections of the facilities used to produce rabies vaccine and plasma derivative products, unrelated to the production of anthrax vaccine.

In the mean time, Michigan Biological Products Institute had applied to the FDA to upgrade its anthrax vaccine production facilities to meet the increased demand resulting from the DOD anthrax vaccine immunization program. The FDA approved the planned upgrade and, in January 1998, the Institute voluntarily stopped production of the vaccine in order to begin the FDA-approved renovations to the vaccine production facilities. It is important to note that the stoppage of production of the vaccine was completely unrelated to the discrepancies noted during FDA inspections of rabies vaccine and plasma derivative products production facilities, and stoppage was completely unrelated to the FDA's letter of intent to revoke the Michigan Biological Products Institute's license.

In 1997, Secretary of Defense Cohen made the decision to implement the anthrax vaccine immunization program to vaccinate all military personnel using lots of vaccine already on hand. Since supplies of the vaccine were limited, the immunization program was divided into three phases. Completion depended on the production and release to DOD of additional lots of vaccine after the production facilities were upgraded. As of early 2002, only the first phase has been implemented, meaning only personnel at risk for exposure to inhalation anthrax in high risk areas (i.e., Korea and the Persian Gulf) will be vaccinated.

Part of the secretary's directive was that each lot of the vaccine would be completely retested using FDA testing procedures to reconfirm potency, safety, purity, and sterility. Each lot had to pass such supplemental testing before it would be administered to Defense Department personnel. The lots undergoing supplemental testing had already passed FDA certification, had been released by the FDA for sale, and had been purchased by the DOD.

Eight lots underwent supplemental testing for potency and were released before a problem with the potency test itself was discovered in the fall of 1998.[49] Since then, the potency testing difficulties have been corrected and the test is now working according to specifications.[50] However, the FDA did not release any additional lots until it is satisfied with the quality of the vaccine and had approved necessary potency test amendments implemented to correct the earlier potency testing problems.[51]

In September 1998, the state of Michigan sold the Michigan Biological Products Institute facilities with the vaccine licensing rights to BioPort as part of an effort to privatize government programs and cut costs.[52] In late 1999, BioPort completed the renovations and applied to the FDA for inspection and certification of the new production facilities.[53] In 2002, BioPort continued to have problems with its renovated facility and still had not received FDA certification.[54]

In the meantime, BioPort had started producing new lots of anthrax vaccine.[55] It is important to note that the new lots produced by BioPort have not been certified or released for sale by the FDA, have not been purchased by DOD, and have not been administered to anyone. Furthermore, the Defense Department will not purchase these lots to begin phase two of the immunization program until the BioPort facility passes the FDA inspection and the FDA has tested, certified, and released the new lots for distribution.[56]

BioPort had a total of thirty-two lots of vaccine in storage for DOD produced before the production facilities were shut down for renovations. In February 1998, the FDA inspected these lots of vaccine, and the Institute voluntarily quarantined ten lots. In addition, one other lot was permanently quarantined due to questions regarding sterility and will not be used. Another fourteen lots were tested at random and found not to contain any squalene.[57]

The rate of vaccination of military personnel via the immunization program had been reduced due to the dwindling supply of vaccine. As of May 2000, seventeen lots of anthrax vaccine, all produced by Michigan Biological Products Institute before the renovations began, had passed FDA certification tests and passed recertification tests as ordered by the Secretary of Defense.[58] Defense officials pointed out on numerous occasions in the media and in sworn testimony that only these seventeen lots have been used for the immunization program.

Defense officials had hoped that BioPort would have obtained FDA approval quickly and new lots tested and released.[59] The FDA had identified thirty deficiencies that needed to be rectified before it would grant certification of the vaccine. In addition, some members of Congress were dissatisfied with BioPort's situation and began to urge DOD to consider designing a government-owned, contractor-operated (termed "GOCO") vaccine production facility.[60] Fortunately, in late January 2002, FDA gave final approval of the Bioport facility and the anthrax vaccine production. Additionally, the military has significantly increased its orders for vaccine and has shared its stockpile for a civilian protection.[61]

In summary, it should be noted that the current vaccine is an FDA-licensed, nonexperimental vaccine. It is more potent and more pure than, but otherwise identical to, the earlier version of the vaccine produced in the 1950s by Merck, Sharp & Dohme. The Institute voluntarily stopped production of the vaccine in order to upgrade production facilities, not due to the results of any FDA inspections. The Institute then sold its anthrax vaccine production facilities to BioPort. In January 2002, Bioport received final approval of its production facilities and is actively producing the vaccine.

DOD-mandated supplemental testing, BioPort's voluntary quarantine of lots previously released by the FDA , and the modifications implemented to improve the quality of testing for potency demonstrate the intense level of interagency scrutiny that exists to ensure that DOD's immunization program attains the highest possible levels of safety for DOD personnel.

EFFICACY

Brachman et al. published a controlled study using the original anthrax vaccine produced by Merck, Sharp & Dohme and supplied by the U.S. Army Chemical Corps in 1962.[62] The study looked at how effectively the vaccine prevented anthrax in a population of wool-mill workers considered to be at risk for contracting anthrax. Historically, about 1 percent of these workers contracted cutaneous anthrax annually. To do the study, volunteers were divided into two groups—one group received the vaccine and the other received a placebo (an inactive substance used as a control that looks like the vaccine but is harmless and has no biological effect). The vaccination schedule used in the study matches the current FDA-approved schedule for vaccinations using AVA. The rate of occurrence of anthrax in the vaccinated group was compared with the rate of occurrence in the group that received the placebo and all other workers not participating in the study.

During the study period there were twenty-six cases of anthrax. One case of cutaneous anthrax appeared in a fully vaccinated individual. Twenty-three cases of anthrax appeared in unvaccinated workers and two in partially vaccinated (meaning they did not complete the series of immunizations) workers. No cases of inhalation anthrax occurred in vaccinated or partially vaccinated workers, although five cases of inhalation anthrax occurred in unvaccinated workers during the study period. Four of these cases were fatal. The frequency of occurrence of inhalation anthrax was not sufficient to determine any statistical significance for how effective the vaccine was in preventing inhalation anthrax.[63]

As already pointed out, the vaccine used in the Brachman study was also a protective antigen vaccine similar to AVA but less potent and less pure since it contained more cell fragments. Because the mechanism to produce immunity is the same for both vaccines, Brachman's study results are relevant when discussing the issue of efficacy of the vaccine. In addition, other surveillance studies using the vaccine, completed since the publication of Brachman's study, confirm AVA's efficacy in preventing anthrax in humans.[64]

Between 1962 and 1974, the CDC collected data measuring the occurrence of anthrax in workers at risk for infection who had been vaccinated with AVA versus nonimmunized workers. The study also tracked any adverse reactions to the vaccine.[65] During this period, an additional twenty-seven cases of cutaneous anthrax were identified, three in partially immunized workers who had only received one or two doses. There were no cases of anthrax in the fully immunized workers.[66] A total of 7,000 workers received more than 16,000 doses of the vaccine.[67] The efficacy data from the Brachman study, using the original protective antigen vaccine, and the CDC study, using the vaccine, were eventually used during the licensing procedures for it.[68]

Between 1974 and 1989, it is estimated that an additional 68,000 doses of AVA were administered to at-risk individuals.[69] There were no cases of cutaneous anthrax in vaccinated individuals, although there continued to be reported cases of cutaneous anthrax in unvaccinated people at risk. In addition, the rate of adverse side effects remained low, comparable to rates cited in the FDA-required package insert that accompanies each vial of the vaccine.[70] Due to the increasing rarity of anthrax infections, the fact that workers at risk for exposure to anthrax spores are immunized, and improvements in working conditions, any additional field studies of anthrax vaccine are unlikely.[71] In conclusion, the clinical data collected over several decades indicate that the vaccine is very effective in preventing cutaneous anthrax and, potentially, inhalation anthrax in humans.[72]

Fortunately, inhalation anthrax in humans is very rare even among unvaccinated workers routinely exposed to anthrax spores. Improvements in the work place plus use of the vaccine in workers at risk for exposure to anthrax spores have essentially eliminated the occurrence of inhalation anthrax.[73] But the rareness of this disease also means it is not possible to collect enough data in humans to determine if the vaccine would prevent inhalation anthrax in humans. In order to do a study in humans, one would have to take volunteers, divide them into two groups, vaccinate one group with the vaccine, the other with a placebo, then expose both groups to lethal doses of aerosolized anthrax spores and track how many in each group contract the disease. Obviously, such a study would be unethical.

Numerous animal studies have been performed to measure the effectiveness of AVA to prevent inhalation anthrax. Granted, there is always a possibility that results in one species of animals cannot be assumed to represent potential results in another species. For example, animal studies suggest that some species are more difficult to immunize against anthrax infections, using AVA, than others. In guinea pigs, the vaccine seems to confer variable protection against certain strains of anthrax, suggesting possible species-dependent differences in the guinea pig's immune system. Guinea pigs seem especially sensitive to one particular strain of anthrax, called the Ames strain, even after they are fully immunized with the vaccine.

On the other hand, AVA confers excellent protection in rabbits and nonhuman primates against the Ames strain, providing near 100 percent protection even after as few as two inoculations, including situations where they are exposed to several times the lethal dose of anthrax spores. Moreover, inhalation anthrax infections in nonhuman primates closely resemble inhalation anthrax infections in humans.[74] Based on the animal studies results and the absence of cutaneous and inhalation anthrax in fully immunized individuals exposed to anthrax spores, it is reasonable to conclude that the vaccine prevents inhalation anthrax in humans.[75] In fact, on December 30, 2003, the FDA released a final ruling that the vaccine was approved as "safe and effective for the prevention of anthrax disease—regardless of the route of exposure."[76]

SAFETY AND SIDE EFFECTS

The side effects and adverse reactions recognized as caused by the vaccine tend to be grouped into four main categories: mild local reactions, moderate local reactions, severe local reactions, and systemic reactions. Mild local reactions are defined by tenderness and redness in an area less than one to two centimeters in diameter and occur about 30 percent of the time. Moderate local reactions are identified by an area of response greater than five centimeters in diameter and occur about 4 percent of the time. Severe local reactions are characterized by extensive swelling (edema) of the arm and forearm in which the vaccine was administered. These occur less frequently than moderate reactions. In general, the rate of local reactions is about twice as high in women than men.[77] Systemic reactions are characterized by fever, chills, nausea, and body aches and occur in less than 0.2 percent of vaccinations.[78] Allergic reactions are even less common, being reported in only one per 100,000 doses.[79]

Normally it takes three doses of the vaccine before an individual begins to develop an immune response and seems to correlate with the observation that reactions to subsequent doses tend to be stronger.[80] Individuals who have had cutaneous anthrax or who have severe local or systemic reactions to the vaccine are not to receive the vaccine.[81] In a study conducted from 1962 to 1974, the CDC tracked the occurrence rates of reactions during the administration of more than 16,000 doses to over 7,000 individuals. The results of this study are the rates reported on the informational package insert accompanying each vial as required by the FDA.[82]

Since AVA was licensed in 1970, there have been numerous reviews documenting the occurrence of side effects attributable to it. An independent civilian advisory panel met in 1985 to review the results of the 1962 to 1974 CDC study.[83] The panel reported that only a few systemic side effects had occurred of which all resolved. Local reactions were typically mild and also resolved.[84] From 1974 to 1989, over 68,000 doses of vaccine were administered to persons considered at risk for contracting anthrax. This would include goat hair workers, laboratory personnel, livestock handlers, and veterinarians. Yet, after more than thirty years of use, no long-term side effects have been reported in association with this vaccine.[85]

Since 1973, the U.S. Army Medical Research Institute of Infectious Diseases (USAMRIID) at Fort Detrick, Maryland, has actively followed 1,590 workers who have received more than 10,000 doses of AVA, again with no reported long-term or chronic side effects. Only 4 percent reported local reactions and only 0.5 percent had any type of systemic reactions. All reactions resolved without any lost work time.[86] Another study conducted by the Canadian Armed Forces reported that in 547 individuals who received the vaccine, rates of reaction were less than the rates listed on the package insert. There were no long-term effects except for one individual who reported a persistent nodule at the injection site.[87]

In addition to the CDC study, the USAMRIID study, and the Canadian study, there are three other separate studies on AVA, examining the rate of occurrence of adverse reactions. In 1997, the Pittman study reported on 508 subjects who were actively followed after they received the vaccine. Local reaction rates were roughly the same as reported by other studies, but Pittman noted a much higher rate of systemic reactions. Twenty-nine percent were classified as mild and 14 percent were classified as moderate to severe. Another study, conducted at Tripler Army Medical Center in Hawaii, reported a rate of mild systemic effects of 43 percent and moderate to severe in 5 percent out of a total of 536 individuals vaccinated. Both studies are significant in that they report moderate to severe systemic reactions much higher than the 0.05 percent to 0.2 percent usually reported, and they differentiate between mild and moderate to severe systemic reactions.[88]

The third study is a DOD study, which reported in May of 1999 that out of 223,000 individuals vaccinated, forty-two experienced adverse side effects, which were reported to the FDA and CDC. Of these, seven either missed more than one day of work or required hospitalization. None of these studies note any long-term or chronic adverse effects attributable to the vaccine and none question the safety of it in their conclusions.[89] In addition, there have been no cases of anaphylactic reactions (severe, potentially life threatening, systemic allergic reactions) reported due to its administration.[90]

There have been multiple review panels, including panels hosted by the FDA, the CDC, the World Health Organization, and the Armed Forces Epidemiological Board. A civilian panel of twenty-one experts from several major medical and research centers led by Dr. Thomas V. Inglesby convened to assess the risk that anthrax could be used as a biological weapon agent. The panel also developed a consensus on the care and management of victims of an anthrax biological weapon attack and examined the safety and efficacy of the vaccine. The panel's results were published in May 1999 in the *Journal of the American Medical Association.*[91]

The panel concluded that the likelihood that anthrax could be used in a terrorist attack is high. The panel also reported that its investigation of the clinical data on the use of AVA showed no serious adverse effects have been causally related to AVA, and it reached a consensus for recommending treatment protocols to care for anthrax victims. The panel also recommended that research should be devoted to developing a next-generation anthrax vaccine that requires fewer doses to immunize humans. The panel's findings correlate with the findings of numerous other review panels examining the medical literature published on the vaccine, which confirm the clinical safety and its efficacy in humans.[92]

In 1990, the FDA and CDC launched the Vaccine Adverse Events Reporting System (hereafter termed "the reporting system"). This is a passive reporting system, meaning success depends on medical personnel, patients, and families taking the initiative to file reports. As of October 1, 2002, 2,124,855 doses of the vaccine had been administered to 529,516 personnel with 1,857 reports submitted to the reporting system. Of these reports, 966 were determined to be actually due to the vaccine—862 were less than serious, 93 reported a loss of more than 24 hours of duty, and 11 were hospitalized for allergic inflammatory reactions at the injection site. No unexpected patterns of adverse events were identified.[93]

In addition to the FDA reviews of the reporting system data, DOD convened the Anthrax Vaccine Executive Committee composed of nongovernment medical experts. This group meets periodically to review the reports from the Vaccine Adverse Events Reporting System.[94] Since its first meeting in 1990, the committee has not identified any unexpected patterns of adverse events among the reports submitted to the reporting system.[95] The committee continues to meet every six weeks to review data reported on the vaccine.[96]

The Anthrax Vaccine Executive Committee concluded it is not possible to attribute to the vaccine all the symptoms reported to the reporting system. But, for the sake of argument, if one assumes that all the reports could be linked causally to the vaccine, the rate of adverse reactions, including serious or severe ones, is still less than 0.03 percent. This is below the rate of 0.05 percent reported by other studies and well below the rate of 0.2 percent listed in the vaccine product information package insert. By way of comparison, the hepatitis B vaccine, required for all healthcare workers, has a systemic reaction rate five times greater than that observed due to the anthrax vaccine.[97] Based on reporting system data, the FDA has concluded that it has no concerns about the safety of the vaccine and "continues to view it as safe and effective for individuals at risk of exposure to anthrax."[98]

On November 19, 2003, the DOD released the results of two independent panels that had studied the illness or death of four individuals that received the anthrax vaccine as well as other vaccinations. Three of the cases found no association from vaccination. The other case, Specialist Rachel Lacy, received five different vaccinations on March 2, 2003. She died on April 4, 2003, with a diagnosis consistent with systemic lupus erythematosus. Neither she nor her physician knew she had any underlying immune disorder. The multiple vaccinations may have played a role in initiating her illness, but determination of which vaccine or vaccines may have been the culprit was undeterminable.[99]

In all, there have been at least thirteen studies conducted in humans assessing the safety of the present anthrax vaccine or its precursor protective antigen vaccine, including those discussed in this paper, covering almost fifty years of clinical experience.[100] The clinical evidence accumulated is consistent from study to study and demonstrates that the vaccine is safe and effective. Anthrax Vaccine Adsorbed quite possibly has undergone more scrutiny that any other vaccine developed for human use, yet it continues to find endorsement in medical textbooks, in the medical peer-reviewed literature, and in sworn testimonies given before congressional panels as a safe and reliable vaccine against human anthrax infections.[101]

UNDERSTANDING THE ARGUMENTS AGAINST ANTHRAX VACCINE ADSORBED

It is possible to group the concerns over the vaccine as follows: concerns over the vaccine's safety and efficacy; concerns regarding proper indications for use; concerns over its manufacture and ingredients; concerns regarding the lack of FDA certification of BioPort's renovated manufacturing facility; concerns regarding licensure (including whether or not the vaccine is investigational in nature); concerns over lack of published peer-reviewed clinical trials; concerns over the development of strains of anthrax that are resistant to vaccination; the apparent high rate of occurrence of symptoms in vaccinated individuals at Dover Air Force Base, Delaware; and concerns over whether the threat justifies the use of the vaccine, since weaponized anthrax has not yet been used against our armed forces. Most of the evidence addressing these concerns has already been presented.

As already discussed, licensure of the anthrax vaccine and the information for the package insert were based on both the Brachman study and data collected by the CDC over a ten-year period on the use of the vaccine in workers considered at risk for exposure to anthrax spores. Furthermore, the Brachman study is not the only place where data on the safety and efficacy of the vaccine has been published. As already noted in this paper, there have been numerous other studies on the safety and efficacy of the vaccine conducted over several years involving tens of thousands of human subjects.[102] Although not all of these studies are individually published as peer-reviewed articles, the data collected by these studies has been examined by review panels and published in several articles that have undergone the peer-review process.[103] Therefore, stating that the Brachman study contains the "published adverse reaction rates" without acknowledging these other sources of data in the peer-reviewed literature is misleading.[104]

Another concern raised by opponents to the immunization program is that adversaries might develop strains of anthrax that are resistant to the vaccine.[105] Some base this on the fact that strains of anthrax have been developed that are resistant to antibiotics. Also, there have been reports that anthrax strains have been developed that may render the Russian-developed live attenuated vaccine ineffective.[106] Neither of these reports means that a strain of anthrax has been produced that is resistant to the present U.S. vaccine.

First, it must be pointed out that developing resistance to antibiotics is not the same as developing resistance to vaccines. Antibiotics (biochemicals produced in nature or synthesized in laboratories that are toxic to bacteria) are completely different from antibodies (complex proteins produced by the inoculated individual's immune cells) that result from vaccination. Bacteria commonly develop resistance to antibiotics through several naturally occurring mechanisms, resulting in the antibiotic (such as penicillin or tetracycline) no longer being toxic to the bacteria.

Anthrax Vaccine Adsorbed, however, induces the inoculated individual to produce antibodies against protective antigen, which also is a protein. In order for anthrax to develop a resistance to the vaccine, the bacteria's genetic code for protective antigen would have to be altered in such a way so the bacteria produces an altered version of protective antigen that the antibodies cannot recognize, but the protective antigen would still have to retain its functional ability to combine with the host's cells and the other anthrax toxins (which are also proteins made by anthrax bacteria) to produce disease.

An adversary intent on producing a strain of anthrax resistant to AVA would, therefore, need to possess highly sophisticated and very expensive genetic engineering capabilities. Needless to say, any genetics program intended to alter anthrax to change the characteristics of protective antigen would be a monumental undertaking and well beyond the reach of most potential adversaries. Not surprisingly, there is no documentation that a strain of anthrax consistently resistant to the vaccine in all species has been produced.[107]

At Dover Air Force Base, Delaware, the number of individuals reporting adverse reactions after inoculation with the anthrax vaccine appears to exceed the rate one would expect based on the published literature. A list of many of the symptoms reported can be found on the World Wide Web.[108] There are several problems, however, trying to make a connection between these symptoms and the vaccine. First of all, there is no discernible pattern to the symptoms. The time of onset between vaccination and the onset of symptoms is highly variable, ranging from a few hours to months. The listings on the Web site do not indicate if these patients got better except in one or two cases.

From a statistical perspective, after almost forty years of clinical experience with AVA, plus several studies documenting its safety, why would there be this sudden cluster of cases at Dover? By way of contrast, the USAMRIID tracked 1,590 individuals who received 10,451 doses of the vaccine over several years, documenting rates of adverse events no higher than those listed in the FDA package insert and no loss of duty.[109] With no recurrent pattern of symptoms and no consistent temporal relation of the development of symptoms to inoculation with the vaccine it is extremely difficult to claim the cases at Dover prove the vaccine is the cause.[110] In addition, the rate of occurrence of any disease (for example thyroid disease) in vaccinated personnel at Dover is equal to or less than the rate of occurrence of the same disease in unvaccinated individuals, and the rate of occurrence of individual symptoms in personnel vaccinated is no higher than the rate expected when vaccinating personnel with any other vaccine, further complicating claims that the anthrax vaccine caused the symptoms.[111]

Without a doubt, it would be wrong to trivialize the symptoms these patients are experiencing. The symptoms are very real and must be addressed in a compassionate, professional manner. But the fact that these individuals are having symptoms and the fact that they received shots does not prove that the vaccine caused the symptoms. In contrast, it is more likely these individuals would have developed the symptoms from which they currently suffer even if they had not received the vaccine.

One writer goes so far as to suggest there should not be any vaccinations of Defense Department personnel until an anthrax-based biological weapon is actually used, even though he acknowledges that historical precedence exists to justify concern that anthrax could be used as a political tool.[112] This approach ignores the ready availability of anthrax spores and the potential for weaponization. There are limitations associated with constant use of personal protective gear with gathering intelligence to provide advanced warning of an attack, and no means exists to detect reliably that an attack with anthrax is occurring. Considering that international conventions historically have failed to prevent proliferation of biological weapons and that it takes time for an individual to develop an immunity against anthrax after vaccination, it becomes apparent that waiting until an attack is imminent before immunizing personnel would not only be ineffective but dangerous.[113] Consequently, immunization against anthrax before an attack becomes imminent is still our best proactive defense to protect personnel from attacks using anthrax-based biological weapons.

There are also allegations that the Defense Department is not doing enough to document the occurrence of reactions or side effects due to vaccination. These allegations are highly critical of the effectiveness and accuracy of the Vaccine Adverse Events Reporting System (hereafter, called the "reporting system") data claiming that the rate of reporting to the reporting system by DOD healthcare workers is low. Some allege health-care workers and physicians were ordered not to report any but the most severe reactions and not to report any symptoms or reactions not specifically listed in the FDA package insert for the vaccine. There is no source or substantiating documentation given for this allegation.

The purpose of the reporting system is to gather ongoing, long-term data on potential adverse reactions due to vaccines that were not identified during limited clinical trials. For example, if the incidence of a particular reaction or severe systemic effect occurring is one in a million, then several hundred thousand or even several million doses may have to be administered before that reaction would be observed. In reality, such extensive, long-term studies are not possible during clinical trials. Furthermore, if evidence exists that the vaccine will prevent more disease and save more lives than any harm caused by the vaccine, it may be regarded as unethical to withhold the vaccine from market to conduct long-term studies. The FDA instituted its reporting system to continue to collect data over the long-term, after vaccines are released for sale, to look for extremely rare adverse effects even though initial studies indicate a vaccine is safe and effective.

The reporting system is passive, meaning that individuals must take the initiative to file a report.[114] There is no one that actively calls or surveys vaccinated individuals to see if they developed any symptoms. In some cases, this could be a disadvantage leading to low reporting rates. Also, it is not possible just by using the reporting system data to establish that a particular vaccine actually caused an event, but, through the identification of possible trends over the long-term, this data is useful to direct new clinical studies to establish causality.

Several facets have been built into the reporting system to facilitate gathering all the facts. For example, anyone, including patients and families, may report any symptom suspected to be due to a vaccine. In addition, medical personnel are routinely reminded through extensive educational programs about the reporting system and the need to report. Furthermore, medical personnel are required to report adverse effects due to vaccines to the manufacturer who are then required to report those.[115]

The reporting system receives over 12,000 reports of possible adverse reactions to vaccines each year. Fifteen percent are considered serious, including those that are life-threatening, result in hospitalization, missed work, or permanent disability. It should be noted that for some childhood vaccines, more reports of potential adverse effects from the vaccine are filed each year than the number of reported cases of the disease the vaccine is designed to prevent.[116] This cumulative evidence suggests that, contrary to the criticisms of anthrax vaccine opponents, the reporting system is highly successful.

The Defense Department has reiterated to medical personnel that they should report any events they feel may be due to the anthrax vaccine to the reporting system. There is no documentation that DOD instructed medical personnel to file a report only when they observe the side effects and reactions listed in the FDA package insert.[117] Instead, DOD encourages all medical personnel to report all events potentially thought to be related to AVA and requires them to report to the reporting system all adverse reactions potentially associated with the vaccine resulting in hospitalization or loss of more than twenty-four hours' duty.[118] Additionally, in 1999, the Air Force Surgeon General directed that any adverse events even suspected by medical personnel to be related to the vaccine will be reported to the reporting system.[119] The allegations that DOD physicians are prohibited from filing reports to the reporting system on any potential vaccine-related event are completely unfounded, ignoring the fact that such prohibitions may be illegal.

In spite of the extensive documentation of evidence addressing the safety and efficacy of AVA in humans, concerns over its use continue to be propagated in the media. Many press release articles confuse facts, combine separate facts, or report facts in such a way as to be potentially misleading. For example, an extensive article published in the *Phoenix New Times* stated that anthrax vaccine production had been halted due to problems with the new BioPort production facilities.[120] Actually, the Michigan Biological Products Institute voluntarily halted production in order to renovate the facility, then later sold it to BioPort. After the sale, BioPort completed renovations but had problems obtaining FDA certification of the renovated facility. While both facts are true, they are not directly, nor causally, related to each other as the *Phoenix New Times* article implies. This article also attempts to raise completely unsubstantiated concerns that there could be birth defects if a man who received the vaccine fathers a child.

Another example is an Associated Press article entitled "Food and Drug Administration inspection cites problems in vaccine production."[121] The article correctly stated the problems were with FDA certification of the renovated facilities, required before new batches of the anthrax vaccine may be sold, but the last sentence of the article gives an unrelated fact that several anthrax vaccine lots failed FDA potency testing. The article did not clarify that these were older lots, none of which had been used by the Defense Department and were not related to the problems with FDA certification on BioPort's more recently renovated production facilities. This could lead one not familiar with the facts to believe there was a direct relationship between the FDA inspections and the lots of the vaccine that failed potency testing where, in fact, no such direct relationship exists.

Understanding the debate over the present vaccine, in large part involves understanding the Internet's effect on public opinion and the challenges the Internet presents to those seeking a scientifically rigorous opinion. The informational World Wide Web sites on anthrax have some potential value, but they can also be the source of significant confusion and misinformation. Some individuals on the Internet go so far as to raise questions regarding the legality of anthrax vaccine immunization program, implying military personnel are duty-bound to disobey it and that the DOD immunization program is a violation of their civil rights.[122] It is important to note that many links found on Internet Web sites opposed to the immunization program connect to on-line source documents that do present the facts regarding AVA. These facts are consistent with the clinical and historical evidence presented above and match the information presented on the DOD anthrax informational Web site.[123] The difference is how the facts are interpreted and represented, often taking and quoting documents out of context, and inserting subjective opinions and editorial comments.

One of the most comprehensive World Wide Web sites opposing administration of the vaccine is entitled "Anthrax Vaccine Links and Information" and provides an extensive list of links to other related sites. Included are links to sites with copies of congressional testimonies, Government Accounting Office reports, summaries of the symptoms reported by personnel at Dover Air Force Base who received anthrax shots, press releases, and other documents of interest.[124]

To illustrate the importance of presentation, one title to a link claims the FDA admits it has never received data on the vaccine's effects on long-term health, potentially leading some to believe the data does not exist. This link connects to a letter the FDA wrote to the executive director for Veterans for Integrity in Government.[125] The letter responds to a series of questions, including whether or not any studies on the long-term health effects of the anthrax vaccine have been performed. It states the data has not been submitted to the FDA, but adds the vaccine had (at the time of writing) been used for more than twenty-eight years in veterinarians, laboratory personnel, industrial workers, and FDA inspectors. The clear intent of the answer is that the studies on the long-term health effects of the vaccine have been performed and the data does exist, but it has not been formally submitted to the FDA.

There is also confusion between present DOD vaccine and the British version of the vaccine. Another link on the "Anthrax Vaccine Links and Information" Internet Web site announces there have been British reports of outbreaks of Gulf War Syndrome after "recent" anthrax vaccinations. It references a British article entitled "Anti Bio-weapon Vaccine for Troops Fails

Safety Tests" from an independent British newspaper, which reports newly produced lots of the British anthrax vaccine failed safety tests.[126] The article cites concerns from British Persian Gulf War veterans that the British version of the anthrax vaccine may have caused Gulf War Syndrome and that further use of the vaccine may cause more to develop symptoms. They claim many fell ill after recent vaccinations, but the article provides no substantiating information. The article further alleges the lots used had expired, and the shelf life had been extended several times.[127]

This link is misleading because the article is about the British version of anthrax vaccine. The British version of anthrax vaccine is not the U.S. vaccine. It is not produced either by Michigan Biological Products Institute or BioPort, does not require FDA licensure, and is not used in the United States. Furthermore, the FDA and British regulatory systems are completely separate. Yet the adversarial Internet site contains no statements to make this distinction.

Many who are opposed to the DOD immunization program have attempted to connect the vaccine with Gulf War Syndrome in spite of the fact that no such causal relationship has ever been demonstrated.[128]

Other links seem intended to provoke an emotional response, such as one with photographs of injection sites with signs of local reactions entitled "Painful Anthrax injection site photos . . . OUCH!" Others refer to the numerous cases of individuals at Dover Air Force Base who claim to have developed symptoms after receiving the vaccine, claiming this proves DOD really knows that the vaccine is not safe. There are also links to support groups and online chat rooms where those opposed to the immunization program may discuss their views or tell their story.

Interestingly, there are also links to other sites opposed to the use of other types of vaccines (e.g., hepatitis B vaccine) or all vaccines in general. This suggests that those opposed to the use of anthrax vaccine are part of a larger movement opposed to the use of all vaccines.

At the forefront of the opposition to the DOD's anthrax vaccine program is an emergency room physician from Maine Dr. Meryl Nass. She has written a number of articles and testified before Congress several times against the anthrax vaccine program and is regarded by opponents to the Anthrax Vaccine Immunization Program as an expert on the vaccine. For example, one link on the "Anthrax Vaccine Links and Information" site makes the claim that DOD officials really do know the anthrax vaccine is not safe. It turns out the link leads to an unpublished article written by Dr. Nass about an informational meeting for one hundred physicians at Fort Detrick in May 1999, where issues about the anthrax vaccine were discussed. Her article implies that military physicians asking policy questions about AVA and Vaccine Adverse Events Reporting System proves the Defense Department does know AVA is not safe. She ends by admonishing the readers to contact their congressional representatives.

Dr. Nass also has her own informational World Wide Web home page about anthrax.[129] The "Anthrax Vaccine Links and Information" site lists her credentials, which includes three years experience studying the anthrax outbreak in Zimbabwe.[130] She is quoted as saying as many as 10 percent of those receiving AVA have gotten sick, although there is no explanation of what that means—whether the symptoms were mild, moderate, severe, localized, or systemic.[131]

In 1999, Dr. Nass published an article reviewing the anthrax vaccine and its potential protective value against a biological attack with weaponized anthrax.[132] While extensively researched and documented, she cites sources that are of questionable veracity. For example, she alleges the Defense Department may have attempted to increase the potency of AVA by secretly adding squalene, citing herself as the source by referring to a letter she wrote to the Army Surgeon General in May 1998.[133] Based on this allegation, she implies a potential connection between Gulf War Syndrome and Defense Department vaccination programs, including AVA, which is the basis for most of the concern with the safety and efficacy of AVA.

She also states in this article "the present human anthrax vaccine probably provides only limited protection for troops facing a BW [*sic*] attack by anthrax."[134] She bases this assertion on the lack of controlled studies in humans that investigate the clinical effectiveness of the vaccine against inhalation anthrax during a biological attack. Yet she presents no clinical data of her own to substantiate her claim that the vaccine may not be effective in preventing inhalation anthrax after a biological attack. In other words, in her opinion, the more than thirty years of clinical data from field trials of anthrax vaccine in workers exposed to anthrax, the absence of inhalation anthrax in the workplace since 1978, and the animal studies that demonstrate AVA's effectiveness in preventing inhalation anthrax are not enough to conclude that the present vaccine may prevent inhalation anthrax after an attack. Instead, she implies the only way to justify using the vaccine to protect against inhalation anthrax would be to design and conduct a study in which humans are deliberately exposed to aerosolized anthrax spores.

No vaccine is perfect, meaning that none is 100 percent safe and effective. But, as has been presented, the clinical evidence suggests that the current anthrax vaccine is safe and effective—probably safer with lower rates of side effects than other vaccines in use today. FDA recently agreed with an expert panel's recommendation to approve the vaccine as safe and effective.[135] That does not mean there is no room for improvement regarding vaccinations against anthrax.[136] The requirement for six inoculations does create a significant logistical problem, especially as supplies of currently retested and approved lots of vaccine run low. But the current requirement for six inoculations is in accordance with the FDA ruling and probably won't change unless studies are done to confirm the vaccine provides protection with fewer doses. Newer vaccines that require fewer doses to confer immunity have been developed but have not been approved for use by the FDA.[137] The 30 percent rate of occurrence of local reactions ideally could be lower, although this rate is already lower than other vaccines currently required by DOD.

A major challenge is how to demonstrate an individual has developed adequate immunity against anthrax after vaccination either with the present or a newer anthrax vaccine without exposing the individual to aerosolized anthrax spores. As discussed previously, it is not ethical to expose individuals to aerosolized anthrax spores to see if the vaccine prevents development of inhalation anthrax. Using animal models may or may not be useful since species differ in their sensitivity to anthrax, and differences in their immune systems may alter the efficacy with which anthrax vaccines confer immunity. Measuring the level of antibodies an individual has circulating in the blood against protective antigen has been shown to be a very unreliable measurement of immunity against anthrax. The next best approach would be to develop a test that could be administered to the individual to indicate the degree of immunity. Currently no such test exists, which is one reason why the FDA recommends a series of six shots of AVA with an annual booster. With such a test, individuals could be screened and only those with inadequate immune responses would require supplemental inoculations, potentially decreasing the required number of doses of vaccine.

It should be reiterated, however, that even though there is room for improvement, none of these issues negates the current value and effectiveness of the vaccine. The risk from taking the vaccine is far less than the risk of being a target in a bioterrorist event or biological warfare attack.

Dr. Nass believes there should be more emphasis on using alternatives to vaccination with AVA to protect troops from anthrax. For example, she suggests there should be more emphasis on the use of protective equipment. The problem with this approach is, due to the lack of real-time detection capability, there is no way for personnel to know when they need to wear the protective equipment, meaning they would have to wear it continually to be effective. Dr. Nass also expresses concern that immunizing troops against anthrax may provoke an adversary to simply pick another biological agent.[138] As previously discussed, other biological agents are more difficult to weaponize, and the likelihood that other agents would be used in an attack instead of anthrax is much lower.[139]

Lieutenant General (retired) James T. Scott recently wrote an editorial that, arguably, does more to place the entire controversy over DOD's anthrax vaccination into proper perspective than any other work examined in this paper.[140] He states that both sides share the blame for escalating this debate out of proportions. Officials from the Defense Department could have done better stating their case for a comprehensive vaccination program in peacetime. DOD's credibility had already been damaged by how it handled the Agent Orange and Gulf War Syndrome issues. This problem is exacerbated by the chronic underfunding of the military health-care system, which is eroding what little confidence beneficiaries may have in military healthcare, and the Defense Department failure to anticipate the effect the Internet would have on spreading disinformation campaigns against the Anthrax Vaccine Immunization Program.

To the opponents who are also service members, Scott writes that it is time to find out the facts. He states service members concerned over the immunization program should be sure the information they possess is based on solid facts. He admonishes them to ask themselves if they are only concerned with the safety and efficacy of AVA or if their concerns run much deeper—that their opposition to the Anthrax Vaccine Immunization Program may reflect that they have lost complete confidence in the military system. If so, it may be time for them to resign.

To military leaders and supervisors, he says the controversy over the DOD's vaccine program is not a test of leadership. The ability to talk subordinates into vaccination versus court-martialing those who refuse is a false test and misses the point. The real issue is how they will restore their subordinates' confidence in the mission, the chain of command, the unit, and each other. This confidence should be based on "rational explanations based on credible evidence."[141] In an all-volunteer force of such high quality people, the "men and women who serve in our armed forces deserve no less."[142]

CONCLUSIONS AND RECOMMENDATIONS

The current anthrax vaccine is a licensed vaccine and has been demonstrated to be clinically safe and effective for preventing inhalation anthrax after exposure to anthrax spores. Based on the findings of the 1985 advisory review panel examining the safety and efficacy of the vaccine, the FDA categorized the vaccine as a "Category 1 (safe, effective, and not misbranded) vaccine."[143] On December 30, 2003, the FDA announced its final order on the AVA, stating it was "safe and effective for the prevention of anthrax disease—regardless of the route of exposure."[144] In spite of the existing documentation of its safety and efficacy, DOD continues to ask outside consultants and panels to review the evidence documenting the safety and efficacy of the vaccine. For example, the Defense Department asked the Institute of

Medicine to review all available data on AVA.[145] One would be hard pressed to identify another vaccine in use today that has undergone more scrutiny than Anthrax Vaccine Adsorbed.

There are significant issues with AVA that should be addressed, including the current dosage regimen, the inability to specifically measure the level of immunity an individual may already possess, and the occurrence of local reactions in 30 percent of those who are vaccinated. In spite of these issues, there is no clinical evidence that DOD's program is considered to be at risk for exposure to anthrax. The risk of serious adverse reactions or permanent injury from the anthrax vaccine is no higher than (and, in fact, is probably lower than) that for any other vaccine commonly in use in the general population today. In contrast, the risks to military personnel from the threat of attack with an anthrax-based biological weapon, plus the high lethality of inhalation anthrax, far outweigh the risks associated with vaccination.

The USAMRIID completed preclinical research on a next-generation anthrax vaccine several years ago. The new recombinant vaccine is now in advanced clinical development. Unfortunately, FDA approval of a new vaccine is still several years away. In the meantime, long-term data collection studies should continue in order to document further the safety of AVA and attempt to identify extremely rare adverse effects that may only become apparent after millions of doses of vaccine have been administered. The Defense Department should also continue with programs to provide long-term follow-up to individuals claiming to have developed symptoms after receiving the anthrax vaccine. These patients' symptoms are real, and they deserve compassionate, professional medical care.

Continuance of the anthrax vaccine program should include an aggressive, active educational and informational program designed to address concerns at all levels, from the top leadership down to the installation level. The Defense Department Web site and its links to other service-specific Web sites are excellent but passive, meaning they depend on people going to these sites to get the facts. What is needed is an active education program where information is actively taken out to the troops.

The DOD programs actively promoting education of all military personnel, using the information on the Internet Web site, could significantly alleviate the suspicions and doubts currently surrounding the anthrax vaccine immunization program. Commander and supervisor involvement at every level of command is essential to rebuilding the confidence military personnel should have in their chains of command. Commanders and supervisors also should be aware of the biased nature of informational Web sites opposed to the program, emphasizing to their personnel the importance of basing any conclusions about the vaccine or the anthrax vaccine immunization program on all the facts. Such proactive educational efforts should prove useful to reverse any negative trends and perceptions emanating from DOD's handling of the Agent Orange and Gulf War Syndrome issues. The Anthrax Vaccine Immunization Program should be viewed as an opportunity for the DOD to demonstrate its commitment to maintaining the health and safety of service personnel while countering any threat to our nation's security from anthrax-based mass-casualty weapons.

CHAPTER 6

Smallpox: A Primer

Brenda J. McEleney

Smallpox is a virus that has plagued humanity for millennia. It was the first and only disease ever intentionally eradicated from the face of this planet, a scourge defeated in a remarkable, never-before-attempted campaign of generosity and cooperation by the nations of the world. Its eradication was a triumphant symbol of science and dogged persistence winning over nature. Moreover, its eradication was a gift to all mankind.

Yet, is it possible that the same hand of man that once rid the scourge of smallpox from the world will be used to unleash this terror again on its unprotected citizens? This chapter, by providing a thorough review of the history, epidemiology, and current risks associated with this dreaded disease, addresses that question and its implications for the American public.

ORIGINS OF SMALLPOX

Smallpox has been described as one of the great scourges of mankind.[1] Every corner of the world has felt its grip and known its devastation. Historians speculate that smallpox first appeared around 10,000 B.C. in the agricultural settlements in northeastern Africa. From there, it probably spread to India via Egyptian merchants. There is evidence that smallpox is at least three thousand years old. It was known in China as early as 1122 B.C. Its scars have been found on the mummy of Pharaoh Ramses V, who died in 1157 B.C., as well as on other mummies from the eighteenth and twentieth Egyptian dynasties.[2,3]

The first known smallpox epidemic was recorded in 1350 B.C. During the Egyptian-Hittite war that year, Egyptian prisoners unwittingly spread smallpox to the Hittites. Even the Hittite King Suppiluliumus I and his heir fell victim to the virus. It devastated their civilization and ensured the Egyptians victory.[4]

Records also show the ancients recognized subsequent immunity in those who survived the disease. Thucydidus noted this curiosity during the Athenian epidemic in 430 B.C. Rhazes, considered the greatest physician of Islam and the Medieval Ages, likewise documented postinfection immunity in A.D. 910, when he recorded the first known medical description of smallpox and its transmission.[5]

Insidiously, smallpox made its way around the world leaving devastation in its wake. The Crusades, the expansion of the Arab world, and the colonization of the Americas—wherever an infected individual came in contact with peoples previously unexposed—contributed to the spread of smallpox. Smallpox reached Europe in the fifth century and was a leading cause of death in the sixteenth and seventeenth centuries. It affected everyone, regardless of age, sex, or socioeconomic status. The commoners of Europe were hit particularly hard. An estimated four hundred thousand died from smallpox every year during the eighteenth century. One-third of the survivors were scarred and many were blinded.[6]

In the 1500s, the Spanish and Portuguese transported the disease to the New World, where it decimated the Aztec and Inca populations in Mexico and South America. Likewise in North America, European colonizers carried the smallpox virus that devastated the native populations there. Sadly, the first documented use of smallpox as a weapon can be attributed to the British, who gave blankets contaminated with smallpox to troublesome American Indians in Quebec in the late eighteenth century to intentionally expose them to the virus.[7]

Not only common folk succumbed to smallpox. The famous and powerful who died from smallpox includes Marcus Aurelius in A.D. 180, King Boranarja IV of Siam in 1534, William II of Orange in 1650, Emperor Gokomyo of Japan in 1654, Queen Mary II of England in 1694, King Nagassi of Ethiopia in 1700, Tsar Peter II of Russia in 1730, and King Louis XV of France in 1774. It is said that President Lincoln was feverish with smallpox when he gave the Gettysburg Address in 1863. Two days afterward, he broke out with the trademark rash.[8, 9]

EPIDEMIOLOGY

Smallpox is a viral disease unique to humans. Highly contagious, it predominantly spreads person to person via inhalation of submicron water droplets (to which viral particles attach) exhaled by infected individuals. However, as with common-cold viruses, the smallpox virus can be introduced into the human body by touching a contaminated object, then subsequently touching one's nose or mouth with the contaminated hand. The virus is not known to enter a body directly through the skin. There is no known animal or insect reservoir or vector.

There are two principal forms of the virus—variola major and, a milder form, variola minor. Variola major historically "resulted in case fatality rates of 30 percent or higher among the unvaccinated [3 percent in the vaccinated], whereas variola minor case-fatality rates were customarily 1 percent or less."[10]

People with smallpox were most contagious from the onset of their papular rash through the first seven to ten days of the rash. Approximately 30 percent of susceptible contacts came down with the disease. As scabs formed, respiratory infectivity waned, but patients were considered contagious until all scabs separated.[11]

The first symptoms of natural infection occurred usually ten to fourteen days after exposure with severe aching, malaise, prostration, headache, backache, and fever. Two to three days later, a macropapular rash appeared on the mucosa of the mouth and pharynx, face, and forearms. The rash then spread to the trunk and legs. Lesions quickly progressed to pustular vesicles. Fever remained throughout the course of the disease, and pain was common as the pustules evolved. About eight to fourteen days after onset, scabs formed and later separated, leaving a pitted complexion. Death usually occurred during the second week. The only way to prevent the spread of smallpox was patient isolation and vaccination.[12, 13, 14]

VARIOLATION AS INOCULATION

Survivors of smallpox—the "speckled monster" in the eighteenth century vernacular—were known to have immunity. For this reason, doctors and others intentionally exposed healthy people to the disease in hopes that they too would become immune. They collected samples from vesicles, pus from pustules, or scabs and introduced them into the nose or skin of healthy humans. This method of inoculation, or "variolation" as it was first called, is believed by some to have originated in China.[15] Mountain hermits there are known to have used smallpox inoculation as early as the tenth century B.C.[16] It became widely popular in China during the period from 1567 to 1572. "In fact, it seems that the operation [of variolation] had been practiced quite discreetly in numerous African countries, in India, in China, and even in Europe for a long time."[17] It was during the seventeenth century that the practice of variolation spread to the Ottoman Empire, where it became common practice.

Lady Mary Wortley Montague, the wife of a British ambassador to the Sublime Porte in the Ottoman Empire, introduced variolation to England.[18] She was a survivor of smallpox, which had disfigured her beautiful face. Because of her personal experience with the disease, the Turkish preventive practice of "engrafting" fascinated her. This procedure entailed making four or five scratches or a puncture in the arm and introducing material from smallpox pustules. To prevent her five-year-old son from getting smallpox, she had him variolated in 1718. After returning to England in 1721, she had her four-year-old daughter immunized in the presence of the king's court doctor. News of the inoculation spread. The procedure was tested in 1721 on six prisoners sentenced to death and six orphaned children and, in 1722, two daughters of the Princess of Wales were variolated. All developed immunity to the virus.[19]

Variolation was the only known way to prevent the spread of smallpox. However, intentionally introducing smallpox virus into the skin could be harmful, if not deadly. Over time, practitioners used a variety of practices to prepare their patients, such as taking of blood, enemas, and strict diet with purging. Edward Jenner, the British physician who developed the first smallpox vaccination, described his preparation for variolation when he was eight years old: "there was taking of blood until the blood was thin; purging until the body was wasted to a skeleton; and starving on a vegetable diet to keep it so."[20] This preparation took two to four weeks, followed by ten to fifteen days of actual sickness from side effects. The effects were severe enough to keep the patient in bed, and convalescence took up to one month.[21] Complicating the process was that inoculation could be fatal. About two people died for every one hundred variolated.[22]

Even with the high risks, variolation spread throughout Europe. While not everyone could afford to receive the inoculation, nobility in Austria, Prussia, France, and Russia were variolated. The procedure soon reached the New World. In 1721, it was used to stop an epidemic in Boston. Now variolation quickly spread throughout the colonies. In 1776, the colonial soldiers under George Washington failed to take Quebec from England because a smallpox epidemic had cut their numbers in half; the British were saved because they had received inoculation. By 1777, Washington ordered all his soldiers variolated. To prevent another epidemic, he also had all new recruits immunized as soon as they entered duty.[23, 24]

ERA OF VACCINATION

Back in England, milkmaids became the unlikely subjects of rudimentary medical research. It had been observed that milkmaids tended to escape outbreaks of smallpox unaffected. Edward Jenner suspected a connection between the pox marks (caused by cowpox) on the milkmaids' hands and their immunity to smallpox. In 1796, Jenner inoculated an eight-year-old boy, John Phipps, with the cowpox virus. Six weeks later, he vaccinated the same boy with smallpox. The boy did not get sick. He repeated the procedure months later with the same results. The boy was immune. Jenner had discovered a crude smallpox vaccine.[25]

Jenner tried to publish his discovery through the Philosophical Transactions of the Royal Society, but the society rejected his "incredible" ideas.

Finally, he resorted to publishing his findings himself, and titled it "An inquiry into the causes and effects of the *variolae* vaccine, a disease discovered in some of the western counties of England, particularly Gloucestershire, and known by the name of the cow pox."[26] While not initially accepted, vaccination with cowpox pustule fluid was eventually tested and confirmed. The era of smallpox vaccination had arrived.[27]

By 1800, vaccination had permeated most of Europe and America, with about one hundred thousand people vaccinated worldwide. Over the next 150 years, healthcare providers all over the world gradually adopted vaccination. Nevertheless, the disease persisted where people went unvaccinated. As late as the 1930s, smallpox infected up to fifty thousand people a year in the United States. An epidemic even broke out in 1947 in New York City when a businessman traveling from Mexico brought smallpox into the city. Within a couple of weeks, thirteen people died. Massive hysteria occurred, and the city vaccinated six million residents. The last case in the United States occurred in 1949 in Hidalgo County, Texas. Nevertheless, the rest of the world continued to experience smallpox well into the 1970s.[28, 29, 30]

ERADICATION

In 1953, the newly created World Health Organization (WHO) suggested that smallpox be eradicated from the human race. They tried again in 1958. Little progress occurred until 1967 when the Union of Soviet Socialist Republics and the United States gave $2.5 million to fund the initiative. D.A. Henderson of the Centers for Disease Control and Prevention headed the campaign. Its goal was to interrupt, permanently, the chain of transmission of smallpox.[31]

When the eradication campaign began, smallpox was endemic to five regions of the world—South America, West and East Africa, India, and Indonesia. The plan was to go to each region and vaccinate the entire population there, but the effort quickly ran short of vaccine. A more economical approach was designed. Surveillance and containment became the new plan of attack. It focused on currently infected households. The process involved finding a case of smallpox, isolating the patient, and vaccinating all the people in contact with or within a short distance, or ring, of the patient. Then medical workers extended the ring of vaccination to a practical distance. They called the process surveillance and containment, or ring vaccination.

The search was enormous. Every single case of smallpox had to be hunted down by a determined medical professional or volunteer. Nevertheless, the strategy worked with dramatic results. By 1971, Latin America was free of smallpox. Indonesia and South Africa followed closely behind. India, next on the list, was a huge success story. In 1973, WHO volunteers traveled to every village in the country. More than 120,000 healthcare workers visited over one hundred million homes. Eighteen months later, smallpox was gone.[32, 33]

The last two remaining strongholds for smallpox were Bangladesh and East Africa. In 1975, the battle in Bangladesh was won.[34] Through 1977, smallpox persisted in the region of Ethiopia, Kenya, and Somalia. The last case in Ethiopia was diagnosed in August 1976; the last in Kenya was February 1977. As for Somalia, the WHO staff and epidemiologists rooted out the last known case of smallpox on October 26, 1977. With the victim in isolation, the chain of transmission was finally broken.[35]

The WHO needed two years with no further reports of smallpox to declare success. Three cases of smallpox did develop in 1978 at the Medical School at the University of Birmingham in England, due to careless handling of the virus stored in its laboratory. However, by the fall of 1979, it was clear that no further natural cases of smallpox were to be found. On May 8, 1980, WHO declared smallpox eradicated.[36]

THE VIRUS LIVES ON

Smallpox may have been eradicated, but its etiological agent, the variola virus itself, continued to exist in many laboratories around the world. The incident in Birmingham in 1978 and the high transmissibility potential of the virus flagged the need for stricter controls. The WHO recommended that all laboratories storing the virus destroy their stocks or transfer them to two WHO-sanctioned, high-security laboratories. These laboratories are currently the Russian State Center for Research on Virology and Biotechnology in Koltsovo, Novosibirsk (Siberia) and the Centers for Disease Control and Prevention (CDC) in Atlanta, Georgia.[37, 38] These are the only two locations in the world where the virus is known to still exist.

Variola has been on death row for years. Three times, the Assembly of WHO recommended dates by which all stocks of the virus should be destroyed—December 31, 1993; June 30, 1995; and June 30, 1999. Each time, as the dates for destruction drew near, scientists, medical providers, and world leaders began to question the prudence of destroying the last of the variola virus. Those in favor of destruction argue the risk of a virus release outweighs the research benefits the live virus provides. They contend the smallpox virus must be destroyed so it can never again threaten mankind. Those who favor maintaining the virus believe the stocks are a counterbalance to terrorism and a source of future research. On May 22, 1999, the Assembly of the WHO granted variola its latest stay of execution, until 2002, to determine if the live virus is still required for research.[39, 40]

VACCINATION AND DIMINISHED PROTECTION OVER TIME

Vaccination with vaccinia was the modern way to protect against smallpox. With its eradication in 1980, the WHO recommended all countries cease vaccinating their citizens.

In the United States, healthcare officials had already stopped vaccination. Because of the implementation of worldwide vaccination and quarantine programs, "the risk of importation of smallpox into the United States was reduced by the 1960s. Consequently, United States discontinued routine, public smallpox vaccination in 1972."[41] Additionally, the vaccination of healthcare professionals and international travelers was discontinued in 1982. That same year, the only active, licensed producer of the vaccine ended production for general use. Finally, in July 1988, the military stopped routine smallpox vaccinations. Consequently, since 1972, very few American citizens have been immunized with vaccinia. This makes our population potentially susceptible to smallpox.[42, 43]

Studies show that receiving one dose of the vaccine provides more than 95 percent of the recipients an antibody titer level of at least 1:10, furnishing protection against smallpox infection. This same level of immunity was found in 75 percent of those receiving a second dose and for up to thirty years for those receiving three doses. While the antibody level that protects against smallpox is unknown, research studies suggest that immunity lasts from five to ten years and lengthens with additional boosters.[44, 45] Substantial but waning immunity may persist in some individuals for more than ten years.[46] Experts generally agree that smallpox vaccinations do not protect an individual for life. Because people born before 1972 received only one shot, it is safe to assume most no longer have any immunity. In essence, this means all U.S. citizens are dangerously susceptible to smallpox.

When the eradication program ended, a number of countries along with the WHO stored enough vaccine for about two hundred million people.[47] The WHO retained only five hundred thousand doses. The U.S. stockpile until very recently consisted of only 15.4 million doses.[48]

Wyeth Laboratories produced the reserve stock of U.S. vaccine in the 1970s. While it is stored at –20° C to preserve its potency, time has taken its toll. Rubber stoppers on vials have begun to crumble, and the vaccine's brilliant green dye has begun to lose its color. CDC officials purport that potency of the vaccine in the vials is nearly at full strength.[49] But Peter Jahling at the U.S. Army Medical Research Institute of Infectious Diseases (USAMRIID) in Frederick, Maryland, says, "50 percent of those doses are thought to be flawed."[50] These vials failed quality control tests because of elevated moisture levels, bringing into question the actual potency of the vaccine. To make matters worse, the stocks of vaccinia immune globulin, the antidote used to treat complications related to vaccination, has turned from clear to pink because the dye from rubber stoppers had leaked into the vials.

Since the anthrax attacks after September 11, 2001, steps have been taken to bolster U.S. defenses against smallpox. In response to this inadequate supply of vaccine, the U.S. government awarded a contract in November 2001 to two companies, Acambis PLC and Baxter Inc., to produce 209 million more doses of smallpox vaccine. Additionally, on March 29, 2002, Aventis Pasteur, a French drug company with operations in Swiftwater, Pennsylvania, announced it had discovered eighty-five million doses of vaccine that had been in storage for years. The vaccine is apparently safe and was donated to the U.S. government.[51, 52, 53] Research has shown that the vaccine can be safely diluted by at least five-fold. With dilution of the existing vaccine and the addition of vaccines from Acambis PLC and Baxter Inc., the U.S. vaccine stockpile will soon rise to over 350 million doses.

U.S. RESPONSE

In response to the concerns noted above, the Department of Defense (DOD) and National Institutes for Health (NIH) have recently stepped up research efforts. Their goals are to develop a new vaccine and replace the current vaccinia immune globulin. In 1996, the DOD started funneling money toward the production of a stockpile of vaccine.[54] USAMRIID, in conjunction with the Salk Institute of Swiftwater, Pennsylvania, had previously adapted the calf-lymph vaccinia vaccine to modern cell-culture production methods and has now conducted some safety and immunogenicity testing in human volunteers. In 1999, with the increased concern about terrorist use of smallpox and the dwindling supply of vaccine, DOD and the Health and Human Services (HHS) began parallel programs to produce more vaccine using the cell-culture process.

In October 1999, NIH initiated an effort to improve civilian defense against bioterrorism. The goal was to address civilian needs not addressed by DOD. They requested research proposals in three areas: (1) discovering and supplying drugs for mass treatment of and/or prevention of smallpox infection,[55] (2) collecting and analyzing the genomes of pox viruses and then providing the information to others through a Web site,[56] and (3) developing a new antidote against vaccinia complications.[57]

On December 13, 2002, the President announced the U.S. smallpox vaccination program. The program called for the creation of Smallpox Response teams made up of healthcare professionals ready to provide assistance in the event of an outbreak. The U.S. military will be required to vaccinate a portion of its members, and civilian healthcare and emergency response members will be offered the vaccine on a voluntary basis. Phase II of the plan will involve offering vaccinations to police, fire, emergency medical technicians and selected others. The implementation of this program has had varied success from state to state.[58, 59, 60]

IMPLICATIONS

Over the past decade, there has been increasing concern that rogue states and terrorists could use smallpox as a weapon. Its potential availability and natural lethality as well as our susceptibility and inadequate stockpiles of deteriorating vaccine make it potentially a very deadly weapon. The potential impact of the intentional release of smallpox is so great that in February 1999, USAMRIID personnel reported smallpox as one of "the two greatest [biological agents] with the greatest potential for mass casualties and civil disruption."[61] Because it could cause the most potential harm if used, CDC moved smallpox to the top of its bioterrorism threat list.[62]

A great fear is that the virus may exist outside the high-security storage laboratories in Atlanta and Siberia. Ken Alibek, a defector who was the former deputy director of the Soviet bioweapons program, reports Russia's smallpox weaponization program was active up until 1992 when President Yeltsin ordered it to end. With the collapse of the Soviet Union, scientists working in the program may have sold samples of the virus or hidden them for later sale to support themselves.[63] A recent unclassified intelligence report concluded that Iraq, North Korea, and Russia may possess the deadly smallpox virus possibly for military use.[64] This assessment was based on information from a senior Soviet defector, blood samples from North Korean soldiers, and Iraq's manufacture of smallpox vaccine.

The susceptibility of our population is equally worrisome. As of 1998, it has been estimated that 42 percent of Americans have never received a smallpox vaccination and less than 15 percent of the population is immune.[65] While the mortality of those in close contact to the virus could be 30 percent, the morbidity, or rate of incidence, would range from 60 to 90 percent.[66] A release of smallpox would be cause for worldwide alarm. It is highly contagious and very stable in the environment. International airline travelers could unknowingly spread the virus around the world within days. Healthcare systems could be overwhelmed if an outbreak were not contained early. Most healthcare providers would not have immunity. Most negative pressure hospital rooms would fill quickly. Citizens would probably insist on vaccination but current stocks will not meet the demand. Municipal plans for dealing with an outbreak are surely shallow, where they exist at all.[67]

Finally, variola's attributes make it one of the most feared biological terrorist or warfare weapon. Outbreaks in Europe in the 1970s illustrate its potential. In the 1970s German outbreaks, as many as ten to twenty second-generation cases resulted from one case.[68] An outbreak occurred in Yugoslavia two years later, in spite of routine vaccination; the first case infected eleven other people, and these eleven each infected an average of thirteen more people.[69] One can only speculate on the extent of an outbreak today when so many people have not been vaccinated and those who have, have retained little immunity. In addition, the worldwide epidemic of HIV-AIDS has both increased the highly susceptible population, since smallpox was eradicated, and would now make mass vaccination almost impossible.

As grave as the situation may seem, there are sources who argue the likelihood of a targeted release of smallpox is relatively small. Terrorists may be able to obtain the virus with state sponsorship and release it covertly, but there has been little interest in biological terrorist weapons historically. W. Seth Carus's review of unclassified terrorist interests, both domestic and international, in biological warfare since the 1950s provided four conclusions:[70]

1. Only a few terrorists have attempted to acquire biological agents and fewer have attempted to use them.
2. The number of incidents involving use or attempted use of biological agents is extremely small, especially when compared to the thousands of known terrorists.
3. The number of known victims from unclassified terrorist attacks is limited to the 751 people who became sick during the 1984 Rashneeshee salad bar attacks. There were no known fatalities.[71] [Aum Shinrikyo, a Japan-based religious cult, produced biological agents and tried to use them. . . . Fortunately, the Aum scientists apparently made mistakes in either the way they produced or disseminated the agents, and so far as is known, no one became ill or died as a result of the biological attacks.[72] The fatalities from Aum Shinrikyo's terrorist attacks on the Tokyo subway system resulted from the chemical agent sarin.]
4. To date, the relatively few terrorist groups that have attempted to use biological weapons have used crude dispensing technology, and with the exception of the late 2001 anthrax attacks in the United States, have used poorly prepared or poor quality biological or chemical agents incapable of inflicting mass casualties. Aum Shinrikyo and the perpetrator(s) of the anthrax-through-the-mail attacks in the United States in late 2001 were the only groups known to have an interest in developing an aerosol capability, and the Japanese cult's biological weapons program has been neutralized.

There are number of factors given to explain the infrequent use of biological agents by terrorists. They include:

1. Dependence on meteorological conditions makes agent delivery unpredictable.
2. Terrorists may fear for their own safety due to the potential for infecting themselves.
3. Terrorists may prefer a more precise weapon for their selected targets.
4. Terrorists may have moral qualms about using biological weapons.
5. Conventional weapons are easier to obtain and employ and may be considered adequate.
6. State sponsors may understand the implication of bioterrorism and promote restraint.
7. There is little precedence for the use of biological agents as terrorist weapons.
8. The technological constraints of obtaining, producing, and dispensing noncontagious agent are significant.[73]

Essentially, there are numerous hurdles to overcome to use smallpox as a weapon. Nevertheless, as long as the variola virus exists in any form—natural or engineered—the threat will be real. Whether the threat is small or large, it is prudent to require more study and research in all facets of a viable defense against the recurrence of smallpox.

CONCLUSION

Smallpox—has it been defeated and eradicated? Or will it be used as a weapon of terror or war? Information derived from unclassified intelligence sources report that smallpox may indeed be in the hands of a few rogue states. Fortunately, one of those states, Iraq, is no longer a threat. The population of the United States, as well of the rest of the world, is all too susceptible to such a smallpox attack were it to occur. While the actual level of the threat can be debated, the consequences of the use of smallpox as a biological weapon would be overwhelming. Once released, smallpox is not only dangerous, it is currently practically unstoppable.[74] Our population, at the moment, is seriously vulnerable.

Steps in the right direction are beginning with President Bush's smallpox vaccination program which includes improving medical surveillance and other means of strengthening our public health infrastructure, development of a modern smallpox vaccine, and production of much larger quantities of vaccine than now exist in the stockpile of the present vaccine. Other important steps should include development of new antiviral drugs, improved diagnostics, and the expansion of education and a stronger tech base research program for medical defense. To do less than this would leave us dangerously vulnerable to future use of smallpox as an adversary weapon of terror or war.

CHAPTER 7

The Prospects for Biological War in the Middle East

Brad Roberts

INTRODUCTION

The proliferation of biological weapons to states in the Middle East has raised questions about whether, when, and how such weapons might be used there.[1] In the absence of systematic investigation of these questions, different views have taken hold in different parts of the Washington policy community. Among defense planners there is a broad-based belief that likelihood of use is high, largely on the view that their military utility is potentially very high—especially for asymmetric conflicts against the United States. Among country and regional experts there is broad-based skepticism that such weapons will ever be used, largely on the view that such weapons are unproven historically and too risky in terms of the harsh responses they might generate. A third view is sometimes expressed among political-military analysts: that such use is likely only in last resort in an effort to assure regime survival—on the model of potential Iraqi biological warfare (BW) use against the Desert Storm coalition, as it has come to be understood subsequently.

Because these different expectations have fundamentally different implications for U.S. policy, in the military realm, and elsewhere, it is important to look beyond these conventional wisdoms to develop deeper insights into the prospects for the use of biological weapons in the region. This paper is aimed at providing answers to a number of key questions:

- How might biological weapons be used in conflicts in the Middle East over the next decade?
- How probable is such use?
- By what rationales might certain types of targets be selected and concepts of operations (CONOPS) elaborated?
- What use scenarios stand out as of highest potential impact?[2]

The best answers to the questions noted above would come from definitive information from within decision-making circles in these countries. What plans have they made for the use of biological weapons? What infrastructure have they put in place? What doctrine have they written and authorized? How do they understand the risks of escalation, deterrence, and counterdeterrence? But definitive information is sorely lacking.

The absence of hard data on the BW topic reinforces the skepticism of those who believe proliferation will not lead to the use of biological weapons. They conclude that scientific and/or technical factors may be shaping BW programs in the region much more so than strategic imperatives. In elaborating this conclusion, they sometimes draw on the experience of the biological weapons producers of the interwar and early Cold War years—when weapons were developed, produced, and stockpiled in secret R&D programs that were at best loosely connected to the military operator, who wrote requirements and fielded and trained with new capabilities.[3] Even the experience of the United States is illustrative here: during the period that it had an offensive biological warfare program, it developed limited BW CONOPS but barely integrated such attacks into war plans.

The absence of hard data on this topic is hardly reassuring. Because these weapons are the object of an international treaty regime—to which many of the states in the Middle East are party[4]—there are political costs associated with publicly describing an extant but illicit capability. There also are costs in terms of the responses of neighbors who might be compelled to create a retaliatory force of their own. Furthermore, the facilities associated with the development and production of biological weapons are notoriously difficult intelligence targets. Moreover, in the 1990s a great deal was learned about the biological warfare activities of at least three states—Iraq, Soviet Union/Russia, and South Africa—and in each case new insights revealed a level of interest, scale of activity, and degree of sophistication in each country's BW activities that had not been expected. In trying to frame these issues, we must also ward against the opposing tendency—in the absence of hard information to inflate a threat. The fact that many states in the region may have an interest in biological weapons does not necessarily imply that each has succeeded in mastering all of the scientific, engineering, doctrinal, and other challenges associated with their effective use in war or that each has also put together the entire infrastructure from preliminary research to deliverable weapons to do so.

One approach to the basic questions posed above is to explore the motivations that drove decision-makers in the region to acquire a BW capability.[5] Such an approach can provide valuable insights into decision-maker mindsets and their perceptions of the potential political utility of biological weapons. But the motivations to acquire may prove rather different from the motivations to use. Strategic circumstances may have changed, new needs arisen, new understandings of the technical possibilities for BW emerged through greater familiarity, or new perspectives developed as a result of wars or other crises in the region. Accordingly, it is necessary to explore *motivations to use* as a topic separate and distinct from *motivations to acquire*. The two approaches can provide complementary insights.

Another approach, often used in the defense planning community, is to argue from the technical characteristics of biological weapons about their likely military applications in the regions. This approach can provide insights into perceptions of the likely operational utility of biological weapons. Such perceptions seem likely to span the full spectrum, from a view of biological weapons as unreliable on the battlefield and hence of low military utility, to a view of such weapons as promise special and indeed unique capabilities for specific types of missions.[6] Here too a complementary approach is useful, combining technical and motivational assessments. Thinking through the technical characteristics of such weapons in combination with motivations to use them may lead to an understanding of potential uses other than those that might have been expected based on motivations to acquire—novel uses derived from an advanced understanding of the scientific and technical potentialities associated with the use of biological weapons.

In the absence of hard data, this must be a speculative task, drawing on inferences from past experience and underlying technical factors. If that speculation is to offer real insights into the key questions, it must also be systematic. Rather than begin with the question "how might biological weapons be used in the region?" this paper begins with a prior question: what types of conflicts are likely in the region? This enables a more focused review of the interests motivating the conflicts and how those interests might shape the propensity to use biological weapons. The time frame here is the decade 2001–2010. The focus is not limited just to known or suspected possessors of biological weapons; indeed, it is reasonable to assume that all actors in the region can acquire biological weapons if they so choose. Moreover, for this survey of conflict potentials, consideration is given to both state and nonstate actors. The core insights we are seeking here relate to state actors, and that is where the conclusions will focus. But the overlapping patterns of violence between, within, and among states are a striking feature of the region.

This paper begins with a series of propositions about the patterns of conflict likely to be seen in the region over the coming decade. The resulting taxonomy is then used to develop some propositions about the likelihood of the use of biological weapons by state and nonstate actors. One scenario has been selected for more in-depth analysis. This analysis elaborates the strategic logic that could lead to the use of biological weapons, including especially the perceived potential benefits and risks of such weapons relative to the other assets, conventional and non-conventional, within the actor's reach. It concludes with a brief review of key insights.

A CONFLICT TAXONOMY

The Middle East is obviously rife with conflict. The history of conflict between states in the region is as old as the existence of the states themselves, as they have juggled for advantage over one another, acquired or contested territory, or fought foreign invaders. Internal conflicts are also as old as the states, given the broad absence of stable institutions of governance. But a close survey of this history suggests that the unrestrained use of violence in the region is exceedingly rare. The use of violence is instrumental in nature and employed by rational actors seeking specific tactical gains or political ends. Understanding those ends is key to understanding the motivations potentially driving the use of biological weapons. To be sure, there are also instances in which that use is more atavistic in nature, driven, for example, by a desire for revenge.

What types of conflicts are likely in the decade ahead? The following "answer" to this question was developed in 1999 and 2000, in close consultation with Western experts on the region.[7] Accordingly, it is a view of the future that pre-dates both 9/11 and the war to expel Saddam Hussein from Iraq—both obvious and important milestones. But the following propositions remain useful as a way to frame an analysis of the possible future use of BW in the region.

1. Wars between states in the region involving the large-scale use of force, and perceived to be calling into question survival of the regime or state, are unlikely in this time frame. This includes large interstate wars analogous to the Iran-Iraq conflict of the 1980s that pitted two well-armed countries against each other for many years in a war of mass casualties and attrition. The ever-brittle Israeli-Palestinian peace process raises a question for many about whether a new drift of events may be unfolding, with a slope toward major war. Such a war could bring Arab states again into confrontation with Israel, which could well pose—or be seen by Israelis to pose—an existential threat to it.
2. Less unlikely are limited interstate wars for limited terms and limited ends, not raising questions of regime or state survival. No one would rule out border or other disputes between Iran and Afghanistan, Syria and Turkey, or even Turkey and Greece, for example.
3. An act of aggression by one state against another that brings about conflict with the United States and a U.S.-led coalition is also a possibility. Iranian military coercion of the Gulf Cooperation Council (GCC) countries, an Iranian attempt to disrupt or close the strait, or a Libyan attack on Egypt (among others) are considered of moderate likelihood.
4. Low-intensity conflicts raising questions of regime legitimacy and survival will continue and may intensify. Possibilities include armed opposition to governments in Iran and antiregime Islamic movements in Algeria, Bahrain, Egypt, Jordan, Syria, and Turkey. The reeruption of the Intifada against Israel is perhaps the stand-out problem here, bringing with it an intensification of violence and new questions about the tactics necessary in a new phase of confrontation, although

renewed conflict here could be transformed into a major interstate conflict as suggested in 1 above if neighboring states are drawn in.

5. Some regimes will attempt to violently and ruthlessly suppress such conflicts. Iraqi suppression of the Kurds in the 1980s is a model that may be followed elsewhere. Examples of concern include Iran, Yemen, and Syria.
6. As peace processes continue in various venues, splinter groups will emerge to militantly oppose a peace deal. Those groups typically seek to escalate the conflict in order to derail the deal and/or to exact revenge. Multiple possibilities exist: Hamas, Hizbollah, or perhaps radicalized Israeli settlers.
7. State support for terrorism outside the region will continue much as before. States in the region have a long history in the use of covert action to accomplish short- or long-term aims within and beyond the region. The U.S. government has recognized Iran, Iraq, Libya, Sudan, and Syria as state sponsors of terrorism. Obviously the U.S.-led Global War on Terrorism has had a substantial though varying impact on the willingness of these states to continue such sponsorship.
8. Transnational terrorism such as that initiated by Al Qaeda on September 11, 2001, will not disappear from the region, nor will it supplant other forms of substate and interstate violence. Such terrorism is employed in service of a revolutionary agenda aimed at expelling Western and especially U.S. influence from the region and at installing regimes of an acceptable type. Whether it will grow over the decade is an open question. Its growth may be inhibited by the interests of states in the region in avoiding retaliation. The dramatic U.S. and world response to Al Qaeda after the September 11 attacks may also serve to discourage some terrorist adventurism in the future. Although most transnational terrorism is apparently not state sponsored, in some instances it is state tolerated.
9. States and regimes will continue to place high value on weapons of mass destruction (WMD) as a coin of power—for their political as much as for their military utility.[8] Such weapons are valued by different regimes for different purposes: whether to compensate for conventional weakness, to otherwise restore a balance of power of some kind, to press a demand for a seat at the negotiating table, to coerce or compel one's neighbors and other potential adversaries, or more generally to compel the outside world to pay attention to local concerns. The prestige value of WMD is as much internal as international for some of these countries. Possession of WMD, whether actual or only rumored, can help to reinforce the power of a ruling faction within the larger elite. Whether the Bush administration's effort to "roll back" Iraqi WMD will ultimately have a positive or negative impact on this factor remains an open question.

The taxonomy in Figure 7.1 may not exhaust all of the conflict potentialities in the region, but it encompasses most of the important factors and trends.

RATING BW LIKELIHOOD

What does the taxonomy shown in Figure 7.1 offer in the way of insights into the questions associated with the use of biological weapons? It helps to link questions of use with questions of strategic intent. It offers a vehicle for

Figure 7.1
Likelihood of Potential Conflicts to 2010

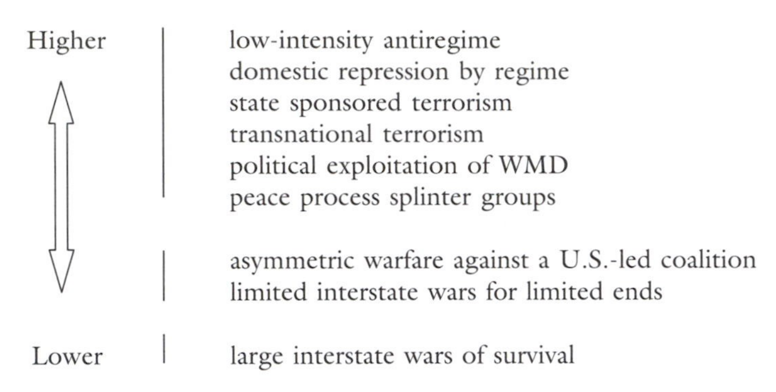

considering whether the most likely conflicts in the region are also the conflicts most likely to see the use of biological weapons.

The logic that would lead to the use of biological weapons seems clearly to be missing in a couple of the conflict potentialities described above. In antiregime, low-intensity conflicts, the use of biological weapons seems quite unlikely. The violent Islamic and other oppositionist movements of concern here are seeking to mobilize public support, to cast existing governments as illegitimate, and generally to create the political conditions that enable them to emerge as successors to the regimes they are attacking. The use of biological weapons could run counter to these interests.[9] The use of a banned weapon—especially its use to generate broad suffering among civilians—could delegitimize these movements in the eyes of their intended domestic supporters and perhaps internationally as well. Some groups depend substantially on international support, such as the groups supporting Palestinian and Kurdish statehood. This may be less true of those Islamic groups that have claimed a holy writ for their chosen tactics. Moreover, in many if not all of the countries where such movements are a concern, there is a significant measure of external, usually covert, meddling; the meddling states have interests that could be damaged if BW use were to result in international condemnation, sanctions, and even military action. A disturbing footnote to this analysis relates to the potential utility of biological weapons for attacks not on humans but on plants and animals; antiregime actors could potentially find such attacks useful for destabilizing a country without unduly risking a punishing reply and perhaps without alienating excessively the target state's human population.[10] Again, this may be less true of some of the Islamic groups, who perceive a strong base of support among those who are politically and economically disenfranchised.

The use of biological weapons for catastrophic effect in border skirmishes and other limited interstate wars also appears to be of low likelihood. Because these are by definition limited wars for limited gains, the use of a weapon of mass destruction would appear to offer few benefits and many risks. Such weapons might be seen as useful for clearing out contested areas of unprotected civilians, especially if they can be used without detection or attribution. From a military perspective, the benefits would likely be limited to possible defeat of the adversary's military forces (assuming effective BW use, in conjunction with other factors, including a conventional ability to exploit whatever advantages might be created by the use of unconventional weapons). The risks could be prompt retaliation by the neighboring state and a spiraling escalation process, as well as a sharp international reaction associated with violating a global treaty and norm. Successful surreptitious attacks would pose fewer such risks.

Some experts believe that an especially sharp reaction to any use of BW is expected in the region. Their argument runs as follows: the failure of the United Nations Security Council to reply in any meaningful way to Iraqi use of chemical weapons in the 1980s precipitated a sudden burst of WMD proliferation in this region, as elsewhere. In order to prevent a similar burst of proliferation in the wake of the next use of biological weapons, and in part as compensation for their failure to respond decisively to Iraqi chemical weapons (CW) use, the council may wish to make a demonstration with its response.[11] Whether the expectation is well founded is an open question; but to some degree the expectation does appear to reflect the thinking of decision-makers in some states in the region about the international repercussions of the use of biological weapons for anything but the most compelling purposes of self-defense in extremis, or regime survival.

At the opposite extreme, in some conflicts in the taxonomy the use of biological weapons appears to be a realistic possibility—indeed, the likelihood might well be high.

A large interstate war invoking questions of the survival of the state or regime would seem likely to see the use of unconventional weapons of whatever type are available to the regime in question.[12] Such weapons might be used only late in the conflict, in strategies aimed at ensuring the survival of the regime—threatened, and perhaps used, as weapons of last resort. It is also conceivable, however, that decision-makers in one or more capitals might conclude that the decisive advantages of such weapons must be reaped early rather than late in any conflict, so as to gain the upper hand in the military confrontation and thus leverage over the end game. The user's risk, of course, would be in generating reprisal and retaliation by the opposing side. This is a risk that is especially pronounced in the BW area, as a victim state could presumably produce retaliatory quantities of weapons in a relatively short period of time. Thus, the first-user would have to expect that early use would decisively terminate the war on favorable terms and eliminate the possibility of counterescalation by the opposing side.

Splinter groups deeply opposed to an emerging peace settlement also seem likely to be interested in biological weapons as a way to destroy the political willingness on one or both sides to make a deal; they might be used to punish their enemies when leaders choose not to, as they make peace; or they might be used to exact revenge against those who would make such a deal.[13] Precisely because biological weapons have not been utilized by politically motivated terrorist groups in their strategies to gain a seat at the table, and legitimacy for their cause, they may be seen as useful by the splinter groups for signaling an escalation of risk and a break with the past to a qualitatively new form of violence. In the Israeli-Palestinian context, the rumored interest of certain segments of Hamas in acquiring chemical weapons is matched by the rumored willingness of Israel to exploit biotechnical and other means to poison its adversaries—perceptions on both sides that may well have weakened the taboo on the use of such weapons within the region.

The use of biological weapons in asymmetric strategies against U.S.-led coalitions also appears likely. Aggressors might see multiple roles for biological weapons in such conflicts, including coercion of the United States and its local allies/partners, warfighting, escalation, and war termination.[14] This subject is explored in greater detail below.

It should be noted that both types of BW use would constitute a significant break from past practice in the region. The fact that terrorists have so far refrained from the use of nonconventional weapons to achieve their aims is striking—just as states have so far refrained from using them to achieve war aims against superior military adversaries. Terrorist restraint in this regard probably has both technical and political explanations. From a technical point of view, they have not benefited from access to the WMD programs of the state sponsors of terrorism, and those few who have been interested in BW apparently have had to master the technical challenges on their own. Those challenges are modest when it comes to the production of bacteriological materials, but are more substantial when it comes to effective storage and delivery of the agents. Moreover, a successful BW terrorist attack would require mastery of multiple skill sets associated with agent selection and production, "weaponization," target selection, training, self-protection, attack operations, and escape.[15]

Technical factors thus may account in part for terrorist restraint in the use of BW, but would not appear to be fully satisfactory as a reason for terrorist nonuse. Thus, it is important also to consider political factors. Terrorist restraint in this regard would appear also to derive from the need to calibrate the use of violence so that it is sufficient to gain attention to a cause and, at the same time, not excessive, in a way that would damage their legitimacy and alienate important constituencies.[16] On asymmetric warfare, the restraint is more difficult to characterize, but would appear to derive from the fact that, within the region, weapons of mass destruction have been understood largely to play a role in deterrence and not operational military art.

Thus, one further "use" must be seen as of potentially high likelihood—the political use of weapons of mass destruction. Such use is already well demonstrated in the region. Saddam Hussein regularly touted his supposed victory in the Persian Gulf War and the ostensible role of biological weapons in preventing the Desert Storm coalition from pressing on to remove him from power. BW capabilities are also spoken of as counters to the nuclear power of states in the region—whether implicitly as a deterrent or explicitly as a capability to be used in retaliation.[17]

This leaves a set of potential conflicts where the role of biological weapons cannot easily be written off, nor can it be predicted as especially likely.

Transnational terrorists have exhibited a strong interest in mass casualty techniques. This has most recently been demonstrated by the Al Qaeda hijacking of four U.S. airliners on September 11, 2001, and ramming them into the Pentagon and two towers of the World Trade Center. Such terrorists are not constrained in the way that traditional terrorist actors have been by the need to calibrate their use of violence. Osama bin Laden has deemed the acquisition of weapons of mass destruction to be a "holy duty."[18] The collateral effects their use would produce could have been seen by bin Laden not as alienating or delegitimizing, but as useful, demonstrating that the U.S. regime in power cannot protect its people. There may also be a particular appeal to biological weapons derived from the special abhorrence they generate; within the region there is a tradition of combating foreign invaders with weapons and tactics that are especially offensive to those invaders. The purpose of choosing such especially offensive techniques is to communicate social rage against that invader. It is also to generate fear, as the invader must contemplate the barbarity of those faced by overwhelming conventional military power. Osama bin Laden also reflects the revolutionary's desire to use violence to raise the stakes in a game that he wants to see accelerate and intensify.[19] In his case, he might also have been attempting to get the United States to strike back in such a way as to alienate and further radicalize the Muslim world, triggering an even wider holy war.

State-supported terrorism outside the region also falls in the middle category. Historically, states have had many good reasons to be restrained in assisting the terrorists they support to master the techniques of mass casualty warfare.[20] Many of the state sponsors of terrorism are also understood to be possessors of chemical and/or biological weapons (CBW), yet none is understood to have opened the CBW arsenal to the terrorist camps. That restraint evidently has something to do with the fear of retribution—as with the technical difficulties and unpredictability of their effects. Looking to the future, the question is how much restraint will they continue to exhibit in this area? They may come to be persuaded that BW attacks are plausibly deniable and thus run little risk of being tracked back to the sponsor. They also may develop techniques for the use of BW for purposes other than mass casualties—perhaps only to sicken in large numbers, with the hope of turning local political will against the United States, for example.

Finally, the use of biological weapons for the purpose of suppressing domestic opposition cannot be ruled out. Indeed, there is a long history in the region, as elsewhere, of the use of poisons to eliminate enemies. Moreover, there is obviously the model provided by Saddam's attack on the Kurds with CW (with allegations that BW was used as well),[21] and the apparent development of a BW agent (aflatoxin) in part for the purpose of waging long-term, covert war against the Kurds. This points to the possible use of biological weapons to exterminate hated groups, especially where they are far from international disease monitoring, or perhaps to deprive them of food and other resources. Here, revelations about the techniques developed by the former apartheid government of South Africa for long-term attack on the black population may prove a stimulus.

Figure 7.2 provides a summary of this discussion of the likelihood of the use of biological weapons in the contingencies identified in the preceding section. Probabilities are expressed in relative and not absolute terms. Absolute predictions are a near impossibility in so complex and volatile a region—and without knowing what is in the hearts, minds, and war plans of decision-makers there. On an absolute scale, it would seem unwarranted to interpret the higher likelihood contingencies as having a high certainty of BW use, but the possibility is plausible and by strategic logic serious. At the other end of the spectrum, interpreting the lower likelihood contingencies as being those in which it is possible to rule out the use of BW would also seem unwarranted. For reasons noted above, the technology of biological warfare may be evolving in ways as to make such uses seem tempting.

Figure 7.2
Likelihood of Use of Biological Weapons

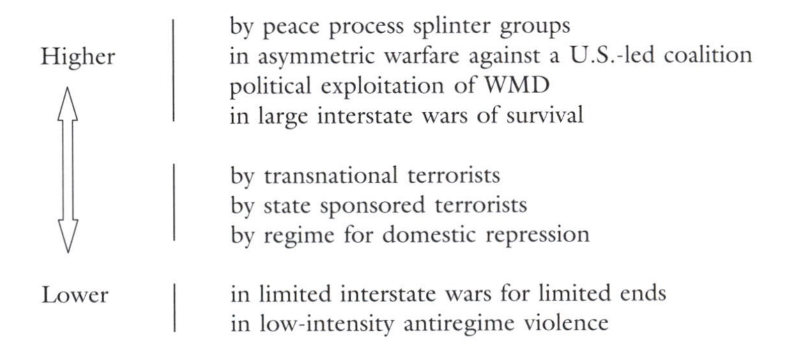

PROBING MORE DEEPLY

This framework of analysis provides some answers to the questions about where and why biological weapons might be used in the region. To consider how they might be used requires exploring specific scenarios in more detail. The following section of this chapter explores one particular scenario: the canonical major theater war problem, in which a local BW-armed aggressor confronts a U.S.-led coalition.

THE CANONICAL MAJOR THEATER WAR

How might a BW-armed regional aggressor use biological weapons to commit and secure that aggression, and to cope with the political-military consequences of a U.S. effort to reverse that aggression? To answer this question requires an understanding of how the aggressor's strategic risk assessment will change during the course of such a war—and of the perceived utility of different military instruments in his tool kit to secure his interests.[22]

Prior to an act of aggression, the enemy leadership is likely to find it useful to isolate the United States to the maximum extent possible in the hope that this will deny it allies, partners, basing rights, and so forth in the conflict to come. This could entail destabilizing countries with which Washington might hope to affiliate itself through the use of proxy groups and domestic terrorism. For this end, as argued above, biological weapons may not look particularly useful. Traditional instruments are well proven and generally effective. The risk that BW may be used for this purpose may be rising, however, if such weapons are understood to offer the possibility of mass casualty attacks with plausible deniability. Moreover, biotechnical developments may make such weapons more easily usable and predictable in their results.

Once the aggressor acts, his primary goal would be to achieve a militarily decisive fait accompli prior to outside intervention. This would present the United States and its allies and partners with a difficult choice between attempting to reverse the aggression at potentially high cost and acquiescing. For this purpose, there would be both incentives and disincentives to the use of BW by the aggressor.

The incentives might include the following: If the aggressor perceives biological weapons to be potentially significant in the conflict, early use may well be seen as more strategically effective than later use. Low lethality attacks on military targets that also spare major population centers may be seen as especially useful in gaining that decisive fait accompli. Such weapons could be seen as useful if the aggression is being undertaken against an adversary with superior conventional warfighting capabilities—or the capability to mobilize them quickly. In this case, likely targets would be in the adversary's depth, with the purpose of slowing his capability to mobilize.

The disincentives might include the following: such use might be seen as increasing the odds that Washington would deem it necessary to respond to the aggression. There might also be concerns about the international backlash that could damage the political prospects for the regime and perhaps direct aid to the victims of the aggression. If an aggressor were to prefer to rely on conventional means for the purposes of achieving a fait accompli, it seems unlikely that he would choose to risk the use of BW solely on a selective basis to achieve his war aims.

Whether or not the effort to achieve a fait accompli succeeds, once having acted the aggressor will have an interest in dissuading formation of a coalition around U.S. leadership and thereby isolating the United States. The aggressor might hope that such isolation would be militarily crippling to the effort to reverse its aggression by denying U.S. intervention forces crucial bases of operation and logistic support. He might also hope that it would be politically crippling, by sowing debate in Washington and especially the Congress about whether the United States genuinely has an interest in intervening in a crisis where locals in the region apparently prefer not to act. In pursuit of such dissuasion, the aggressor would want to inflict some punishment on neighboring civilians—enough to generate fear of more to come, but not enough to make acceptance of the aggression politically impossible. Biological weapons might be seen as too risky for this purpose, given their reputed uncontrollability. But given that they can be used covertly and in plausibly deniable ways, the risk may be seen as worth running.

If the aggressor fails to dissuade coalition formation (or a U.S. decision to act unilaterally), then its interest is in deterring the coalition (or the United States alone) from taking military action, thereby securing the aggression. The deterrent effect of available conventional weapons would not seem particularly compelling. Nuclear weapons could conceivably seem especially useful for this purpose. Biological weapons may well be perceived as closer to nuclear than conventional weapons for this deterrent purpose because of their potential for generating mass casualties among both military personnel and civilian host populations. But again, the aggressor must be concerned with calibrating the use of violence to generate the desired effect (in this case, restraint by Washington and its partners) and not undesired ones (a backlash to his excessive force that casts the aggressor as a dire menace to the region, to be removed from power at all costs). Accordingly, if biological weapons were to be used for this deterrence purpose, it would seem that they might be used on a limited basis against civilian targets so that there is great fear of more suffering to come. U.S. diplomatic personnel in the region would seem lucrative targets, as well as other symbols of American society, such as business interests. Conceivably, the aggressor might also selectively target civilians in Europe, believing that America's NATO allies would pressure Washington to terminate the conflict on available terms so as to end their suffering.

If deterrence fails, the aggressor's interest shifts yet again—to cripple the intervention in its early phases in order to prevent the coalition from exploiting its full military potential and conventional advantages, and thus to create a prolonged stalemate and a basis upon which to negotiate an outcome that protects some or all of the aggressor's gains. For this purpose, chemical and biological weapons may well have a perceived utility that conventional weapons would not. CBW attack on airports and seaports of debarkation, logistic centers, prepositioned equipment, and other host nation support assets could seem particularly beneficial in slowing the arrival of U.S. forces and inhibiting their ability to gather themselves into a coherent fighting force. A creative adversary might reach out of the theater in the attempt to cripple the force flow, with covert, special forces attacks on ports of embarkation in the United States. Such uses of BW would run a very substantial risk from the adversary's point of view: the possible expansion of war aims by the United States and/or its allies to include regime removal. This risk may be especially pronounced if the aggressor attempts to use biological weapons for limited gains but, miscalculating the lethality and effectiveness of his weapons, ends up killing far in excess of the intended numbers. But this risk might not be meaningful to the aggressor as he may have concluded that such a confrontation would necessarily entail questions of regime survival.

If through these means the aggressor is not able to cripple the intervention, and the United States is able ultimately to bring its full conventional power to bear, then the aggressor has an interest in inflicting operational defeat on the coalition's in-theater forces and denying it any advantages of escalation. If the aggressor believes he can do so by conventional means alone, he may well see BW attacks as too risky in terms of generating a nuclear reply from the United States (or perhaps another nuclear-armed coalition partner). But, given the balance of conventional forces in the region and the apparent capability of the United States to defeat any regional adversary if given the time to assemble a force and the capability to fight on its preferred terms, then a conventional victory seems unlikely to be seen as viable by the aggressor. The temptation to escalate would be obvious. It might not seem prudent, given the potential for the United States to counter with a nuclear reply. But a nuclear counter may be discounted by the aggressor on the argument that no act of his so far would warrant the taking of millions of lives by the United States—and Washington's breaking the nuclear taboo. Thus a prediction of the likelihood of BW use at this point cannot be made confidently. If the aggressor possessed nuclear weapons of his own, the temptation to use BW might be rather high. On the other hand, such use could be held in reserve as an escalation option in the hope of dissuading Washington from seeking regime removal as a condition of war termination.

If the aggressor fails to defeat the coalition and prevent it from escalating, his interests shift yet again: to prevent battlefield defeat from becoming strategic defeat in terms of dismemberment of the military, occupation of the country, and/or removal of the aggressor regime by the coalition. At this phase, the aggressor would want to be seen as capable of inflicting very high pain on members of the coalition that press for such strategic defeat. He would want to be able to threaten a "spasm" of attack on civilians among the coalition nations, including the United States.[23] For this purpose, it would seem that missile-delivered weapons of mass destruction could have unique appeal. But if confronted with the need to make good on a threat, which weapon might be seen as the most likely to produce the desired result without generating a backlash? A nuclear attack in this late phase of war would seem highly likely to generate a nuclear reply. Effectively delivered chemical or biological attacks could be seen as offering the leverage necessary to accept the aggressor's offer of "peace," but as far less likely to generate a nuclear reply. On the other hand, the very slowness of their effects would likely be seen as unacceptable in a rapidly unfolding geopolitical crisis.

The conflict dynamics in this war termination phase are a matter of substantial speculation.[24] One possibility is presented in the history of Nazi Germany and Hitler's virtual embrace of the punishment meted out to Germany by the invading powers as just punishment of a people who had failed in creating the thousand-year Reich. By this analogy, a regional aggressor might employ mass casualty BW attacks in the late phases of a war, fully aware of the reprisal to come, but seeing it as a price to be paid for the failure of some grand ambition. Another possibility is presented by those instances in history when professional military leaders chose not to carry out their leader's dictate to take actions tantamount to national suicide. By this analogy, the regime may be motivated to escalate, but the military may be unwilling to do so. It is noteworthy in this regard that in World War II, Germany did not use its chemical weapons in the final endgame, just as Japan did not use its biological weapons.

A final phase must be considered. If the original aggression is reversed, the military is hobbled, and the country loses some measure of sovereignty but the regime escapes the war intact, then the regime's goals would be (1) to prevent a consolidation of regional forces detrimental to its interests, and perhaps (2) to exact revenge against those within and beyond the region (and perhaps domestically) who fought against it. A weak, collapsing regime might be particularly motivated to exact such revenge. For these purposes, biological weapons could be seen as particularly useful, especially given the capability to employ them covertly.

These strategic imperatives for the U.S. adversary, as they evolve through the phases of confrontation, are summarized in Table 7.1.

In sum, in this canonical major theater war scenario, the BW CONOPS an adversary might implement seem likely to be conditioned by the phase of war. At each phase, a specific set of interests is at play, against which questions of risk and benefit will be measured. In some phases, biological weapons seem likely to be perceived as too risky or as not sufficiently promising

Table 7.1
Adversary Strategic Imperatives in Major Theater War Against U.S.

Prior to an act of aggression, to isolate the United States and destabilize its allies/partners.
Once war begins, to achieve a militarily decisive fait accompli.
To dissuade formation of a coalition around U.S. leadership.
To deter any coalition (or the United States alone) from undertaking military action to reverse the aggression.
To cripple any such U.S. intervention in its early phases.
To inflict operational defeat on the coalition's in-theater military forces.
To prevent battlefield defeat from becoming strategic defeat in terms of dismemberment of the military, occupation of the country, and/or removal of the regime.
To prevent consolidation of regional forces detrimental to the regime's interests, while exacting revenge against those who fought against it.

in their results, at least relative to other conventional or unconventional weapons. In other phases, their perceived relative utility could be quite high and the risks seen as manageable. There is little agreement within the expert community about whether the early use of biological weapons would be seen as strategically valuable; some believe that such use would be unnecessarily provocative of the United States, whereas others believe that aggressors would see the benefits of early use to be irresistible. There is also little agreement within the expert community about the likelihood of use later in such a war, in the war termination phase. Some look to the 1991 Persian Gulf War experience and conclude that biological weapons would have been very useful to Saddam Hussein in preventing the coalition from seeking removal of his regime. Others, drawing on other experience in the region, argue that even in the war termination phase, such use is unlikely, as it would make it nearly impossible for the United States to settle for a conclusion to the war that leaves the regime in power.

Given these different motivations to use biological weapons at different phases of conflict, possible CONOPS are necessarily varied as well. When the aggressor's interest in dissuasion and deterrence are most at play, the optimal uses of BW are likely to be selective, surreptitious, and focused on civilians, with the hint of more pain to come. When the aggressor's interests are more operational, the optimal uses are likely to be tied to targets of high campaign significance, such as ports and airfields, and logistic centers (and medical infrastructure), or to deploying forces themselves. The character of BW use, in terms of the type of agent and target selected and the extent of use, would vary according to the phase of war. Only in the war termination phase, when regime survival is most directly at stake, does it seem likely that the aggressor would consider the highest-damage BW attacks on population centers, though even those may look unacceptably risky given the potential for reprisal and retaliation.

This analytical model helps to explain why U.S. military planners were so deeply concerned about possible Iraqi use of biological weapons to try to turn back the U.S.-led effort to expel Saddam from power in 2003. The logic for use in support of regime survival late in war, in combination with Iraq's failure to fully satisfy the U.N. Security Council that it had complied with its disarmament obligations, led to widespread expectations of BW attack. What the model failed to predict was the actual behavior of the Iraqi military and leadership in war. Saddam's non-use of WMD remains unexplained at this writing, as indeed does the entire strategy by which he confronted the United Nations and fought war against the U.S.-led coalition. Whether the model might more accurately capture the possibilities in future conflicts against other BW-armed "rogue" states is a question needing further exploration after the 2003 war.

CONCLUSIONS

Let us return to the four opening questions:

1. How might biological weapons be used in conflicts in the Middle East over the next decade?
2. How probable is such use?
3. By what rationales might certain types of targets be selected and concepts of operations (CONOPS) elaborated?
4. What use scenarios stand out as of highest potential impact?

How might biological weapons be used in conflicts in the Middle East over the next decade? An answer to this question requires an understanding of the types of conflicts that might occur in the region and the political, military, and strategic interests they have for the actors. Not all of the many conflict potentialities in the region present high risk of biological weapons use. Especially in low intensity conflicts and where the use of force is for limited purposes, the use of biological weapons seems likely to be seen as counterproductive. Moreover, it may be seen as unnecessary, as other means are available. Furthermore, many of the regimes in the region have relatively weak control and have consistently shown an unwillingness to employ techniques over which they might lose control and which could be turned back on them. This is an argument to stay with what works.

But there is also a reasonably plausible spectrum of contingencies where the use of biological weapons could look necessary and prudent to the actor. These generally fall within the realm of coercion, deterrence, escalation, and punishment in conflicts where the stakes are relatively high, especially stakes of regime survival. Here the argument must be: don't stay with what you know, because it won't work.

How probable is such use? There is a strong argument that the probability of use is increasing. Most countries have proven incapable of combined arms operations and would not, in any case, be able to provide for the extended resupply of large conventional wars. They have no confidence in their capability to compete militarily against higher-tech conventional forces. So there is rising interest in asymmetric strategies and "special weapons."

To argue that the probability of use is increasing is to make a statement about relative likelihood. What about on an absolute scale? This is far more difficult to gauge. Recall from the introduction the different perceptions of likelihood held by defense planners (who tend to see adversary BW use as inevitable) and country and regional experts (who are highly skeptical of this view). This analysis suggests that both are wrong and that the truth lies in the middle: BW is a likely future condition of conflict but by no means a certainty.

Happily, the most likely conflicts in the region are not the types of conflict where the likelihood of BW use would be rated as high. The most likely conflicts involve nonstate actors or substate groups; the interstate wars that are possible do not appear particularly likely, except perhaps those employing limited means for limited ends. But the "political uses" of biological weapons—whether overtly brandished or quietly rumored—for purposes of reinforcing a regime's stature (and generating fear of it) are already in evidence and promise to become more so in the decade ahead.

From the U.S. point of view, the most important question of probability relates to attack on its own forces and interests with BW. This is seen as probable in a canonical major theater war scenario.

In Northeast Asia, there is the important possibility of a war on the Korean peninsula, which could play out along lines very similar to those sketched out above. But in the Middle East, given the relatively low likelihood of interstate war involving state and regime survival issues, this canonical scenario may be quite unlikely in the decade ahead. *By what rationales might certain types of targets be selected and CONOPS elaborated?* There can be no simple answer to this question. Those rationales derive from the interests at stake in a conflict, as they change during the course of the conflict. They derive also from the actor's understanding of the potential benefits and risks associated with different types of use for different purposes. Where the purpose is to shape the strategic behavior of an adversary, the targets are likely to be vulnerabilities that can be exposed and exploited to induce restraint. For these purposes, CONOPS must be developed that generate fear but not reprisal. The point of coercion is to exploit the fear of more to come to induce restraint, not to kill as many as possible. Where the purpose is to achieve an operational outcome, the targets are likely to be those of campaign significance, such as ports and airfields, just as much as forces deployed on the battlefield, with CONOPS developed to cripple key arriving assets.

In fact, there may be a quite simple answer to this question. It may be that CONOPS are not elaborated beyond what the technical system developer elaborates for delivery of the munition in development. If there is weak linkage between the R&D community and the military operator, as there was in many of the BW programs of the twentieth century, it may be that CONOPS are quite rudimentary and poorly tailored to the specific tactical or strategic imperatives of the types of wars that may actually occur in the region in the next decade. Of course, their elaboration need not be especially time-consuming.

And which use scenarios stand out as of highest potential impact? The scenario explored here (a canonical major theater war) stands out as being potentially the richest in insights for those trying to understand the role of biological weapons in future wars in the region. This scenario focuses on actors whose BW capabilities and understanding of BW can be expected to be relatively mature. And it focuses on wars in which strategic interests could well drive decision-makers to authorize biological attacks. But this does not necessarily make that particular scenario the one with the highest potential impact.

The most devastating uses, exploiting the full potential utility of biological weapons to kill millions, would certainly have far-reaching repercussions. They would generate great anxiety within and outside the region, wherever states neighbor others with rumored programs. They would also generate great urgency about "fixing" the BW problem, and the WMD problem more generally. Unless biological weapons use was clearly either as last resort self-defense or as reprisal, it seems likely that the user would become the object of a major international effort to gain his removal. At the very least, there would be pressure on Washington to do whatever is possible to ensure that such attacks are stopped immediately and definitively.

Arguably, *any* use of biological weapons in the region would have high international impact. It would be seen as setting a dangerous precedent. It also would be seen as another test of the UN Security Council. And it would be seen as the latest challenge to the nonproliferation regime. Finding a way to ensure that the "use" leads to a response that somehow teaches the "right lessons" would likely seem an urgent priority in Washington and elsewhere.

A special kind of importance would attach to a category not so far considered—attacks that might have been prevented or somehow defeated or whose effects could somehow have been minimized if the means had been available to detect and defeat delivery systems and protect against released agent with personal protection systems. In such scenarios, one can imagine a measure of blame falling not just on the perpetrator of the attack but also on those who, in retrospect, are deemed to have failed to take the necessary steps to prevent the attack and minimize its consequences. Thus, there is an argument that a BW attack that is militarily ineffective could still be strategically of great consequence if the simple fact that it was conducted calls into question the value of security relations with the United States.

CHAPTER 8

Assessment of the Emerging Biocruise Threat

Rex R. Kiziah

BACKGROUND: EMERGENCE OF THE LAND-ATTACK CRUISE MISSILE AS A WEAPON OF CHOICE

> The simultaneous proliferation of cruise missile delivery systems and BTW [biological and toxin warfare] production capabilities may pose a serious strategic threat in the future.
>
> Jonathan B. Tucker[1]

The utility of having cruise missiles in a nation's military arsenal was clearly demonstrated to the world between January 16 and February 2, 1991, when U.S. Navy surface ships and submarines in the Persian Gulf, Red Sea, and Eastern Mediterranean launched 288 Tomahawk land-attack missiles (TLAMs) and the U.S. Air Force expended thirty-nine conventional air-launched land-attack cruise missiles (CALCMs) against "strategic" targets in Iraq. These targets included command and control headquarters, power generation complexes, weapons of mass destruction (WMD) facilities, and oil production and refining factories.[2] Although there is some disagreement between official Department of Defense (DOD) sources and outside analyses on the success of these land-attack cruise missile (LACM) strikes, the overall consensus, both official and nonofficial, is that the LACMs proved to be very effective weapon systems. As stated in the DOD's *Conduct of the Persian Gulf Conflict: Final Report to Congress*, "The cruise missile concept—incorporating an unmanned, low-observable platform able to strike accurately at long distances—was validated as a significant new instrument for future conflicts."[3] Just how significant a new instrument the cruise missile would become did not take long to unfold.

Since the 1991 Persian Gulf War, the LACM has become a U.S. weapon of choice in punishing belligerents' transgressions, coercing national leaders to behave according to U.S. wishes, and deterring adversaries' plans against U.S. interests. The following examples, which are not all inclusive, illustrate the extensive U.S. employment of LACMs since 1991.[4] In 1993, to successfully coerce Iraqi President Saddam Hussein to allow United Nations (UN) Special Commissioners inside Iraq to conduct UN-approved WMD inspections, the United States used TLAMs to destroy a suspected nuclear fabrication facility near Baghdad. Five months later, in June 1993, two dozen TLAMs were launched against Iraqi intelligence headquarters in retaliation for an Iraqi assassination attempt against former President Bush. In September 1995, the U.S. Navy used thirteen TLAMs to strike Bosnian Serb air defense targets in northwestern Bosnia after the Serbs shelled the Tuzla airport, a UN-designated "safe area." Once again punishing Iraqi leadership and forcing the Hussein regime to behave as the United States desired, the United States used approximately fifty TLAMs over a two-day period in September 1996 to attack Iraqi command and control networks, Hawk missile batteries, and other selected targets in response to Saddam's assault on Kurdish rebels and the seizure of the northern city of Irbil. Promptly retaliating for the deadly bombings of U.S. embassies in Kenya and Tanzania in August 1998, the U.S. Navy launched seventy-nine TLAMs against Osama bin Laden's three-facility "terrorist university" complex in Afghanistan and the El Shifa Pharmaceutical Factory and Chemical Complex in Khartoum, Sudan, at which bin Laden was suspected of trying to develop WMD. Once again, in an effort to coerce Saddam, in December 1998, the United States began Operation Desert Fox by launching some two hundred TLAMs against targets such as a missile design and production facility in Al Taji; Iraq's Special Security Services headquarters; and one of Saddam's presidential palace sites, Jabul Makhul, suspected of containing command offices, bunkers, and elements of Iraq's WMD programs. Secretary of Defense William Cohen stated, "It would be my hope that following this operation, Saddam Hussein would see the wisdom of finally complying with UN weapons inspections."[5] Most recently, the United States extensively employed cruise missiles (both TLAMs and CALCMs) during the March–June 1999 Operation Allied Force seventy-eight-day air campaign against Serbian President Slobodan Milosevic and his army. In fact, the rate of cruise missile use was so high, that defense planners became very concerned about depleting the inventory.

As the above events illustrate, LACMs have become a centerpiece of the U.S. military instrument of power, and their use has expanded dramatically since the Gulf War. The United States prizes its LACMs for their ability to penetrate enemy air defenses, strike at long ranges (over 1,000 miles from the launch platform for the TLAM), and most importantly, do so without endangering the lives of U.S. armed services personnel. The U.S. LACMs are the ultimate "smart weapons." Not only the United States, but the rest of the world has observed and learned. Given the United States's prominent, overall successful, and escalating use of these weapon systems throughout the

1990s, along with the proliferation of enabling technologies such as precision navigation and guidance, compact and efficient turbojet and turbofan engines, and composite and low-observable materials, it should be no surprise that countries around the world, including the U.S.-labeled rogue nations, desire and are actively pursuing cruise missiles, especially land-attack versions.[6]

Rogue nations value LACMs not only for their long-range, precision strike capabilities using conventional, high-explosive warheads but also for their potential use in delivering chemical and biological warfare (BW) agent payloads. Advances in dual-use technologies such as satellite navigation U.S. Global Positioning System (GPS) and Russian Global Navigation Satellite System (GLONASS) and highly-efficient, small turbofan engines used in aircraft, while allowing the Western nations to improve their long-range, precision strike weaponry, are also enabling lesser developed countries to close the technology gap and begin inserting comparable weaponry into their arsenals relatively "on the cheap" by historical standards and compared to other weapons systems, such as modern aircraft and ballistic missiles. Additionally, with many years of determined efforts that have recently intensified, the United States has pursued theater missile and air defense systems to counter developing and rogue countries' aircraft and increasingly sophisticated ballistic missiles, in particular. Consequently, potential adversaries are acquiring and developing hard-to-detect and -engage LACMs to maintain, and possibly enhance, their capabilities to deter and confront the United States and its allies.

These developments have clearly caught the attention of government officials, defense planners, and intelligence analysts. Dr. Ramesh Thakur, vice rector of the United Nations University, Tokyo, and author of numerous proliferation and arms control articles, stated at a March 1999 arms control conference sponsored by the U.S. Air Force Institute for National Security Studies, "For developing and rogue countries, the balance in cost, accessibility, lethality, complexity, and operational requirements is shifting from ballistic to cruise missiles."[7] More specifically, Donald Rumsfeld, former secretary of defense and chairman of the congressionally mandated 1998 Commission to Assess the Ballistic Missile Threat to the United States, stated in an April 1999 address to the National Defense University Foundation, "The United States must expect such states as Iran, Iraq, and North Korea to acquire or develop cruise missiles over the next few years."[8] Echoing this assessment, the National Intelligence Council's September 1999 unclassified report, *Foreign Missile Developments and the Ballistic Missile Threat to the United States Through 2015*, contains the following, "We expect to see acquisition of LACMs by many countries to meet regional military requirements."[9] Thus, the emerging trend seems to indicate that, in the long term, the greater threat to stability in the various regions around the world of interest to the United States may be cruise missiles instead of ballistic missiles.

This chapter focuses on a subset of the growing threat of cruise missiles by examining rogue nation acquisition and use of LACMs to deliver BW agents against future U.S. military operations in regional conflicts around the world and also against military and civilian targets within the United States and allied countries. The next section discusses some of the motivations and incentives for a rogue state to acquire WMD and their means of delivery, particularly biological weapons, along with highlights of the current assessments of the five U.S.-identified rogue states' BW capabilities. The following section describes the characteristics and key enabling technologies of LACMs and those attributes that make the LACM desirable as a delivery platform for BW agent payloads. Next is an examination of the multiple acquisition and proliferation pathways that rogue and less-developed countries are likely to exploit to obtain LACMs. Also, there is a somewhat detailed discussion of a specific, very plausible indigenous development method that rogue nations could use to develop and deploy a LACM/BW weapon system within a relatively short time period of four to ten years, depending upon the extent of foreign assistance. Lastly, the chapter concludes with a summary of some of the opinions and estimates of the U.S. intelligence community and an overall assessment to answer the question "How likely is it that rogue states will be able to employ cruise missiles to deliver BW agents in future conflicts beyond 2005?"

REASONS ROGUE NATIONS ACQUIRE BIOLOGICAL WEAPONS AND AN ASSESSMENT OF THEIR BW PROGRAMS

> The points to keep in mind about the new world of mass destruction are the following. . . . [T]he roles such weapons play in international conflict are changing. . . . Increasingly, they will be weapons of the weak—states or groups that militarily are at best second-class. The importance of the different types among them has also shifted. Biological weapons should now be the most serious concern, with nuclear weapons second and chemicals a distant third.
>
> Richard K. Betts[10]

MOTIVATIONS AND INCENTIVES TO ACQUIRE WMD

Military and Economic Levers of Strategic Power

There are numerous reasons for rogue countries to pursue WMD and their means of delivery. The most compelling motivation may be that WMD are the only viable levers of strategic power in the post–Cold War world for these nations. They are the rogue regimes' most realistic means to do the three things they desire to do but cannot accomplish with the conventional military forces they are capable of fielding—deter, constrain, and harm the

United States. During the 1991 Persian Gulf War, the United States demonstrated to the world that it had developed overwhelming superiority in conventional military force against any other nation. Although since the Gulf War, the U.S. defense budget has decreased significantly, so have the budgets of most other countries, and no country appears to be narrowing the U.S. superiority gap. Currently, the defense budget of the United States is more than triple the budget of any potentially hostile nation and more than the combined military spending of Russia, China, Iran, Iraq, North Korea, and Cuba.[11] And as Richard Betts, the director of National Security Studies at the Council on Foreign Relations, further notes, "there is no evidence that those countries' level of military professionalism is rising at a rate that would make them competitive even if they were to spend far more on their forces."[12] Rogue nations and other potentially hostile states simply cannot currently, and in the foreseeable future, successfully confront the United States on conventional military terms.

Betts, concisely describes the lesser developed countries' conventional military situation vis-à-vis the United States:

> Rolling along in what some see as a revolution in military affairs, American forces continue to make unmatched use of state-of-the-art weapons, surveillance and information systems, and the organizational and doctrinal flexibility for managing the integration of these complex innovations into "systems of systems" that is the key to modern military effectiveness. More than ever in military history, brains are brawn. Even if hostile countries somehow catch up in an arms race, their military organizations and cultures are unlikely to catch up in the competence race for management, technology assimilation, and combat command skills.[13]

That many countries are fully aware of this situation and see WMD and their delivery vehicles as an effective means of asymmetrically challenging the United States's overwhelming conventional military power is clearly illustrated by the remarks of the Indian defense minister and a former Indian army Chief of Staff in summarizing their country's main lessons from the Persian Gulf War: "Don't fight the United States unless you have nuclear weapons," and "the next conflict with the United States would involve weapons of mass destruction."[14] In essence, WMD can be a weaker country's equalizer to the larger and more advanced conventional forces of the United States and its allies.

Weapons of mass destruction, combined with stand-off delivery systems, provide lesser developed countries with far less expensive, yet qualitatively superior, military and political options for deterring, constraining, and harming the United States as compared to pursuing advanced conventional forces, whose price tag is prohibitive. In other words, WMD and long-range delivery systems allow countries to achieve their regional and strategic objectives "on the cheap." Rogue nations see WMD as an inexpensive means of coercing neighbors, deterring outside intervention, deterring other WMD threats and aggression against their interests, and directly attacking the United States and its allies, if necessary.

Although not a rogue nation, China's actions and rhetoric clearly illustrate the importance of WMD to developing countries. A senior Chinese military officer reportedly stated that the United States would not become substantively involved in a Chinese military move against Taiwanese independence because U.S. leaders "care more about Los Angeles than they do about Taiwan."[15] And obviously believing in the efficacy of their long-range nuclear missile capability in deterring U.S. involvement in what they consider internal matters, during 1996, China launched multiple short-range ballistic missiles in international waters near Taiwan to successively squelch independence movements during Taiwan's first democratic presidential election.

That countries would currently pursue WMD as a less costly and perhaps the only realistic military means of achieving national objectives is similar to the decisions in the 1950s and 1960s of the declared nuclear powers—the United States, Russia, United Kingdom, France, and China—to pursue strategic power "on the cheap" by acquiring nuclear weapons and strategic delivery systems. As an example, the U.S. expenditure on strategic nuclear systems (nuclear warheads, strategic bombers, missiles, and submarines) during the Cold War was, on average, only 10 to 15 percent of the U.S. defense budget.[16]

Technology and WMD Proliferation

The widespread proliferation of enabling technologies and the weapon systems themselves, along with ineffective post–Cold War barriers to their proliferation, are allowing rogue nations to fulfill their desires to cost-effectively acquire WMD and associated delivery systems. In the nuclear arena, India and Pakistan are prime examples of how determined states will pursue and acquire WMD regardless of the international treaties, agreements, and sanctions erected to prevent their acquisition and the subsequent stigmatization of the proliferator by the international community. In all areas of WMD—nuclear, biological, and chemical (NBC) weapons and delivery systems such as ballistic missiles, aircraft, and unmanned aerial vehicles (UAVs)—Iraq surprised the international community with the expansiveness of its WMD programs. These programs continued in spite of pre–Gulf War proliferation barriers, the concentrated attacks during the Gulf War, comprehensive international sanctions, and the unprecedented intrusiveness of the UN Special Commission (UNSCOM) on Iraq, all directed at destroying Iraq's WMD capabilities. Further exacerbating the proliferation problem is the abundance of countries willing to provide foreign assistance, offering WMD and delivery systems for direct purchase, and providing components and technologies for in-country production. The most notorious are China, North Korea, and Russia, who have been actively involved in assisting the U.S.-labeled rogue nations to develop WMD arsenals. Recent information also shows that Dr. Abdul Qadeer Khan, the father of the Pakistani A-bomb, and his associates assisted Libyan, Iranian, and North Korean nuclear efforts.

Difficulties Deterring WMD Use

Another trend enhancing rogue states' desires to acquire WMD and various delivery systems is the erosion of inhibitions on WMD use. Iraq, in particular, has clearly demonstrated the willingness to use WMD on the battlefield. Throughout the 1980–1988 Iraq-Iran War, Iraq employed chemical warfare (CW) agents against Iranian troops. In 1983, Iraq fired at least thirty-three Scud missiles at Iranian targets and is believed to have employed mustard gas on some of the missile launches against Iranian forces. During the last year of the war, in March-April 1988, Iraq attacked Tehran with two hundred Scud missiles, causing approximately one-quarter to one-half of the city's residents to flee fearing that some of the Scuds were armed with poison gas warheads.[17] That these Iraqi WMD attacks and others had a deep and lasting impression on Iranian leaders and their views of the effectiveness and international acceptability of WMD is vividly illustrated with the following 1988 remarks of then President Rafsanjani to some Iranian soldiers:

> With regard to chemical, bacteriological, and radiological weapons training, it was made very clear during the war that these weapons are very decisive. It was also made clear that the moral teachings of the world are not very effective when war reaches a serious stage and the world does not respect its own resolutions and closes its eyes to the violations and all the aggressions which are committed on the battlefield. We should fully equip ourselves both in the offensive and defensive use of chemical, bacteriological, and radiological weapons. From now on you should make use of the opportunity and perform this task.[18]

Also, during the Iraq-Iran War, Iraq became the first country to use nerve agents against an adversary on the battlefield and on its own population as well. And during the 1991 Persian Gulf War, Iraq deployed modified Scuds armed with CW and BW payloads along with other large quantities of CW agents for use by Iraqi troops. Some twenty-five Scuds were armed with BW agents, including ten with anthrax.[19] Saddam also had a dedicated aircraft in a hardened shelter equipped with spray tanks for dispersing BW agents. Had he employed this weapon on the first day of the ground war, the Office of the Secretary of Defense has assessed that over 76,000 of the 320,000 coalition troops southeast of Kuwait City would have died if they had not been vaccinated against anthrax. Apparently, Hussein was deterred from using his WMD by U.S. and Israeli threats of nuclear retaliation.

The credibility of the United States's historically successful, punitive deterrence of WMD by threatening nuclear retaliation may be declining. Richard Betts poses and opines a brief answer to a very relevant and interesting question: "Would the United States follow through and use nuclear weapons against a country or group that had killed several thousand Americans with deadly chemicals? It is hard to imagine breaking the post-Nagasaki taboo in that situation."[20] What if Hussein had used BW agents to kill 76,300 troops at the beginning of the Gulf War? Further addressing the credibility of the United States's nuclear deterrent, Dennis Gormley and Scott McMahon, experts in the area of proliferation of WMD and delivery systems, note:

> This seems to have convinced Saddam Hussein not to use his chemical or biological weapons in 1991. But there are reasons to believe that future threats of nuclear retaliation will neither deter NBC strikes nor reassure regional allies enough that they would permit Western use of their bases while under the threat of NBC attack. Senior U.S. military officers, for example, have declared that they would not condone nuclear retaliation under any circumstances, even if NBC weapons were used against the United States. Although such comments are unofficial, when they are combined with a termination of nuclear testing and the virtual elimination of nuclear planning, it becomes apparent that nuclear deterrence is fast becoming an existential rather than practical option.[21]

Another issue with exercising deterrence to prevent WMD use is that deterrence relies on retaliation, and retaliation requires knowledge of who has launched the attack. Combining a WMD such as a BW agent, which inherently creates difficulties in identifying the source of the resulting disease, with a delivery system such as a long-range LACM, which can be programmed to fly circuitous routes to the target, may provide a rogue state with a nonattributable method of attack, thus eliminating any attempts at retaliation.

National Prestige

A final factor to be discussed as influencing a country's decision to acquire WMD and their delivery systems is national prestige. Robert Gates, a former director of the Central Intelligence Agency, stated the following about WMD, "These weapons represent symbols of technical sophistication and military prowess—and acquiring powerful weapons has become the hallmark of acceptance as a world power."[22] Similarly, referring specifically to the WMD means of delivery, "some regimes in the developing world see a missile force as a talisman which imparts international respect and ushers them into the company of the great powers."[23] For this symbolic effect, the rogue countries and others such as China, India, and Pakistan have primarily focused on acquiring ballistic missiles; however, the performance of the U.S. TLAMs during the Gulf War has perhaps elevated the prestige of LACMs to that of ballistic missiles. As Richard Speier, a consultant for the Carnegie Non-Proliferation Project, has noted, "In the Gulf War the U.S. used three times as many cruise missiles as the Iraqis used ballistic missiles, and our cruise missiles had a very telling military effect."[24] This lesson has probably been well absorbed by potential adversarial countries around the world.

ADVANTAGES TO ACQUIRING BIOLOGICAL WEAPONS

Can Cause Large Numbers of Casualties

Having provided some of the motivations for rogue states and lesser developed countries to acquire WMD and their delivery systems, the following paragraphs highlight some of the reasons why Betts and many others view biological weapons as the most serious proliferation concern. (Table 8.1 captures the salient points of the following paragraphs in a very abbreviated form.) One of the main reasons can be summed up simply with a slight modification to a popular phrase—biological weapons provide "more bang for the buck and effort." As Betts observes, biological weapons combine maximum lethality with ease of availability. Nuclear weapons wreak massive destruction but are extremely difficult and costly to acquire, chemical weapons are fairly easy to acquire but possess limited killing capacity, and biological weapons possess the "best" qualities of both.[25] (Note: Biological weapons most closely resemble a special category of nuclear weapons called "neutron bombs." They harm people, not property, with lethal effects against living organisms.)

Table 8.2 contains examples of pathogens (bacteria and viruses) and toxins that are generally considered to be good BW agents for effective employment as biological weapons. Edward Eitzen, a medical doctor with the U.S. Army Medical Research Institute of Infectious Diseases (USAMRIID), noted that it has been estimated that cruise missile delivery of anthrax under suitable weather conditions could cover an area of comparable size to that of the lethal fallout from a ground-burst nuclear weapon.[26] More rigorously, the Congressional Office of Technology Assessment conducted a study in 1993 investigating the airplane dissemination (assumed to be dispensed in an effective manner) of 100 kilograms of anthrax as an aerosol cloud over Washington, DC, on a clear and calm night (good environmental conditions). The study showed that between one and three million people could be killed—300 times the number of fatalities that could be caused by a similar release of ten times the amount of sarin gas.[27] An earlier 1970 study by the World Health Organization had shown that an attack on a large city (five million people) in an economically developed country such as the United States using 50 kilograms of anthrax disseminated from a single airplane under favorable conditions could travel downwind in excess of 20 kilometers, thus affecting a large area and killing upward of 100,000 people and

Table 8.1
Comparison of NBC Weapons

				Effectiveness			
				Protected Personnel		Unprotected Personnel	
Type	Technology	Cost	Signature	Tactical	Strategic	Tactical	Strategic
Biological	+	–	–	–	–	+	++
Chemical	+	+	+	–	–	++	+
Nuclear	++	++	++	++	++	++	++

++: Very High +: High –: Lower

Source: Lester C. Caudle, "The Biological Warfare Threat," in *Medical Aspects of Chemical and Biological Warfare*, eds. Frederick R. Sidell, Ernest T. Takafuji, and David R. Franz (Washington, DC: Office of The Surgeon General at TMM Publications, 1997), 459.

Table 8.2
Candidate BW Agents for Weaponization

Disease	Causative Agent	Incubation Time (Days)	Fatalities (Percent)
Anthrax	*Bacillus anthracis*	1 to 5	80
Plague	*Yersinia pestis*	1 to 5	90
Tularemia	*Francisella tularensis*	10 to 14	5 to 20
Cholera	*Vibrio cholerae*	2 to 5	25 to 50
Venezuelan equine encephalitis	*VEE virus*	2 to 5	< 1
Q fever	*Coxiella burnetti*	12 to 21	< 1
Botulism	*Clostridium botulinum toxin*	3	30
Staphylococcal enterotoxemia	*Staphylococcus enterotoxin type B*	1 to 6	< 1
Multiple organ toxicity	*Trichothecene mycotoxin*	Dose Dependent	

Source: *The Biological & Chemical Warfare Threat* (Washington, DC: U.S. Government Printing Office, 1999), 2.

incapacitating another 250,000.[28] Additionally, U.S. military scientists verified the order of magnitude effects of BW agent release against urban populations estimated by these studies by conducting combat effects investigations at Dugway Proving Ground, Utah.[29] Thus, when comparing the killing power of WMD, on a weight-for-weight basis, BW agents are inherently more toxic than CW nerve agents, and biological weapon systems can potentially provide broader coverage per pound of payload than CW weapons.[30]

Economically and Technically Attractive

In addition to being extremely lethal and offering nations a feasible alternative to nuclear weapons as a strategic arsenal, biological weapons are economically and technically attractive, or as Betts described, easily available compared to nuclear and chemical weapons. The costs of a BW program are much lower than for nuclear and chemical weapons programs: estimates are $2 to $10 billion for a nuclear weapons program, tens of millions for a chemical program, and less than $10 million for a BW program.[31] Adding to the appeal of biological weapons, almost all the materials, technology, and equipment required for a modest BW agent program are dual-use, obtainable off the shelf from a variety of legitimate enterprises and widely available. And the technical skills required to initiate and conduct an offensive BW agent production program are commensurate with those of graduate-level microbiologists, thousands of whom are available worldwide and many of them trained in the best Western universities.[32]

The most significant technical hurdle to overcome in obtaining biological weapons is weaponization of the BW agents. The primary weaponization concerns are (1) effective dissemination of the BW agent for maximum effect (area coverage and lethality or incapacitation); (2) maintaining the viability and virulence of the BW agent; and (3) selecting the appropriate delivery system and conditions.[33] BW agents should be disseminated as an aerosol cloud for maximum infectivity via inhalation through the lungs and for maximum areal coverage. Obtaining the right aerosol particle size is extremely important. Seth Carus, a world-renowned expert and prolific writer on proliferation issues, notes that aerosolized BW agents of the wrong size could render a BW attack completely ineffective.[34] The ideal particle size ranges from one to five microns in diameter. An aerosol formed from particles in this size range is stable and can be carried downwind over long distances without significant fallout of the BW agent particles. Also, one to five microns is the ideal particle size range for retention in the lungs—particles less than one micron are readily exhaled, and particles greater than five microns are filtered out by the upper respiratory passages and do not make it to the lowest level of the lungs.

BW agents can be produced and aerosolized in either liquid or dry powder form. The liquid form is easier to produce but has a relatively short shelf life (most liquid BW agents can only be stored for three to six months under refrigeration) and can be difficult to aerosolize. Commercial sprayers can be modified for disseminating liquid BW agents, but there are nontrivial issues associated with the clogging of the sprayer nozzles and destroying the agent during the spraying process.[35] Both the shelf life and spraying limitations can be overcome by producing BW agents in dry form through lyophilization (rapid freezing and subsequent dehydration under high vacuum) and milling into a powder of the appropriate particle sizes. Anthrax spores produced in this fashion can be stored for several years.[36] However, producing dry BW agents is extremely hazardous and requires more specialized equipment and greater technical capabilities.

Whether in liquid or dry form, weaponization of BW agents must address and overcome the environmental conditions, which kill or reduce the virulence of the agents. The rate of biological decay depends on numerous factors such as ultraviolet radiation, temperature, humidity, and air pollution.[37] The optimal atmospheric conditions for a BW attack would occur on a cold, clear night with the relative humidity greater than 70 percent. The inversion layer (stable blanket of cool air above the cool ground) would prevent vertical mixing of the aerosol cloud, thus keeping the BW agent near the ground for inhalation.

As clearly indicated above, weaponization of BW agents presents many challenges. Nonetheless, from a proliferation viewpoint, it is important to note that more than forty years ago, the U.S. Army Chemical Corps overcame these challenges and successfully demonstrated and conducted tests of large area and effective dissemination of biological agents.[38]

Clandestine Acquisition

Because of the low costs associated with initiating and conducting a biological weapons program and the dual-use nature of BW research and equipment, a BW program can be carried out clandestinely, disguising the BW activities as legitimate research or completely concealing them. This is a unique feature of biological weapons programs compared to chemical and nuclear weapons programs that may make them particularly attractive to rogue nations. There are no unambiguous signatures that easily discriminate a program that is conducting legitimate biomedical research on highly contagious diseases vis-à-vis a program researching and producing BW agents for offensive military purposes. Adding to the difficulty of uncovering a clandestine BW program is the absence of verification provisions in the Biological and Toxin Weapons Convention. As the Iraqi situation has clearly illustrated to the international community, detecting and understanding the extent of a clandestine BW program are extremely difficult. In January 1999, UNSCOM on Iraq provided a report to the UN Security Council summarizing eight years of extensive investigations and destruction of Iraq's chemical and biological weapons programs. Even with these intensive and powerful (anytime, anywhere) inspections, UNSCOM officials now believe that Iraq, through well-coordinated concealment and deception efforts, may have produced another, as yet unidentified, BW agent in an unreported and unlocated production facility.[39]

Clandestine Use

From an aggressor's perspective, another advantage of biological weapons over chemical or nuclear weapons is that there are currently no highly reliable detection devices available to provide advanced warning of a BW attack, thus allowing a greater probability of large numbers of casualties per weapon use. Additionally, coupled with the delayed onset of symptoms from a BW attack and the fact that these symptoms could easily be attributed to a natural outbreak of disease, biological weapons potentially provide the country employing them plausible deniability. Thus, an attacker may use biological weapons as a precursor to a conventional military attack to wreak havoc and weaken the target forces of a conventionally superior foe with a reduced risk of retaliation and condemnation from the attacked country and international community. (Note: It would likely be possible to identify a large outbreak of something such as anthrax as an almost certain BW attack because large outbreaks of this disease occur rarely, if at all, in nature. However, the outbreak of a common disease regularly found in a given region of the world would possibly be seen at first as a natural outbreak.)

ASSESSMENT OF ROGUE STATE BW CAPABILITIES

As the previous paragraphs have shown, for those nations desiring to acquire WMD, biological weapons offer some technical, economic, military, and political advantages over both chemical and nuclear weapons. Thus, it is understandable (but highly undesirable from a U.S. perspective) that many countries currently possess, are probably actively pursuing, or could potentially develop biological weapons. According to an assessment by the Center for Nonproliferation Studies (CNS) at the Monterey Institute of International Studies, eleven countries have BW programs that range from possible BW agent research activities to production and maintenance of an offensive biological weapons capability.[40] Table 8.3 summarizes the CNS assessment. All five of the U.S.-labeled rogue states—Iran, Iraq, Libya, North Korea, and Syria—are believed to have offensive BW programs.

Iran

Arnold Beichman, a reporter for *The Washington Times*, concludes that Iran's BW efforts are part of its overall campaign to become the dominant power in the Middle East, and in his view, Iran is a greater danger to the world than Iraq.[41] According to Paula DeSutter, a former Senior Fellow for Arms Control and Nonproliferation at the former Arms Control and Disarmament Agency (ACDA), in its quest to become the regional hegemon, "Iran considers the United States to be the primary threat to Iranian interests, and U.S. forces in the region could well be perceived by Iran as lucrative targets for NBC weapons—which Iran will be able to deliver through both traditional and novel means, presenting challenges to U.S. defenses."[42] Furthermore, DeSutter emphasizes that Iran's use of NBC will be particularly difficult to deter and that, in fact, the possibility of the United States failing to deter future Iranian use of WMD is significant.

Some of the reasons for DeSutter's dire assessment were alluded to in the introduction of this chapter. Having been the victims of extensive WMD use, the Iranians emerged from the 1980–1988 Iran-Iraq War determined to develop WMD and missile delivery systems to deter future Iraqi aggression. This desire to develop a WMD deterrent capability was further strengthened by a key lesson learned from the 1991 Gulf War. As was the case for Iraq's military, Iran's conventional forces would not be able to prevent U.S. actions in the region. Thus, Iranian leaders view WMD and their means of delivery as an essential component of the military capabilities required to ensure Iran's security.

Beichman reported that Iranian President Mohammed Khatami has created a science and technology group of advisers, headquartered in the Mahsa Building in Tehran, to supervise his regime's NBC programs. These programs include four different groups currently engaged in producing biological weapons: Special Industries Organization of Iran's Ministry of Defense, Research Center of the Construction Crusade, Revolutionary Guard Corps research at Imam Hossein University, and The Biotechnology Research Center. Additionally, the Iranians have hired Russian, Chinese, and North Korean BW experts to work at these facilities.[43] Based on official unclassified DOD, Central Intelligence Agency (CIA), and ACDA reports, Iran has investigated since the early 1980s both pathogens and toxins as BW agents, produced some agents, and apparently weaponized a small quantity of those produced. Iran is judged to be able to support an independent BW program, possesses the in-house capacity for large-scale agent production, and could have an indigenously developed BW warhead for ballistic missile delivery around the 2000 time frame. Iran is also expected to employ cruise missiles with spray tanks as future BW agent delivery systems.[44]

Iraq

The almost continuous and surprising revelations about Iraq's BW programs, and the phenomenal concealment and deception efforts undertaken to deny information to the UNSCOM from the beginning of its inspections of Iraq's BW activities, clearly show the importance of biological weapons to rogue countries. Richard Butler, the former executive chairman of the UNSCOM, recently commented that of the panoply of Iraq's NBC programs, the BW programs have been the most important to Saddam. Butler remarked:

> Over nine years now, Iraq has consistently made extraordinarily strenuous efforts to hide the biological program—well beyond those they made on missiles or chemicals. Why? Why? No effort was too much to prevent us from getting to the truth. That says to me it was big and nasty.[45]

During these nine years, UNSCOM inspectors, along with the 1995 defection of Iraqi General Hussein Kamal Hassan, have revealed that Iraq's BW program was far more extensive and advanced before the 1991 Persian Gulf War than anyone had suspected.

Iraq produced three bacterial agents (*Bacillus anthracis*, *Clostridium botulinum*, and *Clostridium perfringens*), the fungal toxin aflatoxin, the plant-derived toxin ricin, and the fungal antiplant agent wheat smut and conducted research on other fungal toxins such as *tricothecene mycotoxins*. Iraq also carried out a research program on three viral agents: infectious hemorrhagic conjunctivitis virus, rotavirus, and camel pox.[46] Some of these BW agents were weaponized before the 1991 Gulf War: 166 bombs (100 botulinum toxin, 50 anthrax, 16 aflatoxin); 25 Scud/Al Hussein missile warheads (13 botulinum toxin, 10 anthrax, 2 aflatoxin); 122-millimeter rockets filled with these three agents; spray tanks capable of being fitted to a fighter or remotely

Table 8.3
International Biological Warfare Agent and Weapons Programs

Country	Program Status	Possible Agents
Algeria	Researching biological weapons, but no evidence of production	Unknown
China	Probably maintains an offensive BW program	Unknown
Egypt	Researching biological weapons	anthrax, botulinum toxin, plague, cholera, tularemia, glanders, brucellosis, melioidosis, psittacosis, Q fever, Japanese B encephalitis, Eastern equine encephalitis, influenza, smallpox, mycotoxins
Iran	Researching biological weapons; probably has produced BW agents and weaponized a small quantity	Unknown
Iraq	Previously active research and production program; suspected of retaining clandestine elements of its BW program *prior to OIF. None found after OIF. (CPC Added)*	anthrax, botulinum toxin, gas gangrene, aflatoxin, trichothecene mycotoxins, wheat cover smut, ricin, hemorrhagic conjunctivitis virus, rotavirus, camel pox

Israel	Researching biological weapons, but no evidence of production	Unknown
Libya	Researching biological weapons	Unknown
North Korea	Has researched biological weapons since early 1960s	anthrax, cholera, plague, smallpox, botulinum toxin, hemorrhagic fever, typhoid, yellow fever
Russia	Possible research and production programs beyond legitimate defense activities	Extensive list from "A to Z"
Syria	Researching biological weapons; program may have reached weaponization stage	anthrax, cholera, botulinum toxin
Taiwan	Possible research program	Unknown

Source: Center for Nonproliferation Studies, Monterey Institute of International Studies, "Chemical and Biological Weapons Possession and Programs: Past and Present," n.p.; on-line, Internet, February 14, 2000, available from http://www.cns.miis.edu/research/cbw/possess.htm.

piloted aircraft and spraying 2,000 liters of BW agents over a target area; and artillery shells filled with BW agents.[47]

The bottom line is that even after the targeted destruction of Iraq's BW capabilities during the 1991 Gulf War and the subsequent nine years of UNSCOM discovery and elimination activities, the Hussein regime still possibly possessed a BW capability although little trace of this program has been found after the occupation of Iraq in 2003.

Libya

There is little open-source information available on the current status and sophistication of Libya's BW programs. In its 1997 Annual Report to Congress, *Adherence to and Compliance with Arms Control Agreements*, ACDA reported that there is evidence suggesting that Libya is seeking to acquire the capability to produce BW agents and has the expertise to manufacture limited quantities of biological production equipment for a BW program. Additionally, although the current Libyan BW program is in the research and development stage, the Libyan government is trying to move the program toward weaponization of BW agents.[48] Indicating that Libya may have made progress toward weaponizing BW agents, the CNS assessment of worldwide BW programs contains the following statement from a Russian source: "There is information indicating that Libya is engaged in initial testing in the area of biological weapons."[49]

North Korea

Similar to the case of Libya, there is minimal discussion in unclassified sources about North Korea's BW activities. However, unlike Libya, as Seth Carus observes, North Korea has been conducting BW research since the early 1960s and most likely has capabilities equal to or greater than Iraq's. Carus has rank-ordered the rogue nations' competence in waging biological warfare from highest to lowest as North Korea, Iraq, Iran, Syria, and Libya.[50] The CNS assessment, using DOD and Russian intelligence sources, is that North Korea possesses the biotechnical infrastructure to support a limited BW effort and is conducting military-applied research on anthrax, cholera, plague, smallpox, botulinum toxin, hemorrhagic fever, typhoid, and yellow fever.[51] Recently, the Japanese Defense Agency Chief, Hosei Norota, stated that there were several factories in North Korea that were producing "toxic gas and germs" that could be weaponized.[52] South Korea's 1998 Defense White Paper reports that by 1980, North Korea had succeeded in producing bacterial and viral BW agents, had completed live experiments with these weaponized agents by the late 1980s, and is suspected of maintaining several facilities for producing BW agents and biological weapons.[53]

Syria

Syria has very strong motivations for developing WMD and missile delivery systems. First and foremost, Syria views Israel as an aggressive and expansionist state seeking to fulfill its biblical promises of occupying the lands from the Nile to the Euphrates Rivers as evidenced by Israel's development and possession of nuclear weapons, its heavy armored ground forces, and its powerful air force, which conducted a devastating strategic bombing campaign against Syria during the 1973 war. Consequently, missile-delivered WMD serve as a deterrent to balance Israel's nuclear capabilities and counter the threat posed by Israel's formidable ground and air forces.[54] Concerning its BW capabilities, a U.S. government official briefed in 1995 that Syria's Damascus Biological Research Facility is conducting BW research on anthrax, cholera, and botulinum toxin. Researchers are receiving foreign assistance (possibly from China), and Syria probably has a production capability for their researched BW agents. Furthermore, their BW program may have reached the weaponization stage.[55] Lastly and of particular note, Syria and Iran are cooperating extensively, both technically and economically, on developing offensive BW weapon systems.[56]

LAND-ATTACK CRUISE MISSILES AS BW DELIVERY SYSTEMS

> States able to couple weapons of mass destruction to delivery systems with longer range or greater ability to penetrate defenses can threaten more nations with higher levels of destruction, and with greater likelihood of success.
>
> Office of Technology Assessment, U.S. Congress[57]

CRUISE MISSILE DESCRIPTION

Cruise missile definitions abound in the literature, and no two seem to be the same. A good, fairly comprehensive description of a cruise missile is the following: an unmanned aircraft configured as an antisurface weapon intended to impact on, or detonate over, a preselected surface (land or sea) target; it has an integral means of sustained self-propulsion and a precision guidance system (usually autonomous but possibly requiring limited external input from a human operator); aerodynamic surfaces are used to generate lift to sustain the missile's flight; and the missile autonomously achieves a sustained cruise phase of flight at a predetermined level relative to overflown terrain or water.[58] Given these characteristics, cruise missiles can be considered a subset of armed, unmanned aerial vehicles (UAVs) or standoff weapons.

It is important to note that cruise missiles differ significantly from ballistic missiles. A ballistic missile is an unmanned rocket that is powered only during the initial phase (ascent) of its trajectory, reaches exo-atmospheric heights if it is a longer-range missile, and traverses the majority of its trajectory unpowered (i.e., ballistically). Unlike a cruise missile, ballistic missiles cannot usually be guided after launch. (Some of the more advanced ballistic missile systems are armed with guided reentry vehicles.) Thus, at the risk of oversimplification, a ballistic missile is essentially a rocket, and a cruise missile is an aircraftlike system although it may be rocket-powered. However, most cruise missiles, especially the longer range systems, use air-breathing engines—pulsejet, ramjet, turbojet, or turbofan—and can even be propeller-driven. Cruise missiles can fly as slow as 100 kilometers per hour (kph) (62 miles per hour) or at supersonic speeds greater than Mach 3 (Mach 1 is 1,200 kph at sea level) depending on design and intended mission. Most travel at aircraftlike speeds in the mid- to high-subsonic range. Cruise missile flight ranges span from 20 kilometers (km) to over 3,000 km.[59] Their flight profiles also vary widely. Some fly at high altitudes for fuel savings and increased range, then descend to approach the target; others fly the entire profile at low altitude. The more sophisticated cruise missiles produced by the United States, Russia, and France can fly courses of varying altitudes and azimuths to evade enemy air defenses.

Typically, cruise missiles are categorized according to the intended mission and launch mode instead of their maximum range, which is the classification scheme for ballistic missiles. The two broadest categories are antiship cruise missiles (ASCMs) and LACMs.[60] ASCMs are the most widely deployed cruise missiles; currently they are in the military arsenals of seventy-three countries.[61] As noted by Seth Carus, they are the most important naval weapons possessed by many of these countries: "The punch provided by ASCMs has made it possible for Third World countries to maintain relatively powerful naval forces that rely on comparatively inexpensive missile-armed patrol boats or small corvettes."[62] ASCMs are designed to strike small targets, that is, ships at sea at relatively long ranges (up to approximately 500 km) and thus are terminally guided to ships with high accuracy. The terminal guidance systems are active or semiactive radar, radar-homing, infrared, television, or home-on-jam.[63]

LACMs are designed to attack mobile or fixed, ground-based targets. The basic components of a LACM are the airframe, propulsion system, navigation and guidance system, and warhead. Basically, the LACM airframe is an elongated, cylindrical missile/aircraft structure with short wings and rudders and constructed from metals and composite materials. The propulsion system (rocket or air-breathing engine) is located in the rear; the navigation and guidance system is located in the front; and the fuel and warhead are typically located in the midbody.[64] (See Figure 8.1.) Guidance of a LACM is usually a three-phase process: launch, midcourse, and terminal guidance. During launch, the inertial navigation system (INS) guides the LACM. In

Figure 8.1
Schematic of the Components of a Land-Attack Cruise Missile

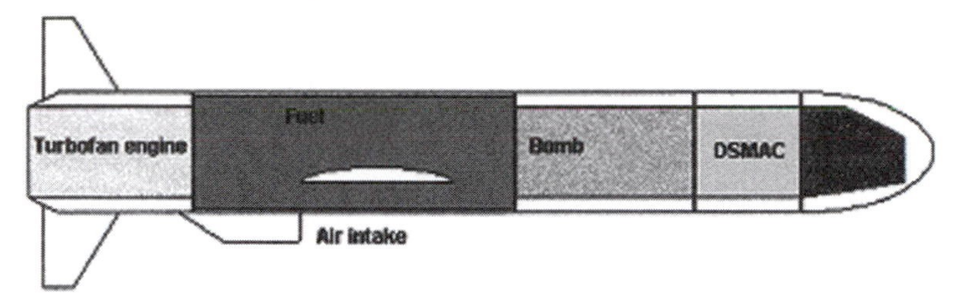

Source: Marshall Brain, "How Cruise Missiles Work," n.p.; on-line, Internet, March 25, 2000, available from http://www.howstuffworks.com/cruise-missile.htm.

the midcourse phase, a radar-based terrain contour matching (TERCOM) system and/or satellite navigation system (such as the U.S. GPS or Russian GLONASS) correct for the inherent inaccuracies of the INS.[65] Upon entering the target area, the terminal guidance system is used and consists of one, or a combination, of the following: GPS/GLONASS, TERCOM with more accurate terrain contour digital maps, Digital Scene Matching Correlator (DSMAC) or a terminal seeker (optical- or radar-based sensor).[66] The mission ranges of LACMs currently in the military arsenals around the world span from 50 to more than 3,000 km, with most designed to travel at high subsonic speeds. Figure 8.2 is a sketch of LACMs produced by various countries.

CRUISE MISSILE TECHNOLOGIES

Coinciding with the "eye-opening" performance of the U.S. TLAMs during the 1991 Persian Gulf War was the beginning of the elimination of substantial technological barriers to Third World countries producing accurate LACMs. Specifically, until the late 1980s, accurate LACMs required sophisticated guidance and navigation technologies—stand-alone, accurate and complex INS, TERCOM, and DSMAC—that were well controlled by the Missile Technology Control Regime (MTCR) and thus only available to a few countries such as the United States, the United Kingdom, Soviet Union, and France.[67] Now there are critically enabling technologies available commercially that will allow rogue states to acquire militarily as well as politically effective LACMs: precision navigation and guidance technologies (GPS, Differential GPS [DGPS], GLONASS); mission planning tools (high-resolution [1 meter]) satellite imagery and sophisticated Geographical

Figure 8.2
Land-Attack Cruise Missiles of Various Countries

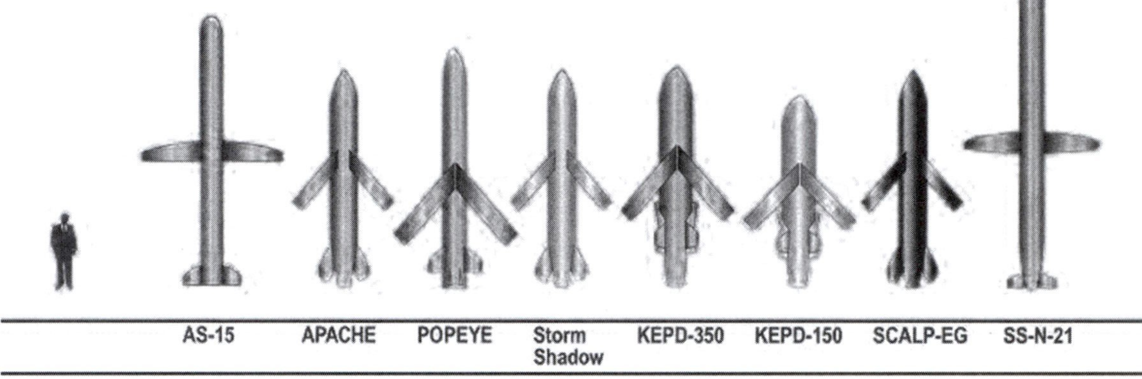

Source: National Air Intelligence Center, *Ballistic and Cruise Missile Threat*, NAIC-1031-0985-99 (Dayton, OH: Wright-Patterson Air Force Base, April 1999), 16.

Information Systems (GIS); high-efficiency, reduced-volume air-breathing engines; more efficient fuels; and composite and low-observable materials.

The commercial availability of accurate satellite navigation updates has allowed Third World countries to leapfrog probably fifteen years of development for long-range, fairly accurate LACMs. Relatively inaccurate and widely available $50,000 INS systems can now be combined with low-cost GPS receivers (a few hundred dollars at most) to achieve the navigational accuracies of stand-alone, fairly accurate INS systems produced only for Western commercial aircraft and costing roughly $150,000.[68] GPS, DGPS, and GLONASS receivers can be incorporated into all guidance phases of a flight—launch, midcourse, and terminal. Used in combination, these technologies allow Third World countries to develop LACMs that are robust with respect to GPS degradation and can deliver a payload to within a few meters of the intended target. Commercial DGPS systems are available worldwide and can improve the accuracy of GPS Coarse/Acquisition (the GPS signal available to all users and providing accuracies around 30 meters [m]) guidance by an order of magnitude.[69] Additionally, GLONASS, used in conjunction with GPS, improves robustness and accuracy of the guidance system. Honeywell and Northwest Airlines have developed and tested integrated GPS-GLONASS receivers for commercial airline use and have achieved accuracies below 20 m.[70]

GPS, DGPS, and GLONASS guidance technologies provide sufficient LACM accuracies for delivery of both conventional and NBC payloads without the need for a Third World country to employ TERCOM- or DSMAC-like systems, which require extensive digital maps. However, a Third World country may want to develop a LACM that flies at very low altitudes and maximizes terrain masking in order to increase in-flight survivability and penetration of air defenses. Such low-altitude flight capabilities would require accurate digital map-making capabilities that, until recently, were prohibitively costly. Now such capabilities are commercially available and within affordable ranges for some lesser developed countries. A Third World country can purchase 1-m resolution satellite imagery, add accurate GPS/DGPS position information with GIS, and produce very accurate 3-D digital maps.[71]

Other LACM-enabling technologies are the increasingly efficient fuels and turbojet and turbofan engines available on the international marketplace that provide Third World countries the capability of producing cruise missiles with ranges of at least 1,000 km.[72] Additionally, commercially available radar absorbing structures, materials, and coatings along with infrared suppression techniques can greatly reduce the signatures of a Third World country's cruise missiles. Incorporation of these technologies into LACMs significantly and disproportionately complicates U.S. and allied air defense efforts should these LACMs be used in regional conflicts.

DESIRABLE ATTRIBUTES OF LAND-ATTACK CRUISE MISSILES

Besides accessibility to the technologies as described, there are many advantageous characteristics of LACMs as weapon systems that motivate lesser developed countries with limited monetary resources to acquire or develop them as part of a balanced military strike force, which includes combat aircraft, ballistic missiles, and cruise missiles. One particularly desirable feature is their relatively small size, especially compared to aircraft and ballistic missiles. Coupled with the LACM's aerodynamic flight to the target (as opposed to ballistic dynamics), which eliminates the need for stabilization at launch, LACMs are easily deployable on a wide variety of platforms—ships, submarines, aircraft, and small fixed or mobile land-based launchers. This flexibility in carrier platform translates directly into increased survivability before launch. Unlike a combat aircraft, a LACM is not restricted to operating from airfields, which, during conflict, are extremely vulnerable to preemptive attacks by the adversary. Also, on land, LACMs are much easier to hide from opposing forces and more mobile than ballistic missiles (no presurveyed launch site required), further enhancing a rogue nation's ability to conduct "shoot and scoot" launches, which the Iraqis executed with great success against the United States during the Persian Gulf War in spite of the United States's intensive "Scud hunt" operations.

A very interesting and potential sea-based exploitation of the LACM's small size has been discussed by Dennis Gormley.[73] Even a bulky, fairly large 500- to 700-km range LACM (8.5 m in length, 0.8-m body diameter, 2.4-m wingspan), that a rogue nation such as Iran might be expected to indigenously produce by the 2005–2010 time frame (discussed in more detail in the next section), can fit into a standard 12-m shipping container along with a small erector constructed for launching the LACM directly out of the container. The international maritime fleet consists of thousands of commercial ships using these containers, and on any given day, about 1,000 ships are transiting the Atlantic. Only 4 percent of these ships are scrutinized by customs upon docking in U.S. ports. Furthermore, the United States ports handle thirteen million shipping containers annually. A range of 500 to 700 km allows a rogue country deploying such a ship-based LACM to remain outside the 200-mile territorial waters zone and strike the majority of the key population and industrial centers in both Europe and North America. Such a threat is extremely challenging, posing both a very difficult monitoring challenge for the intelligence community and challenges for establishing adequate defenses. Gormley states in a Spring 1998 *Survival* article that "the non-governmental 'Gates Panel,' in reviewing NIE [National Intelligence Estimate] 95–19, . . . concluded that not nearly enough attention was being devoted to the possibility that land-attack cruise missiles could be launched from ships within several hundred kilometers of U.S. territory."[74]

Perhaps in response to this criticism, the Intelligence Community's most recent (September 1999) unclassified NIE on the ballistic missile threat to the United States through the year 2015 states:

> A commercial surface vessel, covertly equipped to launch cruise missiles, would be a plausible alternative for a forward-based launch platform. This method would provide a large and potentially inconspicuous platform to launch a cruise missile while providing at least some cover for launch deniability.[75]

Another benefit of the LACM's relatively small size and design is the resultant increased survivability of the missile during flight. Because of its small size, a LACM has inherently low visual, infrared (IR) and radar signatures. The reduced radar observability, referred to as a reduced radar cross section (RCS), makes the missile difficult for air defense radars to detect, identify, track, and engage, especially compared to the conventional combat aircraft in a rogue state's arsenal. Complicating the problem for the air defenses, a LACM can readily be made more difficult to detect with the application of low-observable materials. The simplest approach would be to apply radar-absorbing coatings to the airframe surface and incorporate an IR reduction cone around the engine. The airframe could also be constructed with radar absorbing polymers and nonmetallic composites to minimally reflect radar energy. Or, requiring the most technical skill, the shape, structure, composition, and integration of subcomponents of the LACM could be designed and constructed from the beginning with very low observability as the goal.

The impact of reduced observability can be dramatic because it reduces the maximum range from missile defenses that an incoming LACM can be detected, resulting in minimal time for intercept. To illustrate, a conventional combat aircraft, such as an F-4 fighter, has an RCS of about 6 square meters (m^2), and the much larger, but low-observable B-2 bomber, which incorporated advanced stealth technologies into its design, has an RCS of only approximately 0.75 m^2.[76] A typical cruise missile with UAV-like characteristics has an RCS in the range of 1 m^2; the U.S.'s Tomahawk air-launched cruise missile (ALCM), designed in the 1970s utilizing the fairly simple low-observable technologies then available, has an RCS of less than 0.05 m^2. The U.S. AWACS radar system was designed to detect aircraft with an RCS of 7 m^2 at a range of at least 370 km. Using the physics of radar detection, which dictates that detection range varies with the object's RCS raised to the one-fourth power, the AWACS radar could detect the typical, nonstealthy cruise missile at a range of at least 227 km, and the stealthy cruise missile would approach air defenses to within a range of 108 km before being detected. Traveling at a speed of 805 kph (500 mph), air defenses would have only eight minutes to engage and destroy the stealthy missile and seventeen minutes for the nonstealthy missile. Furthermore, a low-observable LACM can be difficult to engage and destroy even if detected. According to Seth Carus, a Soviet analyst assessed that cruise missiles with RCSs of 0.1 m^2 or smaller were difficult for surface-to-air missile (SAM) fire control radars to track.[77] Consequently, even if the SAM battery detects the missile, it may not acquire a sufficient lock on the target to successfully intercept. Even IR tracking devices may not detect low-observable LACMs, and IR-seeking SAMs may not home in on the missile. To further thwart engagement, a LACM could employ relatively simple countermeasures such as chaff and decoys.

Further increasing its survivability, a LACM can avoid detection by air defenses through programmed flight paths on which the LACM approaches the target at extremely low altitudes, blending its small signatures into the large ground clutter, and also takes advantage of terrain masking. Technologies that enable "terrain hugging" flight—radar altimetry, precision guidance and satellite navigation, computerized flight control, high-resolution satellite imagery, and digitized terrain map making via sophisticated GIS—are becoming increasingly available from commercial sources at affordable costs. These technologies also enable the longer range LACMs to be programmed to fly lengthy and circuitous routes to the target to minimize their exposure to air defense systems and perhaps eliminate the exposure altogether.

Another approach to penetrate air defenses that is afforded by the operational flexibility of the LACM is to launch multiple missiles against a target simultaneously from varied directions, overwhelming air defenses at their weakest points. Also, a rogue state could launch both theater ballistic and cruise missiles to arrive simultaneously at the designated target. The different characteristics of these two approaching missiles—high-altitude, supersonic ballistic trajectory of the ballistic missiles and low-altitude, subsonic flight of the cruise missiles—could stress and overwhelm the capabilities of the most advanced air defense systems. A Joint Chiefs of Staff official interviewed by an *Aviation Week & Space Technology* reporter commented, "A sophisticated foe might be able to fire 20 or 30 [Scud-type] battlefield ballistic missiles, followed by aircraft that pop up to launch waves of cruise missiles. The resulting problem for U.S. defenders would be staggering in complexity."[78] And a former senior planner for Operation Desert Storm commented, "During Desert Storm, if the Iraqis could have fired even one cruise missile a day—with a two-city block [accuracy]—into the headquarters complex in Riyadh, we would have been out of commission about half the time."[79] Complicating the defender's situation even further, the attacker could time the LACM strikes to coincide with the return of the defender's aircraft, thereby greatly complicating an already difficult problem for the defender of identifying friend from foe. As stated by a senior official at the Pentagon's Joint Theater Air and Missile Defense Office, "The challenge with ballistic missiles is hitting them . . . . With cruise missiles, it's figuring out whether it's friendly or not."[80]

Enabled by the increasing commercial availability of advances in key technologies for all components of a LACM—airframe, propulsion, guidance and navigation, and warhead—the combined accuracy and range attributes of LACMs now exceed those of ballistic missile systems at far less cost per weapon system. For example, LACMs can be developed with similar-sized warheads and ranges as those of substantially more complex ballistic missiles but at less than half the cost (approximately $250,000 or less versus $1,000,000) and with at least ten times the warhead delivery accuracy (10–100 m circular error probable (CEP) compared to 1,000–2,000 m CEP).[81] By carrying different warheads, a LACM provides a rogue nation more cost-effective capabilities for deep strike of heavily defended targets such as airfields, ports, staging areas, troop concentrations, amphibious landing areas, logistics centers, and command, control, communications and intelligence nodes. Additionally, since the accuracy of the LACM is significantly better than a similar-range ballistic missile, the probability of destroying or damaging the target is much higher. Furthermore, the range of a LACM is extended by the range of its platform, which gives it the capability to attack targets well beyond the range of a comparable ballistic missile. Also, as is the case for ballistic missiles, the LACM attacks are carried out without risking the loss of aircrew lives.

As a delivery system for WMD, LACMs are ideally suited for disseminating BW agents. As would be the case for aircraft dissemination, a subsonic LACM, using an aerosol sprayer embedded in its wings and built-in meteorological sensors coupled to the guidance and control computer, could alter its flight profile and release a line source of BW agent tailored to the local topography, micrometeorological conditions, and shape of the target, thus maximizing the resultant lethal area of the BW payload. The advantage of employing a LACM for BW agent delivery as opposed to an aircraft is that a pilot's life is not risked; the disadvantage is forfeiture of pilot improvisation. According to Gormley, "The lethal areas for a given quantity of CBW [chemical or biological warfare agents], and this is a very, very conservative calculation, are at least ten times that of a ballistic missile delivery program. This judgment reflects the results of extensive modeling and simulation."[82] In Gormley's simulation, an optimal pattern of distribution of CBW agents using submunitions was assumed for ballistic missile delivery. For LACM delivery, both worst-case and best-case distributions were averaged for the comparison. The increased lethality area for a LACM-delivered CBW payload is primarily attributable to the aerodynamic stability of the LACM and the capability of distributing the CBW agent payload as a line source. It is interesting to note that the United States investigated using the Snark cruise missile for delivery of BW and CW agent payloads as early as 1952, and through the early 1960s funded projects developing dissemination systems for cruise missiles and drones.[83]

In addition to achieving significantly more effective dissemination of BW agents, subsonic LACM delivery is simply technically less challenging than supersonic ballistic missile delivery. There are considerable technical difficulties with packaging BW agents within a ballistic missile warhead and ensuring that the agent survives and is disseminated as an aerosol at the correct height above the ground.[84] The reentry speed is so high during the descent phase of the ballistic missile's trajectory that it is difficult to distribute the agent in a diffuse cloud or with the precision to ensure dissemination within the inversion layer of the atmosphere. Also, the high thermal and mechanical stresses generated during launch, reentry, and agent release may degrade the quality of the BW agent. U.S. tests have shown that, without appropriate agent packaging, less than 5 percent of a BW agent payload is viable after flight and dissemination from a ballistic missile.

There are a few other operational features of LACMs that may make them economically and militarily appealing to a lesser developed country building strike capabilities with very limited defense resources. Compared to aircraft and ballistic missiles, LACMs require less support infrastructure and have lower operations and maintenance costs. They can reside in canisters, which makes them significantly easier to maintain and operate in harsh environments. Furthermore, since they are unmanned, the need for expensive pilot and crew training is eliminated.

PROLIFERATION PATHWAYS FOR LAND-ATTACK CRUISE MISSILES

> Until recently, the problem of cruise missile proliferation centered on antiship—not land-attack—systems. But now there is growing concern that the developing world will acquire land-attack cruise missiles. . . . Should such strike systems proliferate into the arsenals of rogue states, they could present serious challenges to U.S. force planners in a variety of military contingencies.
>
> K. Scott McMahon and Dennis M. Gormley[85]

In estimating the time frame by which rogue nations may acquire threatening LACMs as BW payload delivery systems, many factors must be considered. Three important factors were discussed in the previous sections of this chapter: (1) the motivations and incentives for countries to acquire WMD (biological weapons, in particular); (2) the operational and economic advantages of LACMs as part of a precision strike force; and (3) the commercial availability and proliferation of key enabling technologies for accurate, long-range LACMs. Another major factor is the multiple and varied acquisition paths available to rogue nations. Three major proliferation pathways that are likely to be used by rogue states are (1) the direct purchase of complete LACMs from another country; (2) indigenous development of LACMs, with or without outside assistance; and (3) conversion of ASCMs or UAVs to land-attack weapon systems.

DIRECT PURCHASE

The quickest way for a rogue country to obtain LACMs is to purchase them directly from producer nations. In the past this acquisition path was unavailable because the only producers of complete LACM systems were France, Russia, and the United States, and they did not export their missiles. However, within the next decade, the number of countries besides the United States that produce LACMs will jump from two to nine.[86] Table 8.4 summarizes this rapid growth in the number of LACM-producing countries and the systems currently under development. Most of the LACMs under development will incorporate low-observable technologies, have modular designs that readily facilitate range and payload modifications, will have multiple navigation and warhead options, and will be deployable from a variety of platforms.[87] Many of these countries, including France and Russia, will probably make their LACMs available for export, especially given the increasing desires of the more industrialized countries to export advanced weapon systems because of shrinking domestic military sales during the recent years of declining defense budgets. Market analysts project that six thousand to seven thousand LACMs could be sold by 2015, excluding U.S., Russian, and Chinese sales.[88]

Halting the export of LACMs will be extremely difficult because of the serious shortcomings of the MTCR, the only international export control arrangement that actively attempts to control the proliferation of cruise missiles, their subcomponents, and key enabling technologies.[89] MTCR members voluntarily pledge to adopt the regime's export guidelines and to restrict the export of items contained in the regime's annex. Category I of the MTCR annex requires member states to make a strong presumption to deny exports of UAVs and cruise missiles (and their key subsystems, technologies, and production facilities) carrying 500-kg payloads to ranges of 300 km or more. Category II urges member discretion in exporting dual-use components and complete missiles capable of 300-km ranges with any payload.

From a LACM proliferation viewpoint, the most serious problem with the MTCR is that there is no approved methodology among the MTCR members for determining the Category I range and payload threshold for cruise missiles.[90] Determining a cruise missile's range is not straightforward because of flight profile variability and ease in trading off range and payload to improve mission performance. Therefore, judging whether a LACM is Category I or Category II is very difficult and leads to different interpretations and disagreements among the members, thus weakening the regime's ability to control LACM export. Additionally, the MTCR places only very weak controls on the export of low-observable technologies. The regime also permits exports to support both civilian and military manned aircraft. The guidance systems, INSs, flight controls, autopilots, avionics, jet engines, and other components and technologies for many of these aircraft are usable in cruise

Table 8.4
Non-U.S. Land-Attack Cruise Missiles

System	Country	Launch Mode	Warhead Type	Maximum Range (kilometers)	Initial Operational Capability
Chinese cruise missile	China	Undetermined	Conventional or nuclear	Undetermined	Undetermined
APACHE-A	France	Air	Conventional submunitions	160+	1999
SCALP-EG	France	Air & ship	Conventional/ penetrator	480+	2002
KEPD-350	Germany/ Sweden/ Italy	Air & ground	Conventional/ unitary	350+	2002
KEPD-150	Germany/ Sweden/ Italy	Air & ship	Conventional/ unitary or submunitions	160+	2002

Popeye Turbo	Israel	Air	Conventional/ unitary	320+	2002
AS-15	Russia	Air	Nuclear	2,400+	Operational
SS-N-21	Russia	Submarine	Nuclear	2,400+	Operational
Russian conventional cruise missile	Russia	Undetermined	Conventional/ unitary or submunitions	Undetermined	Undetermined
MUPSOW	South Africa	Air & ground	Conventional/ unitary or submunitions	200+	2002
Storm Shadow	United Kingdom	Air	Conventional/ penetrator	480+	2002

All ranges are approximate and represent the range of the missile only.
Source: National Air Intelligence Center, *Ballistic and Cruise Missile Threat*, NAIC-1031-0985-99 (unclassified) (Dayton, OH: Wright-Patterson Air Force Base, April 1999), 20.

missiles.[91] Finally, there are no provisions in the regime for enforcement of its terms or sanctions for violations. Essentially, the door is wide open for lesser developed countries to purchase highly capable LACMs, and unless international controls on cruise-missile exports can be strengthened, this pathway may become the major source of advanced LACM proliferation.

Although no known direct transfers of complete LACMs have yet occurred, France is considering exporting a 140-km range, 520-kg payload variant of its very sophisticated, state-of-the-art, stealthy Apache LACM.[92] The Apache is modular in design and will be produced in three variants, all of which use the same 1,200-kg airframe. The Apache with its 1,200-kg airframe being considered for export can carry a 500-kg payload beyond 300 km, clearly making any variant of the Apache an MTCR Category I cruise missile. However, to date, the United States has been unsuccessful in convincing the French that the advertised Apache variant is Category I.[93] With regard to stealth, the Apache is Tomahawk-level or better. Additionally, it uses a millimeter-wave radar system similar to TERCOM, allowing for low-altitude flight profiles, incorporates GPS midcourse guidance updates, employs a terminal seeker with a radome (which reduces the active signature of the terminal guidance system), and has a reported accuracy of 1- to 2-m CEP.[94] Gormley warns, "Should such a system fall into the wrong hands, it would provide not only design insight into an advanced-technology missile, but also a robust threat system capable of challenging the most advanced air defenses."[95] Just as disturbing is the precedent that the French, charter members of the MTCR, would establish for fellow members if they are ultimately successful in exporting the Apache. Some of the other MTCR members may follow the French lead and export LACMs in violation of Category I. For example, the Spanish company CASA initiated a program to develop and produce an LACM with characteristics similar to the French Apache and has stated its intentions to compete its LACM against the Apache in what it sees as a lucrative export market.

The Russians are also trying to export sophisticated LACMs. At the Moscow Air Show in 1992, Russia offered for sale a shorter-range version, 500–600 km with a 410-kg conventional payload (just under the MTCR Category I payload threshold), of their 3,000-km AS-15 strategic LACM. This missile, referred to as the Raduga Kh-65SE, incorporates INS, GLONASS updates, and TERCOM-like systems to achieve a reported accuracy of less than 20 m. Figure 8.4 is a marketing brochure for this potential Russian LACM export. Subsequently, at the 1993 IDEX Defense Exhibition in Abu Dhabi, the Russians displayed a further scaled-down version of the Kh-65SE with a quoted range of 280 km, slightly below the MTCR Category I range threshold of 300 km.[96] Taiwanese sources reported that the Russians tried to sell this LACM to the Chinese, but it is not clear whether any sales were made.[97] With a Kh-65SE China would

Figure 8.3
French Apache Land-Attack Cruise Missile

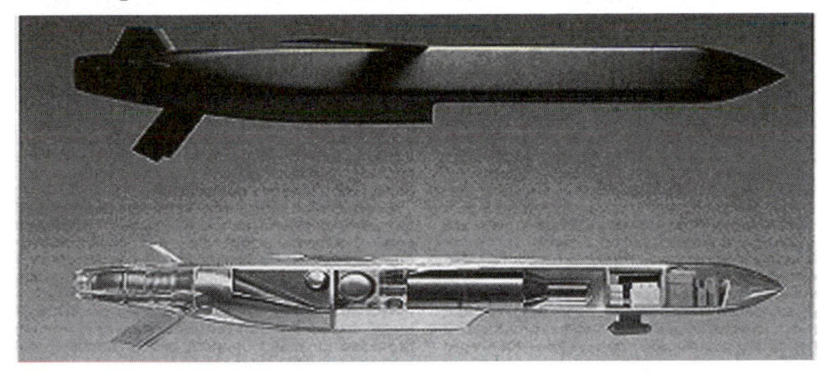

Source: Jean-Paul Philippe, "Matra to Develop APTGD Missile: A New 'Stealth' Cruise missile for France," *Military Technology* 19, no. 2 (February 1995), 60.

Figure 8.4
Marketing Brochure for Russia's Kh-65SE Cruise Missile

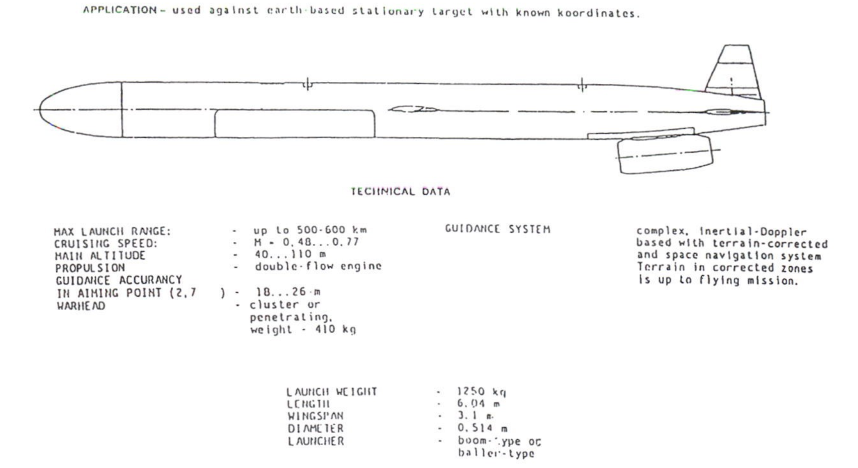

Source: K. Scott McMahon, "Cruise Missile Proliferation: Threat, Policy, and Defenses," presentation to the American Institute of Engineers Conference on Missile Defense, March 5, 1999.

have access to advanced Tomahawk-like LACM technologies, such as navigation and guidance, stealthy airframe design, and low-volume, high-efficiency engines.

Also, apparently the Kh-65SE would only need modifications to carry additional fuel and could then achieve ranges up to 3,000 km.[98] Given the Russians' desperate economic situation and the need for hard currency, one can expect that they will continue to vigorously market their LACMs as the demand from lesser developed countries increases.

Even more ominous than the current situation with the French and Russian attempted maneuverings around the MTCR to export advanced LACMs are recent developments in China. China is reported to have developed and recently deployed a short-range LACM, designated YJ-22, with a range of 400 km, estimated CEP of 50 m or less, integrated INS and GPS/GLONASS guidance and navigation, and capable of being launched from air, land, or sea platforms. It is believed to be an advanced development (modified airframe and better engine) of the YJ-2/C-802 turbofan-powered ASCM, which is itself a reverse-engineered version of the exported French Exocet ASCM.[99] Additionally, it was reported in the August 14, 1999, Hong Kong *Sing Tao Jih Pao Daily* (Internet version) that China has developed a "killer" LACM, similar to the U.S. Tomahawk LACM, with the following specifications and characteristics: 2,000-km range; 5-m CEP; can fly as low as 15–20 m above land or water; carries conventional or nuclear payloads; can be land- or sea-launched; and uses digital maps and topography matching, inertial guidance, GPS auxiliary correction, and other auxiliary guidance.[100] Both Chinese cruise missiles were likely developed with the aid of Russian and Israeli cruise missile technologies exported to China. In 1995, Dr. Chong Pin Lin, a Republic of China government official and People's Liberation Army expert, stated that China had purchased Russian cruise missile manufacturing technology and had hired a Russian cruise missile design team, locating the team in the Shanghai area. It is also believed that China has had access to the cruise missile expertise of the Russian Raduga and NRP Machinostroyenia Bureaux teams in the areas of radar and IR signatures control and may have received help from the Israelis in these same areas.[101] China has presumably acquired a U.S. TLAM that crashed in Afghanistan during the 1998 strikes against Osama bin Laden.[102] Lastly, China and Israel are codeveloping an air-launched, estimated 385-km range, 450-kg payload LACM based on the Israeli Delilah antiradiation attack drone, which probably incorporates INS, GPS, and IR navigation and guidance.[103] Unfortunately, even though they are stated adherents to the MTCR, the Chinese have a well-documented history of ignoring the restrictions of the MTCR and freely exporting missiles of all types.

As a final example of countries that have LACMs and are willing to export them, Taiwan's Hsiung Feng II, 170-km range, 75-kg payload, turbojet-powered cruise missile can be used both against ships and land targets. The Taiwanese reverse-engineered this missile from the U.S. Harpoon ASCM. They have offered the Hsiung Feng II for export.[104] The bottom line is that France, Russia, China, Israel, and others can proliferate LACM technologies and the missiles themselves within (or outside) the guidelines of the MTCR. Therefore, the direct purchase of advanced LACMs is a serious proliferation concern and clearly has the potential of becoming a major source of LACM proliferation to rogue nations and other Third World countries.

INDIGENOUS DEVELOPMENT

Although indigenous development is the most lengthy and technically difficult proliferation pathway, many countries pursue this route for acquiring LACMs in order to be self-sufficient and independent from foreign suppliers. Also, they desire to be a player in the lucrative international military sales arena. As Amy Truesdell, a researcher at the Centre for Defence and International Security Studies, University of Lancaster, UK, notes, "Indeed, China, North Korea, Iran, and Iraq have all proven that they will invest whatever it takes to decipher imported cruise-missile technology to use as the basis for indigenous programs."[105]

Greatly assisting these countries and others in their endeavors is the rapidly decreasing investment, both in resources and time, required for indigenous development as a result of the globalization of the civilian and military aircraft industries. The airframe structures, guidance and navigation systems, and propulsion systems for manned aircraft and cruise missiles are basically interchangeable. Furthermore, there currently exists a "buyer's market" in the worldwide aerospace industry. Developing countries are aggressively taking advantage of this opportune climate to acquire supersonic aircraft with turbojet and turbofan engines and to secure offsets with their purchases that provide them indigenous aircraft maintenance and production facilities.[106]

Another factor shortening the indigenous development cycle is the set of readily available cruise missile enabling technologies discussed previously. Truesdell aptly notes, "When one considers the fact that the cost of GPS receivers continues to plummet, computing power continues to grow, digital mapping software is readily available, and the supersonic aircraft now being exported are propelled by turbojet and turbofan engines, it is clear that the necessary ingredients for indigenous land-attack cruise missile manufacturing programs currently exist."[107] The willingness of countries such as Russia, China, and Israel to provide foreign assistance also demonstrably affects lesser developed countries' abilities and time frames to acquire indigenous LACM development and production capabilities. Commenting on the seriousness of ballistic and cruise missile proliferation, Donald Rumsfeld stated:

> Technology transfer is happening across the globe. People who want to get access to these capabilities can in fact do so. . . . Every country can get some kind of help from somebody, and to the extent they want it, they can get it.[108]

Lastly, the lesser developed countries are increasingly cooperating in a substantial fashion among themselves in the acquisition of strategic and tactical weapon systems. Dr. William Graham, former director of the White House Office of Science and Technology Policy and a member of the 1998 congressionally directed Rumsfeld Commission, believes that "if all help from Russia, China, the U.S., Europe, and Asia were ended today and the developing world was left to its own devices, they would still move forward quite rapidly because among them they have very substantial information, data, facilities, capabilities, and intelligence."[109] Graham also notes that, at any given moment, the West is educating approximately one hundred thousand foreign graduate students, many of them from the countries the United States is trying to prevent from developing long-range offensive missiles.

Of the currently designated rogue nations, the most unclassified information on cruise missile programs and capabilities for indigenous manufacture of LACMs exists for Iran, pre-OIF, and Syria. Table 8.5 summarizes the cruise missiles in the rogue nations' arsenals and those that are being developed indigenously. Iran has acquired a wide variety of short-range, sophisticated ASCMs from multiple exporters. Some of these can also be used in the land-attack role. Since 1989 and with Chinese assistance, Iran has indigenously produced the HY-1 Silkworm and HY-2 Seersucker ASCMs.[110] Additionally, Iran may also be establishing production facilities for ASCMs based on the Chinese C-801 and C-802 cruise missiles. In 1995, Tehran announced it had test-fired an indigenously produced ASCM. Iran is currently developing an improved Silkworm system with a range of 450 km at its Chinese-built plant at Bandar Abbas, again with Chinese assistance. This missile, if developed as a land-attack variant, which some sources indicate the Iranians have claimed, would be able to strike Saudi Arabia and all the Persian Gulf states.[111] An interesting, unconfirmed report from the perspective of Iran's future cruise missile capabilities is that Iran acquired a U.S. TLAM that was fired at Bosnian targets but did not detonate. If this acquisition actually occurred, Iran, especially with Chinese assistance, would probably be able to reverse-engineer a sophisticated LACM. Various assessments indicate that Iran will integrate GPS into guidance systems, develop improved engines for longer ranges, and incorporate low-observable technologies in its continuing development and production of cruise missiles. First generation LACMs would probably be based on the Chinese Silkworm and C-802 ASCMs currently fielded by Iran. By 2010, Iran is assessed to be capable of producing long-range cruise missile delivery systems and packaging BW agents in spray tanks within these systems.[112]

Concerning Iraq's pre-OIF indigenous cruise missile manufacturing capabilities, the FAW series of ASCMs are domestically produced versions of the short-range Chinese Silkworm ASCMs. The FAW 150 and 200 are longer-range (up to 200 km), delta-winged versions of the HY-2 Silkworms. Before the 1991 Gulf War, Iraq first revealed its indigenously produced Ababil LACM, which was developed from the Italian Mirach-600 remotely piloted vehicle. This system is turbojet powered and has a range of 500 km and payload of 250 kg. Also, before the 1991 Gulf War, Iraq had under development a ramjet-powered, Mach 3 cruise missile with a range of up to 800 km.[113] In 1998, UNSCOM discovered that Iraq had been acquiring the 900-km Polish BZM18 UAV with the possible intent of modifying the system for delivery of CBW payloads.[114] Despite fears that Iraq had already deployed cruise missiles and UAVs equipped with CW or BW warheads, none have yet been found so equipped in the aftermath of Operation Iraqi Freedom.

Reportedly, Syria was particularly impressed with the performance of the U.S. TLAMs during the 1991 Persian Gulf War and is believed to be developing its own cruise missile for future deployment with both conventional and unconventional payloads.[115] First-generation missiles would most likely be developed from currently fielded ASCMs such as the SSC-1b Sepal. However, other LACMs could be produced given Syria's intensified cooperative efforts with Iran. Of particular note, if Iran did acquire the U.S. TLAM from Bosnia, it is very possible that the technical information gleaned from the TLAM was shared with Syria.

CONVERSION OF ASCMS TO LACMS

In addition to direct purchase and indigenous development of LACMs, rogue states and other lesser developed nations will likely pursue conversion of ASCMs into longer-range LACMs because of the commercially and readily available LACM enabling technologies and the large number of ASCMs—more than 75,000—that have proliferated worldwide and currently reside in the world's military arsenals. Of the proliferated ASCMs, the older, first-generation Russian Styx and its Chinese derivative the Silkworm family (HY-1, HY-2, and HY-4), are better suited for modification to LACMs.

Because of their relatively large size and simplicity of design compared to the more modern ASCMs such as the French Exocet and U.S. Harpoon, they are inherently easier to modify. Also, the sizable volume provides space for transformation and additional fuel, thus allowing for significant range extension.[116] The most direct route for ASCM conversion into a longer-range LACM consists of transforming the turbojet-powered Chinese HY-4 Sadsack.

Table 8.5
Rogue Nations' Cruise Missiles and Development Programs (Pre-OIF)

Country/ System	Supplying Country	Type	Launch Method	Maximum Range (km)	Payload (kg)	Status
Iran						
YJ-1/C-801	China	AS	A/G/S	40	165	In Service
AS-11 Kilter	Russia	LA/AS	A	50	130	In Service
AS-9 Kyle	Russia	LA/AS	A	90	200	In Service
YJ-2/C-802	China	AS	A/G/S	95	165	In Service
HY-2 Silkworm	China/ North Korea	AS	G/S	95	513	In Service
SS-N-22 Sunburn	Ukraine	AS	S	110	500	In Service
RGM-84A Harpoon	U.S.	AS	S	120	220	In Service
HY-4/C-201	China	AS	A/G/S	150	500	In Service
HY-2 (Mod) Silkworm	Domestic/ China	AS	G/S	450	500	Development
Iraq (pre-OIF)						
YJ-1/C-801	China	AS	A/S	40	165	In Service
AS-11 Kilter	Russia	LA/AS	A	50	130	In Service
Exocet AM-39	France	AS	A	70	165	In Service
FAW 70/150/200	Domestic	AS	G/S	70/150/200	500	In Service
Armat	France	LA	A	90	160	In Service

HY-2 Silkworm	China	AS	G/S	95	513	In Service
C-601/Nisan 28	China	AS	A	95	500	In Service
AS-6 Kingfish	Russia	LA/AS	A	180	1,000	In Service
AS-5 Kelt	Russia	LA/AS	A	400	1,000	In Service
AS-4 Kitchen	Russia	LA/AS	A	400	1,000	In Service
Ababil	Domestic	LA	A	500	300	Development
North Korea						
SS-N-2a/P-15 Styx	Domestic	AS	S	43	513	In Service
HY-1/HY-2 Silkworm	Domestic	AS	G/S	95	513	In Service
Modified Silkworm	Domestic	AS	G/S	160+	Unk	Development
Syria						
SS-N-2c Styx	Russia	AS	S	85	513	In Service
SS-N-3b Sepal	Russia	AS	G/S	450	1,000	In Service

AS: Antiship; LA: Land-Attack; A: Air; G: Ground; S: Sea

Source: Humphry Crum Ewing et al., *Cruise Missiles: Precision & Countermeasures*, Bailrigg Memorandum 10 (Lancaster, UK: Centre for Defence and International Security Studies, 1995), 34–41. Center for Nonproliferation Studies, Monterey Institute of International Studies, "Cruise Missiles and Unmanned Aerial Vehicles Deployed in the Middle East," n.p.; on-line, Internet, February 8, 2000, available from http://www.cns.miis.edu/research/wmdme/crui_dep.htm.

Although the HY-1 and HY-2 ASCMs could also be converted into LACMs, the transformation would be more complicated and require more sophistication and technical skills, because the HY-1 and HY-2 use liquid-rocket engines, which would need to be replaced with turbojets or turbofans. Other desirable features of the HY-4 Sadsack are that it has a range of 150–200 km, carries a payload of 500 kg, cruises at a maximum speed of 0.78 Mach, and can be air-, ship-, or truck/trailer-launched. The Sadsack is easily accessible to any country and is already in many countries' arsenals. Moreover, China is advertising for export a multipurpose HY-4 variant dubbed the C-201W and is developing an improved HY-4, the XW-41, which is expected to have an increased range of 300 km.[117] Neither of these ASCMs are restricted exports under the MTCR, and China is quite willing to sell them to anyone offering to buy.

To investigate how rogue nations such as Iran, North Korea, or Syria and other developing countries could convert an ASCM into a LACM, along with the costs and technical skills required for such a transformation, a team of scientists and engineers conducted a paper study on transforming the HY-4 ASCM into nominal 500-, 700-, and 1,000-km range LACMs for delivery of BW agents.[118] The team consisted of a small number of aeronautical and propulsion engineers, aerosol dispenser and weapons effects specialists, and proliferation analysts. The conversion of the HY-4 into a 300-kg payload, 500-km range LACM/BW (or biocruise) weapon system, which will be called the Biocruise-500, required four modifications: (1) replacement of the autopilot and radar subsystems with a land-attack navigation system costing only an estimated $40,000 and constructed from commercially available GPS-GLONASS integrated receivers, radar altimeter, inertial measurement unit, flight management computer, electronic servos, and DC power system with alternator; (2) installation of extra internal fuel tanks for additional fuel; (3) installation of wing tip sprayers for BW liquid agent release; and (4) development of guidance software for the most efficient dispersal of the agents. The 1,000-km range LACM, the Biocruise-1000, required reduction of the BW payload to 120 kg and the additional and more complicated modification of lengthening the existing HY-4 fuselage to carry more fuel. This paper study led to the conclusion that China, Iran, Iraq, North Korea, and Pakistan possess the ability to convert the HY-4 into Biocruise-500s or 1000s. Furthermore, with limited outside assistance, a resourceful and creative proliferant like Iran could probably produce the Biocruise-1000 within seven to ten years. If the outside assistance were more substantial, including experienced technicians, senior engineers, and advanced production equipment, the time might be halved to four or five years. The cost of the Biocruise-1000 was estimated to be between $250,000 and $350,000, substantially less than the $500,000 to $1,000,000 price tag for the Iraqi Al Hussein ballistic missile. Obviously, this paper study illustrates the plausibility of rogue nations rapidly acquiring LACMs/BW weapon systems of significant range, which could be used to seriously threaten U.S. and allied regional military operations and the U.S. and allied homelands.

SUMMARY AND ASSESSMENT OF THE BIOCRUISE THREAT

> A number of countries have the wherewithal to develop the capability to launch cruise or ballistic missiles from forward-based platforms, such as a service ship or freighters . . . well before 2010.
>
> Col. James Ward[119]

From the perspective of a rogue nation facing the formidable conventional military power of the United States and its allies, an LACM, especially if equipped with a BW agent payload, is a very politically and militarily cost-effective weapon system. Politically, the mere threat of using a system such as the Biocruise-1000 with a payload of 120 kg of anthrax against a major U.S. or allied city could deter the United States from becoming involved in a rogue nation's aggression against a neighbor or bid for regional hegemony. Militarily, such a WMD delivery system, especially if low-observable technologies and simple endgame countermeasures such as chaff and decoys have been incorporated, has a good chance of penetrating air defenses and accurately delivering its payload, thus causing large numbers of casualties. And a weapon system such as the Biocruise-1000 is cost-effective, especially when compared to similar range ballistic missiles and to the costs of conventional combat aircraft. As such, a less-developed country with limited defense resources could purchase larger numbers of the LACMs and use them in mass to even further complicate the air defense problem for the United States and its allies.

With the commercial explosion of critically enabling technologies for precise navigation and guidance; sophisticated mission planning; low-weight, high-efficiency propulsion; and air defense penetration, the development of a biocruise weapon system is now within the reach of the rogue states. Iran, Iraq, and North Korea have continually demonstrated in the past that they are determined and resourceful acquirers of weapon systems that will provide them with strategic leverage against the United States and its allies. The rogue nations have multiple acquisition paths that can provide them with highly capable LACMs, such as direct purchase of advanced LACMs from various countries, to include France, Russia, and China; indigenous development, with or without outside assistance; and development of a highly capable LACM via the relatively low cost and technically straightforward conversion of an ASCM, such as the Chinese HY-4 Sadsack. Given all these proliferation conditions, which clearly favor the rogue states and not the United States and its allies, the probability is quite high that by the 2005 time frame, one or more of the rogue nations will possess a 500- to 1,000-km range biocruise weapon system capable of delivering BW agent payloads in a highly effective manner against United States and allied military operations in regional conflicts around the world and also against military and civilian targets within the United States and allied countries.

Just as disturbing, these rogue nation capabilities will likely emerge with little if any warning. The National Intelligence Council's 1999 *Foreign Missile Developments and the Ballistic Missile Threat to the United States Through 2015* report states:

> A concept similar to a sea-based ballistic missile launch system would be to launch cruise missiles from forward-based platforms. This method would enable a country to use cruise missiles acquired for regional purposes to attack targets in the United States. . . . We also judge that we may not be able to provide much, if any, warning of a forward-based ballistic missile or land-attack cruise missile (LACM) threat to the United States. Moreover, LACM development can draw upon dual-use technologies.[120]

Not only are the rogue nation developments of strategically significant LACMs difficult for the intelligence community to assess and predict, Director of the CIA, George Tenet, recently testified before the Senate Select Committee on Intelligence that the U.S. intelligence services may be incapable of monitoring the proliferation of nuclear, chemical, and biological expertise and technologies. Tenet also stated that now, more than ever, "we risk substantial surprise."[121] Add to these sobering assessments the disturbing knowledge that some of the rogue states have clearly demonstrated that they will use WMD against an adversary, and that the United States and its allies are not likely to deter such use, one can understand the seriousness of the emerging biocruise threat and the concerted U.S. and allied efforts that must be applied in the near term to adequately address this threat.

CHAPTER 9

Next Generation Bioweapons: Genetic Engineering and Biological Warfare

Michael J. Ainscough

INTRODUCTION

The history of warfare and the history of disease are unquestionably interwoven. Throughout the history of warfare, disease and nonbattle injury have accounted for more deaths and loss of combat capability than from actual battle in war itself. The most striking example is the great influenza pandemic during World War I that killed 20 million people or more worldwide in 1918.[1] Although this was a naturally occurring event, what if a country could create a biological agent that could yield the same catastrophic loss of life on the enemy? That, in essence, is the potential effect of applying genetic engineering for biological warfare (BW) or bioterrorism (BT).[2]

Today, we face not only natural diseases (including emerging infectious diseases), but also threats of BW or BT, possibly with genetically engineered agents that may resist known therapies. In simple terms, genetic engineering is the process of human intervention to transfer functional genes (DNA) between two biological organisms. In the BW/BT context, it is the manipulation of genes to create new pathogenic characteristics (increased survivability, infectivity, virulence, drug resistance). Organisms with altered characteristics are the "next generation" biological weapons.

In this century, it is widely predicted that advances in biology and biotechnology will revolutionize society and life as we know it. At the same time, the "black biology" of biotechnology, which can be used to create biological weapons, will be one of the gravest threats we will face. In this era when cloning and "designer genes" are topics of the evening news, much has been written about biowarfare and bioterrorism resulting from genetically altered microbes, and it is often difficult to discern fact from fiction. This chapter has two purposes. The first part consolidates accounts of genetic engineering from sources close to the former Soviet Union's BW program. The remainder of the chapter discusses near-term future capabilities of genetic engineering and biological warfare from an American perspective. The "next generation" of biological weapons made possible through genetic engineering will be asymmetric weapons par excellence.

THE FORMER SOVIET UNION'S BIOLOGICAL WARFARE PROGRAM

Biopreparat

Despite signing the 1972 Biological and Toxin Weapons Convention (BWC), it is now certain that the former Soviet Union (FSU) continued a clandestine and illegal offensive biological weapons program until at least the early 1990s. Biopreparat (a huge military program with civilian cover as a pharmaceutical research facility) was organized to develop and weaponize biological agents for BW.[3] It employed approximately half of the Soviet Union's 60,000 BW workers in more than 18 facilities and in the 1980s had an annual budget equivalent to tens of millions of U.S. dollars.[4] Unlike the American offensive BW program (1942–1969) that worked primarily with organisms that were not contagious in humans (e.g., anthrax and tularemia), the Soviet BW research and development program also sought out the most contagious and lethal bacteria (e.g., plague) and viruses (e.g., smallpox) known to man.[5]

Because Biopreparat and other Soviet BW research facilities operated under the highest security classification of "Special Importance" (higher than Top Secret), the U.S. intelligence community did not even know it existed until 1989 when a top ranking scientist from the BW program defected to the United Kingdom.[6] From his extensive debrief, and subsequent collaboration by three other defectors from the program, we now know detailed information on the genetic engineering successes and other advances in Russian microbiology. Obviously much of the data remains classified, but the four defectors' accounts have been documented to some extent in various unclassified books and articles. This chapter discusses their open-source accounts.

Pasechnik

In October 1989, Dr. Vladimir Pasechnik, the first primary source from inside the Soviet program, defected to England.[7] A top Soviet microbiologist and director of the Institute for Ultra Pure Biological Preparations in Biopreparat, he described the extensive organization of biological research and production facilities in the program.

In addition to confirming that the Soviet Union had an offensive BW program in violation of the 1972 BWC, he disclosed that the Soviets had an "extensive genetic engineering program aimed at developing new kinds of biological weapons against which the West would be defenseless."[8] His institute's top priority was to increase the lethality of plague and tularemia, and at the same time make them more resistant to antibiotics and temperature extremes. By introducing specially engineered plasmids into successive generations of tularemia cultures, the strain became resistant to all known Western antibiotics.[9] The dried, powdery super-plague became the Soviet weapon of choice (twenty tons in stock at all times) and was loaded on various munitions. The use of BW had been integrated into Soviet special war plans for a range of tactical operations where they would have been delivered using spray tanks and cluster bombs and strategic operations where intercontinental ballistic missiles (ICBMs) and strategic bombers would have carried plague, anthrax, or smallpox.[10]

Pasechnik also detailed work on perfecting other new strains of bacteria and viruses that would aerosolize well for use in weapons.[11] After thirty years of experimentation, Soviet scientists had solved the problems of fragile microbe survival in major atmospheric pressure changes and temperature extremes during missile flight by fitting BW rockets with astronaut cabin-like protective systems. They solved the "destruction on explosion" problem by selecting the hardiest strains and calculating the required redundant quantity needed based on explosive testing done in Biopreparat and other BW research labs.

In summary, Pasechnik had disclosed that the Soviets (1) had genetically engineered bacteria and viruses, (2) weaponized the microbes in a powder form, (3) loaded them onto various munitions, and (4) integrated BW into their doctrine and had specific plans for use of BW.[12]

"Temple Fortune"

In the spring of 1992, a lower-level bench scientist who had worked on plague research in Pasechnik's lab also defected to the United Kingdom.[13] He has remained undercover and is referred to by code-name "Temple Fortune." He fully corroborated Pasechnik's previous account, and then updated the British on Soviet BW work in the thirty-month interval from Pasechnik's departure to that of "Temple Fortune." President Mikhail Gorbachev had ordered the termination of biological offensive programs in 1990, and despite the fact that President Boris Yeltsin had also announced (by televised address to the Russian people and in a personal commitment to President Bush) termination of the program, research on new forms of plague had secretly continued.[14]

"Temple Fortune" stated that, in addition to being even more resistant to multiple antibiotics, the improved super-plague would be nonvirulent in its stored form, but could be easily converted into a deadly antibiotic-resistant form when needed for weaponization.[15] The genes that cause plague virulence are located on a plasmid. What he was describing was a binary biological weapon, where benign bacterial plague cells would be mixed with virulence-enhancing plasmids immediately before loading on a weapon, and the transformation would take place in a small bioreactor on the weapon itself.[16]

Alibekov

In late 1992, shortly after "Temple Fortune's" defection, Dr. Kanatjan Alibekov became the third defector from the Russian BW program.[17] As the Chief Scientist and First Deputy Director (number-two man) of Biopreparat and an infectious disease physician/epidemiologist, he was the highest ranking defector ever from the program. Dr. Alibekov anglicized his name and now goes by Ken Alibek. In 1999, Alibek published *Biohazard*, a first-hand detailed account of his experiences. Alibek disclosed a virtual encyclopedia of intimate details on Biopreparat from the top down: personnel and facilities, history of the offensive research, medical and microbiological discoveries, special production methods, weaponization techniques, aerosol testing, Russian BW defensive innovations, prior deceptions and secret plans, and the future direction of the program.[18]

Alibek confided that Soviet biologists in the 1960s and 1970s were already interested in using genetics and gene manipulation to produce BW agents. In 1973, President Leonid Brezhnev established the "Enzyme" program to modernize the BW program and develop genetically altered pathogens.[19] Early in his career, Alibek had been in charge of developing Biopreparat's first vaccine-resistant tularemia bomblet.[20] By 1986, his team had also tripled the potency of the "battle strain" of anthrax (Strain 836).[21] He was the first to weaponize glanders and supervised the first Soviet tests with the Marburg virus (an Ebola-like virus).[22]

Alibek disclosed that, by 1992, the Russians possessed a grand total of *fifty-two* different biological agents or combination of agents, including deadly Marburg, Ebola, and smallpox viruses, that could be weaponized. The most infectious and easiest to manufacture and transport microbes were labeled "battle strains."[23] The favorite "battle strains" were anthrax (Strain 836), Pasechnik's super-plague, and a special Russian strain of tularemia (Schu-4). By 1991, Alibek stated that Russian scientists had "improved" all three of these so that they could overcome all immune systems and current medical treatments.[24] In May 1998, Alibek testified before the U.S. Congress:

> It is important to note that, in the Soviet's view, the best biological agents were those for which there was no prevention and no cure. For those agents for which vaccines or treatment existed—such as plague, which can be treated with antibiotics—antibiotic-resistant or immunosuppressive variants were to be developed.[25]

Although Biopreparat had worked with a highly virulent, rapidly infectious "battle strain" of smallpox (India-1) since 1959, they began research in 1987 to develop an even more virulent smallpox weapon, and tested it in 1990.[26]

In his book *Biohazard*, Alibek wrote about using plasmids to increase virulence or antibiotic resistance in bacteria.[27] This corroborated Pasechnik's and "Temple Fortune's" prior statements. He also discussed transfer of a gene for myelin toxin to *Yersinia pestis* (plague bacteria); however, this agent was reportedly not yet weaponized. He said that a new Moscow-based company named Bioeffekt Ltd. had offered, by mail order, three strains of tularemia produced by "technology unknown outside Russia" (i.e., genetically engineered strains). Techniques for the development of genetically engineered strains were also for sale.

Most astounding of all, Alibek revealed that genetic engineering research was underway to create entirely new life forms.[28] The goal of hybrid "chimera" viruses was to insert genes from one virus into another to create an even more lethal virus. Alibek stated that the Russians had created the first chimera virus from inserting DNA from Venezuelan equine encephalitis (VEE) virus into vaccinia virus (genetic structure almost identical to the smallpox virus).[29] Chimeras of VEE, Ebola, and Marburg genes inserted into the actual smallpox virus were in the research phase when he left in 1991.

Near the end of his book, Alibek talks about how biotechnical knowledge was shared with other countries.[30] For many years the Russians taught courses in "genetic engineering and molecular biology for scientists from Eastern Europe, Cuba, Libya, India, Iran, Iraq, and other countries." In fact, Cuba had set up a pharmaceutical company near Havana and was producing interferon from a genetically altered bacteria that contained an inserted plasmid.

Popov

Sergei Popov, a department chief in the Soviet bioweapons program, also left Russia in 1992. Unlike the previous defectors, he was not immediately debriefed, and for eight years conducted research in immunology and pharmacology in the United States. After Alibek's *Biohazard* was published, Popov identified himself as a former Soviet bioresearcher and was finally interviewed.

Popov, a Ph.D. biochemist, described his research to synthesize genes for insertion into viruses and bacteria and also his work to insert viruses inside bacteria (bacteria pro-virus concept).[31] By splicing a myelin-producing gene into *Legionella* (Legionnaires disease), the altered bacteria could produce a delayed neurologic syndrome in lab animals. He also told of a strain of plague that was resistant to multiple antibiotics and anthrax that was resistant to both vaccine and multiple antibiotics.

Bioweaponeer Diaspora

Since the demise of the Soviet Union and its BW program, many bioscientists have had difficulty finding new professional employment in Russia. As a result, thousands have emigrated around the world. The four defectors noted here came to the West, but others were lured to the highest bidder countries not necessarily aligned with the United States's interests. The FSU bioweaponeers who remain in Russia and those who have dispersed to other countries are potential sources for biologic specimens and BW knowledge.

Yeltsin and Sverdlovsk

In 1979, an accidental release of anthrax spores from the BW facility at Sverdlovsk (now Yekaterinberg, Russia) killed at least sixty-six people. In 1998, a DNA sequencing study done on preserved samples from eleven victims revealed the simultaneous presence of up to four distinct genetic variants of *Bacillus anthracis.* These findings indicate that at least some level of engineering of military anthrax had taken place, because only one strain would likely be found after a natural outbreak.[32] The Soviet Union at the time denied the existence of a military program, and the official in charge of the province where the incident occurred was none other than Boris Yeltsin.

More than a decade later, after becoming president of Russia, Boris Yeltsin visited Britain in 1992. In a public speech, discussing biological warfare research, he stated that the Russians "had undertaken research on the influence of various substances on human genes." Yeltsin's statements substantiated the existence of a previous Soviet genetic engineering research program.[33] Yeltsin, as Russia's president, later issued a public decree outlawing the entire Russian BW research and production program.

Scientific Reports

In 1995, Russian scientists presented a study at a conference in Britain that they later published in the British medical journal *Vaccine* in December 1997.[34] They reported that they had successfully transferred genes from *Bacillus cereus* into *Bacillus anthracis* cultures, making the anthrax resistant to Russian anthrax vaccine (at least in hamsters). This raised the obvious question about effectiveness of the American anthrax vaccine. American agencies sought to obtain a sample of the more potent Russian anthrax strain.[35] Unable to do so, in early 2001 the Pentagon made plans to duplicate the Russian work and genetically engineer its own modified strain for biodefense purposes.[36]

Implications

Biological-type weapons have been used many times in history. Humanity's ancient enemies are, after all, microbes.[37] What is new today is the tailored development of more contagious and lethal pathogens and the increasing number of states and terrorist groups that may have access to the knowledge or cultures of them.[38] The above accounts from Russians knowledgeable about their BW programs indicate active research and success in genetic engineering, chimera agents, and binary biologicals. From public record accounts, we know that the FSU used genetic engineering techniques in their massive offensive BW program.[39]

Because the FSU classified its offensive BW program as "Special Importance" (higher than Top Secret), it is clear that they considered BW missiles to be as valuable as their nuclear missiles.[40] Because of the protective military secrecy, it is plausible that even many top-ranking Soviet/Russian officials did not know the full extent and details of the offensive program nor have control over it.[41] This Mafia-like secrecy may explain Gorbachev's and Yeltsin's confusions, hesitancies, and contradictions when talking to the West about treaty violations.[42] Incredibly, Pasechnik claimed that he had never been told about the existence of the Biological and Toxin Weapons Convention and learned of it first from his British debriefers.[43] Indeed, despite Yeltsin's decree to dismantle the FSU's offensive BW program, many intelligence analysts suspect that it is still viable, hidden deep in the military structure, which is reluctant to surrender its BW secrets.[44]

Major General John Parker, the former commander, U.S. Army Medical Research and Materiel Command, acknowledged that "bioterrorists could just re-engineer diseases such as anthrax to negate the effect of existing vaccines."[45] Some western intelligence experts believe a Russian genetic engineering program such as Alibek described is still in its infancy.[46] The pace of recent discoveries in molecular biology makes it imperative to contemplate new BW threats.[47] Advances in "the dark side" of biotechnology predict a future of antibiotic-resistant bacteria, vaccine-resistant viruses, and the creation of completely new pathogens (chimeras).[48] The expertise and technology to create lethal new strains of viruses and bacteria are available at most major universities around the world. Some American scientists predict that we have some twenty years before genetic engineering will effectively make current biological defenses completely ineffective and obsolete against BW attacks. Science fiction may become science fact within two decades.[49]

The threat of a war with ICBM exchange with Russia has been greatly reduced in recent years. However, as nuclear and BW missiles were decommissioned and Biopreparat and portions of the rest of the BW scientific infrastructure were dismantled, many Russian scientists were suddenly unemployed. There is concern that knowledge of genetic engineering, or even cultures of highly infectious agents (sold, stolen, or smuggled), may have been transmitted to "nations of concern" or terrorist organizations. If true, such leaks, combined with the ease of flow of technology and information around the world, would result in a proliferation of capability that makes biological weapons use increasingly likely in major theater wars, smaller scale contingencies, and terrorist events.[50]

A biological weapon consists of both the biological agent and its means of delivery. Growing microbes is easier than weaponizing or disseminating them. As Larry Johnson, former deputy director of the State Department's Office of Counter-Terrorism, said, "producing these weapons requires infrastructure and expertise more sophisticated than a lab coat and a garage."[51] However, terrorists may attempt to recruit former biological weapons researchers to obtain information on weaponization techniques. Well-funded terrorist organizations might be able to buy the Russian scientists they need. A small subset of terrorist groups is likely to possess the technical know-how needed to carry out an effective biological attack.[52] Unless they are able to buy knowledge or microbe cultures from large programs, such as the former Soviet BW program, it is unlikely, though not impossible, that small terrorist units would have access to or produce genetically engineered biologicals.

GENETIC ENGINEERING, BIOTERRORISM, AND BIOWARFARE

Revolutions in Medicine and Military Affairs

The techniques of genetic engineering began to be developed in the 1970s.[53] In the 1980s, genetic engineering was already a global multibillion-dollar industry.[54] In the last decade of the twentieth century, the knowledge of molecular biology increased exponentially. The recent revolution in molecular biology may have incidentally unleashed a new threat to mankind in the form of genetically engineered pathogens, which could be used to develop many new offensive biological weapons. The same biotechnology that has promised to save lives by treatment of many human diseases also has a dark side that could be misused for the development of deadly bioweapons. The future of this "black biology" is the subject of the remainder of this chapter.

The revolution in molecular biology and biotechnology can be considered as a potential Revolution in Military Affairs (RMA). Andrew F. Krepinevich noted ten RMAs in the history of warfare.[55] Four elements are required for a RMA: technological advancement, incorporation of this new technology into military systems, military operational innovation, and organizational adaptation in a way that fundamentally alters the character and conduct of conflict. The 1991 Gulf War has been seen as introducing the space/information warfare RMA. From the technological advances in biotechnology, biowarfare with genetically engineered pathogens may constitute a future such RMA. The Russians have integrated BW into their doctrine, but fortunately there is no present evidence that they have had any occasion to practice it in the past few decades.

Lieutenant General Paul Van Riper, USMC (Ret.), former commanding general, Marine Corps Combat Development Command, asserts that we are at the front end of strategic change and that there are currently multiple RMAs in progress.[56] It is difficult to assess their impact and meaning while they are still works in progress. Indeed, only time can prove that a technological innovation will contribute to a RMA. It may take twenty or thirty years until we fully understand their significance. It is currently believed by some that the next true major threats to our national security are in information and biological warfare.[57] We are arguably farther along in the information warfare RMA than a biowarfare RMA. Ironically, genetic engineering is becoming routine and commonplace while weaponization of biologicals is currently a less developed art. However, the recent spate of anthrax-laced letters sent through the mail communicates the message that terrorists can be very creative in their delivery methods.[58]

Whether or not biotechnology contributes to a future RMA, it certainly is revolutionizing medicine. The human genome has been sequenced. Gene therapy, which will allow the replacement or repair of faulty genes, promises to be the Holy Grail of modern medicine.[59] The techniques of molecular genetics, genome sequencing, and gene splicing therapy have dual-use potential. Paradoxically, the same biotechnology for developing a new drug or new vaccine may be used to develop more virulent bioweapons. The same science that can be used to save lives may also be used to take lives. The rise of biotechnology knowledge presently parallels an increase in the willingness of terrorists to inflict mass casualties and increased devastation.[60] Following the historical pattern of interaction between warfare and disease, these two relatively new phenomena of unprecedented biotechnology and terrorists willing to inflict mass casualties will very likely intersect in history. The anthrax attacks in the United States following the September 11, 2001, terrorist attacks on the twin towers of the World Trade Center and the Pentagon likely are previews of coming events.

Emerging Infectious Diseases

Richard Preston's 1997 novel *The Cobra Event* was a fictional scenario of bioterrorism with a genetically engineered supervirus.[61] President Clinton's reading of this novel sensitized him to the bioterrorist threat. He looked more deeply into the BW/BT threat and subsequently issued two Presidential Decision Directives to address national security deficiencies related to biological and chemical terrorism and warfare.[62] In the wake of the September 11 terrorist attacks on the World Trade Center and the Pentagon, and the multiple anthrax-tainted letters subsequently sent to national legislators, the governor of New York, and news media offices, President Bush established the Homeland Security Council to coordinate a national effort of some forty diverse agencies and organizations that were already involved in homeland security.

Because we do not know what new diseases will arise, we must always be prepared for the unexpected.[63] The Centers for Disease Control and Prevention (CDC) in Atlanta is the nation's lead agency for disease epidemics and tracks naturally occurring emerging infectious diseases worldwide. The CDC has traveled all over the world and investigated outbreaks of Ebola hemorrhagic fever, Marburg virus, hantavirus, Severe Acute Respiratory Syndrome (SARS), Asian avian influenza (bird flu), and other emerging diseases.[64] These were challenging natural outbreaks of pathogens that had not been previously known to man. An outbreak of a biologically engineered pathogen might create a similar situation and may have an even greater disease potential (contagion and mortality) than recently discovered naturally emerging diseases. The epidemiological investigations of these emerging infectious diseases and other outbreaks serve as templates for responses to future biowarfare and bioterrorist events.

Natural versus Biologically Engineered Pathogens

In late 2001, anthrax spores in letters mailed through the U.S. Postal Service resulted in more terror than actual morbidity. In the three months following the anthrax letter attacks, five people died of inhalational anthrax and a total of eighteen others had contracted some form of the disease.[65] Over 50,000 people took broad-spectrum antibiotics, and many more people purchased antibiotics for future prophylaxis. "Anthrax anxiety" was reported on the nightly news. Hundreds of thousands of the "worried well" deluged the medical care system.

Yet, as bad as anthrax-by-mail was, an outbreak of a biologically engineered pathogen could be potentially even more devastating. Although highly lethal, the anthrax of September 2001 was determined to be a well-known strain and it was not contagious (spread from person to person). Although anthrax spores are highly stable and can remain viable for years, compared to other pathogens a relatively large number of organisms is required to cause illness.[66] These facts may explain why investigators found traces of anthrax spores in many office buildings and post offices, but only a few people actually contracted the disease. Furthermore, if evidence of an anthrax attack is determined (as was the case just after September 11), people can be screened for exposure and/or treated with antibiotics that are highly effective if taken before symptoms begin. There is also an FDA-approved vaccine for anthrax.

Genetically engineered pathogens would likely prove to be a more difficult challenge than the 2001 anthrax attacks. Most likely they would be novel in characteristics with either higher transmissivity, communicability, or antibiotic resistance. Such "tailoring" of classical pathogens could make them harder to detect, diagnose, and treat. In effect, they would be more militarily useful.[67] Obviously, a vaccine would not be available for a novel pathogen. Biological warfare expert Steven Block outlines other qualitative differences and attributes possibly expected from genetically engineered pathogens. They could be made safer to handle, easier to distribute, capable of ethnic specificity, or be made to cause higher morbidity or mortality rates.[68]

The entire DNA sequence of the smallpox genome is known, and some scientists fear that it has already been genetically manipulated.[69] Although the only authorized laboratories in the world for smallpox are the CDC in Atlanta and the Russian State Research Center for Virology and Biotechnology in Koltsovo, it is believed that cultures may exist elsewhere in the FSU and possibly have been transferred to other nations of concern or to nonstate organizations.[70] Ken Alibek described in his book *Biohazard* that the FSU was working on genetic modifications of smallpox in 1992.[71] Because it was eradicated from the world's population in 1980, any release of even the original form of the disease would affect millions of people and constitute an epidemic of worldwide concern. Certainly, a biologically "improved" strain of smallpox would be ominous.

Offensive Biological Weapons Capabilities

The Office of the Secretary of Defense has identified countries that maintain various levels of offensive biological warfare capabilities or research facilities. This list includes Russia, China, Iraq, Iran, North Korea, Syria, Libya, India, and Pakistan. The Henry L. Stimson Center also lists Egypt, Israel, and Taiwan as countries of "proliferation concern."[72] Also, the Al Qaeda network reportedly sought to buy biological agents.

Most developed nations maintain some level of defensive capability against biological warfare and bioterrorism. This typically includes deployment military mission-oriented protective posture (MOPP) gear and civilian hazardous material (HAZMAT) responder "space suits." Also important are vaccines and antibiotics stockpiled against the BW/BT threats. The United States Department of Defense maintains a defensive capability. In 1969, President Nixon issued an executive order to unilaterally and unconditionally renounce biological weapons. Our program was terminated and stockpiles were destroyed.[73] The closure of our offensive program has had a serious and limiting effect on our ability to develop medical defensive measures, such as our capability to develop appropriate vaccines, antibiotics, and other treatments.[74]

Biowar and Bioterrorism

As our adversaries look for "asymmetric"[75] advantages, biological weapons are always a consideration. Bellicose national leaders and terrorists, allured by the potentially deadly power of biological weapons, persevere in seeking to acquire them. Yet, curiously, when biological weapons have been employed in battle, they have proved to be relatively ineffectual. They have been undependable and uncontrollable.[76] Because they have been difficult to deploy reliably, their military value has been marginal.[77] Stabilizing biological agents and deploying them, either overtly with sophisticated weaponry or covertly without endangering the perpetrator or friendly forces,[78] requires expertise not widely held. Possibly, with the capabilities of biological engineering and a new generation of weapons, this may change.

Nation-state and nonstate actors obviously have differing capabilities, requirements, and expectations for biological weapons. Whereas military troops often train to operate in chemical and biological environments, vulnerable civilian populations do not have either the protective equipment or defensive training for a biological attack and would therefore be the most likely target in a bioterrorist attack. It is increasingly likely that nonstate terrorists will use biological attacks as appears to be the case in the anthrax mail attacks following the September 11 attacks on the Pentagon and the World Trade Center towers.[79]

In the event of an attack with a genetically engineered pathogen, it would likely require some time to sort out whether we were confronting simply a naturally occurring event or one triggered by those with a sinister motive.[80] Identification of the cause may be delayed. Initially, there may not be a high index of suspicion. The disease may not be recognizable if it takes the initial form of a familiar complex of symptoms. Most physicians have never seen patients with anthrax or smallpox, and few have had training to diagnose the most likely bioterrorism pathogens. For example, one of the U.S. postal workers who died of anthrax in late 2001 was diagnosed as having a harmless viral syndrome and released from a physician's care. In the initial stages of an investigation, it might be difficult to determine if the outbreak is a naturally occurring event, an act of terrorism, or an act of war. For example, the first inhalational anthrax victim in Florida in late 2001 was initially thought to have been infected from natural exposure because he was an outdoorsman. It may be difficult for investigators to determine the source of the pathogen or the mechanism of exposure. It took some time before anthrax spores from letters were connected to the first anthrax cases. At the time of this writing, the perpetrator of the events in the United States and the source of the anthrax remain unknown.

A terrorist attack with a biologically engineered agent may unfold unlike any previous event. The pathogen may be released clandestinely so there will be a delay between exposure and onset of symptoms. Days to weeks later, when people do develop symptoms, they could immediately start spreading contagious diseases. By that time, many people will likely be hundreds of miles away from where they were originally exposed, possibly at multiple international sites. Acutely ill victims may present themselves in large numbers to emergency rooms and other medical treatment facilities. In this scenario, medical professionals would be "on the front lines" of the attack. If the pathogen was highly contagious, medics would then become secondarily infected. Unsuspecting hospitals would become contaminated and soon overwhelmed. This would necessitate the quarantine of a large number of people, with the situation exacerbated by the declining numbers of medical caregivers. The media would contribute to public anxiety. Civil disorder and chaos may ensue. We have very little experience in coping with such an epidemic. Advanced warning of an impending specific bioterrorist incident, especially with a genetically engineered BW agent, will be extremely rare—similar to an emerging disease outbreak. Unless we happen to have excellent intelligence, we can only be prepared to respond after the fact.[81]

SIX PATHS TO ENHANCE BIOTHREATS

At about the same time *The Cobra Event* became popular in 1997, the United States Department of Defense released *Proliferation: Threat and Response*, which identified trends in biological warfare capabilities. These included the increasing use of genetically engineered vectors and the growing understanding of both infectious disease mechanisms and the immune defense system.[82] An annex to *Proliferation: Threat and Response* stated, "the current level of sophistication of BW is comparatively low, but there is enormous potential—based on advances in modern molecular biology, fermentation, and drug delivery technology—for making sophisticated weapons."[83] The most recent Report of the Quadrennial Defense Review (September 2001) also recognizes that "the biotechnology revolution holds the potential for increasing threats of biological warfare."[84]

Also in 1997, a group of academic scientists met to discuss "the threat posed by the development and use of biological agents." This JASON[85] Group provides technical advice to the U.S. government and "facilitates the contributions of scientists to problems of national security and public benefit." Their meeting concentrated on the near-term future threat of biological warfare, specifically on genetically engineered pathogens and weapons.

The JASON Group that met in 1997 grouped potential genetically engineered pathogens into six broad groups of potential futuristic threats.[86]

- Binary biological weapons
- Designer genes
- Gene therapy as a weapon
- Stealth viruses
- Host-swapping diseases
- Designer diseases

The biotechnology exists today for some of these possibilities. Indeed, some genetically engineered agents may have already been produced and stockpiled.

1. Binary Biological Weapons:[87] Analogous to a binary chemical weapon, this is a two-component system consisting of innocuous parts that are mixed immediately prior to use to form the pathogen. This process occurs frequently in nature. Many pathogenic bacteria contain multiple plasmids (small circular extrachromosomal DNA fragments) that code for virulence or other special functions. The virulence of anthrax, plague, dysentery, and other diseases is enhanced by these plasmids. What occurs naturally in nature can be artificially conducted with basic biotechnology techniques in the laboratory. Virulent plasmids can be transferred among different kinds of bacteria and often across species barriers.

To produce a binary biological weapon, a host bacteria and a virulent plasmid could be independently isolated and produced in the required quantities. Just before the bioweapon was deployed, the two components would be mixed together. The transformation of the host organism back into a pathogen could conceivably take place after a weapon is triggered and during transport/flight. "Temple Fortune" indicated that scientists in the FSU had mastered this technique.

2. Designer Genes:[88] The Human Genome Project has decoded the alphabet of life and provided a human molecular blueprint.[89] Likewise, the complete genome sequences are now known for 599 viruses, 205 naturally occurring plasmids, 31 bacteria, 1 fungus, 2 animals, and 1 plant.[90] Many of these genomes have been published in unclassified journals and on the Internet. To the bioweaponeer these are essentially blueprints that would enable him to make microorganisms more harmful.[91] Now that the codes are known, it seems only a matter of time until microbiologists develop synthetic genes, synthetic viruses, or even complete new organisms. Some of these could be specifically produced for biological warfare or terrorism purposes.

Perhaps the most obvious way to increase the effectiveness of any biological warfare pathogen is to render it resistant to antibiotics or antiviral agents. Some bacteria naturally develop resistance to antibiotics fairly quickly. Many antibiotic-resistant genes have been identified. The best known of these is the gene that codes for beta-lactamase, the enzyme that defeats the action of penicillin. Such genes could be activated or introduced into other pathogens.

Entire viruses may similarly be created, analogous to the natural mutation of the influenza virus. A new strain of influenza could be created by induced hybridization of viral strains, simply swapping out variant or synthetic genes. Slightly altering a common virus like influenza to make it deadlier might be easier than manipulating more rare or biologically complicated pathogens.

For a bioweaponeer, the databases of increasing numbers of microbial genomes provide a virtual "parts list" of potentially useful genes for a genetic "erector set" to design and produce a new organism. It is possible to pick and choose the most lethal characteristics.[92] Some think it may be possible to create an entirely new organism from scratch. Some animal viruses are so small that their entire genome could be stitched together, at least in principle, from machine-synthesized fragments using current technology. Mycoplasma, an organism that causes pneumonia in humans, has the smallest known bacterial genome.[93] Genetic analyses of strains of mycoplasma indicate that only 265 to 350 genes are essential under laboratory growth conditions. Thus, it may be possible to create an entirely synthetic "minimal genome"[94] organism in the near future. If a streamlined cell of this type were available, it would be an attractive template to build a bioweapon.[95]

As stated previously about viruses, although it may be possible to create life artificially from a set of component parts, this would probably be beyond the sophistication of most bioterrorists. It would be extremely difficult to engineer all of the desired "attributes" into a single pathogen and still have an organism that transmitted effectively and predictably. It would be much more likely that an existing pathogen would be subtly genetically modified to be more difficult to detect, more virulent, or more resistant to drugs, all within the capabilities of today's biotechnology.[96]

3. Gene Therapy as a Weapon:[97] Gene therapy will revolutionize the treatment of human genetic diseases. The goal is to effect a permanent change in the genetic composition of a person by repairing or replacing a faulty gene. Genes have already been spliced into bacteria to produce "human" insulin in large quantities.[98] The eventual goal is to splice a gene that codes for the production of insulin into human pancreatic tissue to cure diabetes. Similar research is progressing on adding in the missing gene to prevent the symptoms of cystic fibrosis. However, the same technology could be subverted to insert pathogenic genes.

There are two general classes of gene therapy: germ-cell line (reproductive) and somatic cell line (therapeutic). Changes in DNA in germ cells would be inherited by future generations. Changes in DNA of somatic cells would affect only the individual and could not be passed on to descendants. Manipulation of somatic cells is subject to less ethical scrutiny than manipulation of germ cells.

This concept has already been used to alter the immunity of animals. The vaccinia virus (a poxvirus used to make immunization against smallpox) has been used as a vector to insert genes into mammalian cells. This genetically engineered virus has been used successfully to produce an oral vaccine to prevent rabies in wildlife.

Research for similar gene splicing in humans continues for possible vectors to carry the replacement genes to their targets.[99] As has been done for animals, there is potential for human "vaccination" against certain diseases, or as a targeted delivery capability for therapeutic drugs or cytotoxic effects.[100]

One class of experimental vectors is the retroviruses, which permanently integrate themselves into human chromosomes.[101] HIV, which causes AIDS, is a retrovirus. So it should not be hard to understand that gene therapy might have sinister capability.

The vector concept was used by Australian researchers to splice a single foreign gene and create a lethal strain of mousepox virus.[102] The genetically manipulated virus completely suppressed the cell-mediated response (the arm of the immune system that combats viral infections) of the lab mice.[103] Even mice previously vaccinated against the natural mousepox virus died within days of exposure to the super virus. Mousepox (which does not infect humans) and smallpox are related viruses. If smallpox were to be similarly genetically manipulated, our current vaccine may not protect against it. These vectors are not yet very efficient in introducing genes into tissue cells. But if a medical technique is perfected, similar vectors might eventually be used to insert harmful genes into an unsuspecting population.[104]

Techniques for cloning tissues and embryos continue to advance. Reproductive (germ-cell) cloning aims to implant a cloned embryo into a woman's uterus leading to the birth of a cloned baby. Therapeutic (somatic cell) cloning aims to use genes from a person's own cells to generate healthy tissue to treat a disease. For example, such cloning could be used to grow pancreatic cells to produce insulin to treat diabetes, or to grow nerve cells to repair damaged spinal cords.[105]

Already sheep, mice, swine, and cattle have been cloned. However, success (defined as births of live animals) rates are low.[106] Initial cloning work with human embryos to produce omnipotent stem cells has been reported.[107] Theoretically, the stem cells could in turn grow into virtually any cell type and serve as replacement tissue in diseases like diabetes.[108] Researchers have also used a virus to insert a jellyfish gene into a rhesus monkey egg and produced the first genetically altered primate.[109] The use of embryos and germ cells has raised many ethical questions.

4. Stealth Viruses:[110] The concept of a stealth virus is a cryptic viral infection that covertly enters human cells (genomes) and then remains dormant for an extended time. However, a signal by an external stimulus could later trigger the virus to activate and cause disease. This mechanism, in fact, occurs fairly commonly in nature. For example, many humans carry herpes virus, which can activate to cause oral or genital lesions. Similarly, varicella virus will sometimes reactivate in the form of herpes zoster (shingles) in some people who had chicken pox earlier in life. However, the vast majority of viruses do not cause disease.

As a biological weapon, a stealth virus could clandestinely infect the genome of a population. Later, the virus could be activated in the targeted population, or a threat of activation could be used as blackmail.

Oncogenes are segments of DNA that, when switched on, can initiate wild cellular growth and misbehavior—the hallmarks of cancer. Some viruses have segments of DNA that can mimic oncogenes and directly, or perhaps through bioregulators or host genes, cause cancer. These changes may take years for clinical effect, but the concept may still be considered by bioterrorists.[111]

5. Host-Swapping Diseases:[112] As previously stated, the vast majority of viruses do not cause disease. In nature, animal viruses tend to have narrow, well-defined host ranges. Unlike bacteria, viruses often infect only one or just a few species. When a virus has a primary reservoir in an animal species, but is transmissible to humans, it is called a zoonotic disease. Animal viruses tend to have a natural animal reservoir where they reside and cause little or no damage. Examples of reservoirs include birds for the West Nile Virus, water fowl for Eastern equine encephalitis, and rodents for hantavirus. The bat is thought to be the reservoir for Ebola virus, and the chimpanzee is thought to have been the original reservoir for the HIV virus that causes AIDS. When viruses "jump species" they may occasionally cause significant disease. These examples illustrate that manageable infectious agents can be transformed naturally into organisms with markedly increased virulence.[113]

When this happens naturally, the process results in an emerging disease. If it were to be induced by man, it would be bioterrorism. In the laboratory of inspired, determined, and well-funded bioterrorists, an animal virus may be genetically modified and developed specifically to infect human populations. Emerging diseases could have serious implications for biological warfare or terrorism applications.

6. Designer Diseases:[114] Our understanding of cellular and molecular biology has advanced nearly to the point where it might be possible to propose the symptoms of a hypothetical disease and then design or create the pathogen to produce the desired disease complex. Designer diseases may work by turning off the immune system, by inducing specific cells to multiply and divide rapidly (like cancer), or possibly by causing the opposite effect, such as initiating programmed cell death (apotosis). This futuristic biotechnology would clearly indicate an order-of-magnitude advancement in offensive biological warfare or terrorism capability.[115]

The concepts and mechanisms of the six classes of biological innovations that could be weaponized, as outlined by the JASON Group and discussed above, have some overlap. These classes were meant to identify a spectrum of conceivable bioterrorist threats based on current or near-future biotechnological capabilities. They were not meant to be all-inclusive or mutually exclusive of possibilities.[116]

Malcolm Dando, another authority on biological warfare, asserts that benign microorganisms might be genetically engineered to produce BW toxins, bioregulator compounds, or venoms.[117] Pathogens may also be genetically manipulated to enhance their aerosol or environmental stability, or defeat current identification, detection, and diagnostic capabilities.

SIX WAYS SCIENCE CAN IMPROVE BIODEFENSE

Biological warfare and bioterrorism are multifactorial problems that will require multifactorial solutions. We need our best critical thinkers and biological researchers to solve this constantly evolving problem. Fortunately, the same advances in genomic biotechnologies that can be used to create bioweapons can also be used to set up countermeasures against them. There are six areas where biotechnology will likely make significant contributions:

- Understanding the human genome
- Boosting the immune system
- Understanding viral and bacterial genomes
- Bio-agent detection and identification equipment
- New vaccines
- New antibiotics and antiviral drugs

1. Understanding the human genome.[118] The Human Genome Project will have a profound influence on the pace of molecular biology research and help solve the most mysterious and complex of life's processes. New biotechnology should allow the analysis of the full cascade of events that occur in a human cell following the infection with a pathogen or the uptake of a toxin molecule. Circumstances that cause individual susceptibility to infectious diseases will become clear. Currently, the functions of nearly half of all human genes are unknown. Functional genomics studies should elucidate these unknowns and enable design of possible new strategies for prevention and treatment in the form of vaccines and antimicrobial drugs.

There have been reports of biological agents that target specific ethnic groups.[119] Although "biological ethnic cleansing" is a theoretical possibility, most experts are skeptical of this potential.[120] Analysis of the human genome sequence to date has failed to reveal any polymorphisms[121] that can be used to absolutely define racial groups. Several studies have shown that genetic variation in human populations is low relative to other species and most diversity exists within, rather than between, ethnic groups.

2. Boosting the immune system.[122] The complete sequencing of the human genome also provides a new starting point for better understanding of, and potential manipulation of, the human immune system. This has a tremendous potential against biological warfare.

After years of effort in the FSU to genetically engineer pathogens for biological warfare, Ken Alibek and Sergei Popov are now working to protect against the use of biological agents. At Advanced Biosystems, Inc., they are researching mechanisms to boost the immune system to defend the body against infectious diseases. One initial project is conducting cellular research that could lead to protection against anthrax. Similar immunological research in other labs has great promise to heighten the general human immune response to microbial attack in an effort to move beyond the "one bug–one drug" historical approach.

3. Understanding viral and bacterial genomes.[123] The genome projects for various microorganisms will explain why pathogens have the characteristics of virulence or drug resistance. A "minimal genome" was discussed previously in this paper. Creating a minimal genome would be an important milestone in genetic engineering as it would prove the capability to create organisms simply from the blueprint of their genomes. This research may provide insight into the very origins of life, bacterial evolution, and understanding the cellular processes of more complex life forms.

Bacteria may also be modified to produce bioregulators against pathogens. For example, *E. coli* has been genetically engineered to produce commercial quantities of interferon,[124] a natural protein that has antiviral activity against a variety of viruses. Xoma Corporation has patented a bactericidal/permeability-increasing (BPI) protein made from recombinant DNA (genes inserted into DNA sequences) technology that reverses the resistance of some bacteria to some widely used antibiotics. The search is on for other bioactive proteins that can affect the human response to infections.

4. Rapid/accurate bio-agent detection and identification techniques and equipment.[125] Biotechnologists need to continually develop more definitive, rapid, and automated detection equipment, regardless of whether or not bacteria have been genetically engineered. The capability to compare genomes using DNA assays is already possible. It is reasonable to contemplate a DNA microchip that could identify the most important human pathogens by deciphering bacterial and viral genomes. This detector could provide information on the full genetic complement of any BW agent even if it contained genes or plasmids from other species, had unusual virulence or antibiotic-resistance properties, or was a synthetic organism built from component genes. The ability to quickly identify and characterize a potential BW agent with a single test will greatly reduce the delays in current detection methods.

Geneticists deciphered the genome of the anthrax bacteria contained in the terrorist letters after September 11, 2001. DNA tests confirmed that the anthrax in every letter was the Ames strain.[126] Forensic scientists also looked for human DNA that might be inside the letters. The information was used for both the criminal investigation (gene clues that might help track back to the perpetrator or origin of the culture) and for further medical research for diagnosis and treatment.[127] Gene sequencing techniques (molecular fingerprinting) for anthrax and other microbes will undoubtedly contribute to future forensics and diagnostics.

5. New vaccines.[128] Vaccines stimulate humoral[129] immunity, the production of specific antibodies for specific pathogens. The availability of many pathogen genome sequences has already led to development advances

in new vaccines for some meningitis and pneumonia bacteria. Researchers have genetically engineered viruses in an attempt to create novel vaccines that would stimulate immunity against multiple diseases with a single treatment.[130] A California laboratory, Maxygen, is combining proteins from related pathogens in hope of developing vaccines that could provide broad protection.[131] Several other laboratories also have initiated genome-enabled efforts investigating ways to boost cell-mediated immunity against those pathogens for which it might be most effective. As yet, this approach has not been as successful as the development of vaccines but, as a result of genome sequencing, having knowledge of all available antigens has been enormously valuable.

6. New antibiotics and antiviral drugs.[132] Advances in microbial genomics hold great promise in the design of new antimicrobial drugs. Current antibiotics target three processes in bacterial cells: DNA synthesis, protein synthesis, and cell-wall synthesis. From deciphered genome information, any other protein essential for cell viability is a possible target for a new class of antibiotics. Although the first such antibiotics may be "silver bullets" for a specific infectious agent, the information gained may lead to broad-spectrum antimicrobial agents.

If the 1950s were the golden age of antibiotics, we are now in the early years of the age of antivirals.[133] With viral genomes decoded, scientists will soon decipher how viruses cause disease and which stage of the disease-producing process might be vulnerable to interruption. Insights gleaned from the human genome and viral genomes have opened the way to the development of whole new classes of antiviral drugs.

Researchers at Saint Louis University replicated the Australian work on genetically engineered lethal mousepox. Their research, funded by a federal biodefense grant, also identified a combination of anti-viral drugs that was effective treatment for the genetically engineered strain. This data will be applied to smallpox and other viruses.

CONCLUSIONS

Genetically engineered pathogens constitute the "next generation" of biological warfare agents. Evidence indicates that the Russians have genetically engineered biological warfare agents. Ken Alibek's original debriefings were so shocking that some military and intelligence personnel preferred to believe that he was exaggerating.[134] As his statements about genetic engineering and FSU capabilities began to be substantiated, however, the reality began to sink in. Such genetic innovations obviously enhance adversarial offensive biological warfare effectiveness and complicate our defensive capability. Because we cannot know with certainty the specifics of these agents (lethality, communicability, and antibiotic resistance), it is imperative that we prepare for the unexpected. Two quotes come to mind. George Orwell said, "Life is a race between education and catastrophe." Further, Gene Kranz said, "Failure is not an option."

Although biologically engineered weapons may currently be less of a concern than their naturally occurring counterparts, the threat they pose can only increase as technology develops.[135] We are only in the initial stages of a revolution in biotechnology.[136] Historically, the available state-of-the-art biotechnology has been used in offensive BW programs (i.e., FSU applied the technology of the 1970s and 1980s). Biotechnology is the ultimate double-edged sword. Once knowledge is attained, there is no going back.[137] As is the case with most powerful technologies, they can be employed for good or evil.[138] We must proceed with caution when developing new life forms.[139] As new organisms are introduced into our delicate bio-equilibrium, we cannot fully predict all potential consequences to the biosphere. The same technology that is used to benefit mankind may paradoxically pose a threat to our military forces and civilian populations either by accident or by sinister forces. It is possible today to genetically engineer microorganisms for specific positive medical and industrial purposes. It is likewise possible to genetically engineer pathogens for biological warfare purposes. It seems likely that such weapons will be used in our lifetimes. Inevitably, sometime, somewhere, someone seems bound to try something with genetically engineered pathogens.[140] If they are ever released, they will pose an ominous challenge for medical care and governmental response.

The use of biological warfare agents on the battlefield against the United States has been restrained in recent history. There have been many declarations and conventions to attempt to define international norms and to regulate the use of biological weapons. In the end, the *law of war* is somewhat of an oxymoron.[141] Several signatories of the 1972 BWC, including Iraq and the former Soviet Union, have participated in activities outlawed by the convention.[142] These events demonstrate the ineffectiveness of the convention as the sole means for eradicating biological weapons and preventing further proliferation. Ultimately, the most effective deterrent to their use has turned out to be fear of retaliation.[143] During the 1991 Gulf War, it is believed that Iraq was deterred from using biologicals and chemicals because Saddam Hussein feared nuclear or otherwise overwhelming retaliation.[144] We cannot be sure that future enemies will be so intimidated. Certainly, nonstate terrorists actors will not be deterred as easily. Biotechnology has made it possible to inflict mass casualties using only small scale special operations that can evade detection in attempt to avoid retribution. In asymmetric warfare, biological weapons are seen as a "great equalizer."

The probability of a terrorist use of a genetically engineered biological agent on a given city is very low, but the consequence of such an event would obviously be very high.[145] With maximum casualties the likely goal, metropolitan areas are at the highest risk.[146] This dilemma is the challenge of local communities, which are sensitive to the need for preparedness, but have finite resources. Local communities must have a plan and sufficient medical and public health resources accessible to sustain a response for up to twenty-four hours. A robust federal assistance would be made available promptly, but it would not be immediate. Historically, dozens of federal entities fiercely competed for the missions and money associated with the unconventional terrorism response.[147] The Homeland Security Department is charged to coordinate a more efficient network of disaster response capability.[148] At present, all military and civilian populations throughout the world are vulnerable to a BW attack.[149] We remain grossly ill-prepared to respond to an epidemic caused by a novel genetically engineered biological agent.

The twentieth century was dominated by physics, but recent breakthroughs indicate that the next one hundred years likely will be "the Biological Century."[150] There are those who say "the First World War was chemical; the Second World War was nuclear; and that the Third World War—God forbid—will be biological."[151]

Chapter 10

A Biological Warfare Wake-Up Call: Prevalent Myths and Likely Scenarios

Jim A. Davis

> Yet, this is still a dangerous world, a less certain, a less predictable one. . . . Many have chemical and biological weapons. Most troubling of all, the list of these countries includes some of the world's least-responsible states.
>
> President George W. Bush[1]

The likelihood that biological weapons will be used against our nation continues to rise. Many in the recent past have considered the talk of such horrific weapons as only hype to justify funding for certain programs for the Department of Defense (DOD), other governmental agencies, or government contractors. The stark reality of September 11, 2001, when hijacked airliners were used as missiles and of the anthrax attacks that followed, changed that perception for many. However, since we have not yet suffered a mass casualty biological warfare (BW) event, there are others that still dismiss the scenario as highly unlikely.

If this view is persuasive to U.S. decision-makers, it will impede the nation's ability to prepare for or prevent such an event. Until very recently, the lack of focus on this subject had resulted in a lack of appropriate funding and accountability. There are six important myths that have caused some senior military and other government leaders to develop an inappropriate view of this threat.

It would be valuable to those that recognize the nation's vulnerability to BW to know the most likely scenarios we should expect to encounter. Such informed speculations and visualization allow us to prepare before the event or possibly even to prevent it. This chapter describes six common myths about BW and three of the most likely future BW scenarios we may face.

WHY POSTULATE?

> The tendency in our planning is to confuse the unfamiliar with the improbable. The contingency we have not considered seriously looks strange; what looks strange is thought improbable; what is improbable need not be considered seriously.
>
> Thomas C. Schelling[2]

The United States has limited funds to spend on social and military programs. The military budget is currently 3 percent of the U.S. Gross National Product (GNP) as compared to 6 percent of the GNP during the late 1980s.[3] The most devastating terrorist attack ever perpetrated against the United States on September 11, 2001, not only cost many lives, but the economic impact exceeds hundreds of billions of dollars in direct replacement costs, lost revenues, and costly response efforts. Yet the human impact and economic impact of September 11, 2001, will be dwarfed if adversaries effectively deploy mass casualty biological weapons against the United States. Unless we focus appropriate dollars and a coherent national plan to prepare for, or better yet, prevent such actions, the United States likely will suffer an enormous economic impact that could even cause our demise as a superpower.

WILL THERE REALLY BE AN ATTACK?

There are at least six reasons that explain why individuals (including senior civilian and military leaders) do not believe a mass casualty BW attack will occur. These individuals have given little credence to the BW threat because they believe one of these six false assumptions or myths.

Myth One: There never really has been a significant BW attack.

This contention is blatantly counter to historical fact. On the contrary, even before the fall 2001 anthrax terrorism in the United States, biological warfare and bioterrorism have occurred on multiple previous occasions. This makes it plausible that they will again be used in the future. Additionally, more countries today have active BW programs than at any other time.

Military organizations have used biological weapons many times. One BW event occurred in 1346 when the Mongols spread plague (*Yersinia pestis*) at the Battle of Kaffa. More recently during the French and Indian War, the British used smallpox (*Variola*) against the Delaware Indians and also are alleged to have used smallpox against American Revolutionary War forces under George Washington's command.[4] The Germans used anthrax (*Bacillus anthracis*) and glanders (*Pseudomonas mallei*) against the horses and mules of the U.S. army and its allies in WW I. The Japanese used typhoid (*Salmonella typhi*) in WW II in direct attacks on approaching Russian forces.[5] They also used over sixteen different BW agents (among which were plague and anthrax) on Chinese forces and citizens, U.S. prisoners of war, British detainees, and others. Ken Alibek, former head of the civilian branch of the USSR offensive biological program, has unearthed information that leads him to believe that the Soviet army may have used tularemia (*Francisella tularensis*) to halt the oncoming German Army in WW II.[6] The *Textbook for Military Medicine*, published in 1997, states there were an estimated 10,923 deaths from chemical and biological warfare (CBW) use by the Soviet Union in Afghanistan, Laos, and Kampuchea (Cambodia) between 1974 and 1981.[7] And in 2001, the U.S. Senate and other U.S. government offices were attacked through the mail system by letters filled with lethal anthrax spores milled to the 1- to 5-micron size that can inflict death from inhalation. The fact is, biological warfare has been an accepted practice for a number of states for a long time.

Myth Two: The United States has never been attacked by a BW agent.

This was a common assumption held by many before the recent spate of anthrax incidents. The fall 2001 anthrax attacks on U.S. Senate offices, news agencies, and other targets should shatter this myth. Counting the 2001 anthrax attacks, there are at least six known instances in which BW has been used against United States citizens or resources. These are, in addition to the four already mentioned, the alleged British use of smallpox in the Revolutionary War; the Germans use of glanders against U.S. Army horses and mules in WWI; the Japanese use of multiple biological agents against their foes in WWII; the recent anthrax attacks in the United States; the Aum Shinrikyo cult's failed attack on two U.S. naval bases, Yokosuka and Yokohama, with botulinum toxin in 1990;[8] and a sixth occurred in 1984 when the Bhagwan Shree Rajneesh cult contaminated 10 restaurant salad bars in Oregon with salmonella, infecting at least 750 local citizens.[9] This BW attack, like the naval base attacks, was not discovered until several years after the event. These last two examples lend credence to the possibility, as proliferation experts such as Seth Carus from National Defense University agree, that the United States may have unknowingly fallen victim of other BW attacks in the past that we know nothing about.[10]

Myth Three: You have to be extremely intelligent, highly educated, and well funded to grow, weaponize, and employ a BW agent.

An individual's (or group's) financial status or brilliance is probably no longer a major roadblock to acquiring significant BW capability. Dr. Tara O'Toole, deputy director for the Center for Civilian Biodefense Studies at Johns Hopkins University, believes we have probably crossed over the threshold from "too difficult" to accomplish to "doable by a determined individual or group."[11] It is true that there are certain technical hurdles in producing and weaponizing BW agents, but there are many thousands of highly educated microbiologists or other health science professionals worldwide that are capable of growing, weaponizing, and employing a BW agent. Much of the technical information is now readily available on the Internet, in libraries, and through mail-order channels that provide "how-to" manuals. For example, Steve Priesler, with a degree in chemistry, has written such a manual, available on the Internet for only $18.[12] This manual, titled *Silent Death* by "Uncle Fester," tells the reader where to find agents such as *Bacillus anthracis* and *Clostridium botulinum*, how to grow them, how to weaponize them, and how to employ the agents to kill small or large numbers of people depending on your goal.

Myth Four: Biological warfare must be too difficult because, when it has been tried, it has failed.

Most of the biological warfare attempts mentioned in this chapter resulted in deaths or casualties. However, not all attempts in the past have been successful. For example, the Aum Shinrikyo sprayed two U.S. naval bases in Japan in 1990, but this was not discovered until 1995 after incarceration of its leaders, when some of the cult leaders confessed. It is not known exactly why their attack failed, but there are thousands of U.S. sailors and dependants who never knew they were one breath away from dying if the Aum Shinrikyo had been a bit more skilled. Although this Japanese cult may have failed to master the technological hurdles in the early 1990s, over a half a century earlier several nations had already learned a great deal about how to effectively make and use these weapons. The Japanese began their BW program in the early 1930s and used it against their opponents in WWII. The United States, Great Britain, and the USSR started BW programs during the 1930s and 1940s. These countries all were able to develop significantly large and potent BW programs. Indeed, basic BW technology has been proven and has been around for sixty years. This was long before the era of genetic engineering and the mapping of genomes. Although some of the secrets from these programs were probably not readily available to the Aum Shinrikyo cult, the decade of the 1990s brought with it a proliferation of information and biotechnological advances. Now, in the twenty-first century, technological barriers are no longer as formidable as they once were. Today it is thought by some experts that a determined group or individual can independently develop their own BW mass casualty weaponry.[13] To say "it has not been successful," based on the Aum Shinrikyo's inability to kill Americans with botulinum toxin or the Aum's other failed attempts to kill Japanese with anthrax,[14] is a weak argument, especially in light of all the previously successful BW attacks in past conflicts.

Myth Five: There are moral restraints that have kept, and will keep, BW agents from being used.

Although past history does not validate this argument, it is true that most states have not developed or used BW agents. For example, the United States had an offensive BW program from 1942 to 1969, but it never used BW agents. The USSR had enough BW agents weaponized to kill the world several times over and yet exhibited restraint. It may be that the various political, military, and moral constraints against BW use have prevented biological warfare on a mass scale to the present time, but it appears that we are now entering a new era. Jessica Stern, in *The Ultimate Terrorists*, outlines four techniques of "moral disengagement" that individuals and groups have used to justify their use of mass casualty weapons.[15] On February 26, 1993, terrorist Ramzi Yousef and several other Muslim terrorists exploded a bomb intended to topple the World Trade Center twin towers and kill at least 250,000.[16] The blast, although not completely successful, killed 6, injured more than 1,000, and inflicted costs in excess of $600 million.[17] Then, on April 19, 1995, Timothy McVeigh committed the worst act of domestic terrorism by an American citizen when he bombed the Alfred P. Murrah Federal Building in Oklahoma City. More than 550 people were targeted, and the resulting tragedy left 168 dead and hundreds of others wounded.[18, 19] In another incident, on September 11, 2001, international terrorists destroyed the twin towers of the World Trade Center, ruined over twenty adjacent buildings, and significantly damaged the Pentagon by hijacking and crashing U.S. commercial airliners into these icons of American society.

In less than two short hours, these brutal acts of terror killed approximately 3,000 innocent civilians and military personnel while injuring many thousands and bringing U.S. air travel to a temporary and very costly halt.[20]

We can look to the emergence of organizations such as Al Qaeda, Osama bin Laden's group, and see that previous moral constraints for massive civilian deaths are no longer applicable. They have launched a "holy war" against the United States and are not reticent to inflict heavy casualties on U.S. citizens even if it entails the loss of their own lives. In fact, according to the "holy war" paradigm propagated by bin Laden, great honor is supposed to accrue to those who die killing many "infidels." Thus, "morality" can be marshaled as a reason both to limit BW use or to advocate mass killings, depending on the decision-maker's values and perspectives.

Myth Six: The long incubation period required for BW agents before onset of symptoms makes BW useless to users.

As stated earlier, there have already been multiple BW attacks. To a savvy biological weaponeer, the incubation period can be used as an advantage rather than a disadvantage. Two scenarios illustrate this. Scenario one is an anthrax attack on a military installation that could render it nonfunctional within seventy-two hours. The first clinical cases of anthrax would probably manifest themselves around twenty-four hours, with subsequent case numbers increasing rapidly. If anthrax were used, conventional military attacks on the installation around three to four days after the BW attack would likely be successful because defenders would be laid low by the disease. Moreover, the attackers would not have to be overly concerned about significant secondary infections from their infected adversaries or large amounts of residual spores in the environment because of the nature of the *Bacillus anthracis* organism.

Scenario two involves an adversary attacking a population or military installation with Q fever (*Coxiella burnetii*). With a two- to ten-day incubation period, the attacker would have time to escape the area before it was recognized that there even had been an attack. Five to ten days after the attack, the adversary could announce this nonlethal weapon was used as a "show of force and resolve" and demand whatever concession he was after. There would be no concern of secondary infection getting back to the adversary or the adversary's allies because Q fever is not communicable. Likewise, the low fatality rate would take away the justification of massive retaliation but still leave a heightened fear within the attacked population because of proven vulnerability.

WHAT WOULD MOTIVATE A BW ATTACK ON THE UNITED STATES?

There are four primary motivations that might drive an adversary to attack the United States with a BW agent. Either might be enough for a rival government, organization, or individual to levy this heavy tax on the United States, but the threat increases when both of these motivations intersect.

The first motivation might be to gradually *erode U.S. influence* as a world superpower. There are adversaries such as North Korea, Iran, or the Al Qaeda organization that desire more influence in their region. Some are infuriated that American "infidels" have increased their presence in the Middle East from just a few in 1949 to over 200,000 U.S. military personnel in 2004.[21]

Second is the desire to reduce a competitor. There are emerging powers in the world that see the United States in a love/hate relationship. They realize that trade with the United States is helping them to become economically sound, but they would ultimately like to take a piece of the economic action from the United States. These nations might want to inflict damage to the United States's economy (e.g., via agroterrorism) to, in their minds, level the playing field in a way that would minimize damage to their own economy and help them to a greater market share. Third, religious differences may motivate attacks. Religious terrorist groups such as Osama bin

Laden's Al Qaeda declare that they have a religious obligation to drive out and destroy the infidels in the name of "Allah."

The fourth motivation could be categorized as *envy, revenge, and hate.* At a time when the United States is integral in stimulating the global economy and thereby improving the standard of living for millions in the world, the great prosperity coupled with the "transparency" of the United States inflames millions around the world with envy and/or hatred. The United States has 5 percent of the world's population yet uses 24 percent of the world GNP.[22] Some individuals may want to inflict revenge because of what they perceive the United States or its "puppet nations" have done to them individually or to their family or group. Many of these individuals are taught from childhood to hate the United States. This prejudice often grows as they see images on television that portray the United States as an immoral and violent society. Such attitudes can foster terrorism and biological arms may be seen as an effective means for poor men to strike at the United States.

POSSIBLE FUTURE BW SCENARIOS

This author believes that three of the most likely BW scenarios that the United States and its allies might face in the future are the following:

- An agroterrorist event against the United States
- A BW attack on U.S. and allied troops in the Middle East
- A bioterrorist attack against a large population center in the United States or an allied state.

Scenario One: The Agroterrorist Scenario

> Agricultural targets are "soft targets," or ones that maintain such a low level of security that a terrorist could carry out an attack unobserved. Biological agents are small, inexpensive, and nearly impossible to detect. A terrorist may choose to use BW against agriculture simply because it is the easiest and cheapest way to cause large-scale damage.
>
> Anne Kohnen[23]

As was articulated by Mark Wheelis, a senior microbiologist at University of California, Davis, many of the moral constraints that might inhibit an adversary can be overcome if he were to use agroterrorism.[24] By effectively inflicting damage to the U.S. agricultural industry with three to five BW agents over a few years, the U.S. economy could become chaotic. For example, the United Kingdom suffered a severe disruption in day-to-day life in 2001 when foot-and-mouth disease broke out, forcing the slaughter of hundreds of thousands of livestock. Estimated cleanup and economic loss is assumed to reach $30 to $60 billion.[25] Belgium suffered an apparent agroterrorist event when dioxin was discovered in chicken feed.[26] This resulted in boycotts across Europe and Asia of Belgian meat products that cost their economy nearly $1 billion.[27] Such an incident in the United States could potentially jeopardize $140 billion in pork, beef, and poultry exports yearly.[28] Table 10.1 is a chart from the Monterey Institute of International Studies of certain nations and contains a breakout of some of their offensive agricultural BW capabilities.

One of the benefits of this type of attack is that the adversary may never be identified unless he so desires. Since the goal is not to achieve attention, but to promote the demise of and inflict pain on the United States, the perpetrators most certainly would enjoy the daily news of turmoil in the United States from a safe distance. They could enjoy watching the successful completion of their plan as their contagious weapon operated on its own (i.e., *The gift that keeps on giving* . . .). Before a perpetrator was willing to use this style of BW attack(s), he would have to recognize it might take years to achieve his objective. Some in the world may be willing to wait to see their strategic plans carried out over this longer period of time.

Scenario Two: BW Attack on Forces in the Middle East

The goal of this attack would be to ultimately have the United States withdraw its military forces from the region and/or reduce its aid to allies like Israel. The Middle East has the highest number of states with biological weapons of any region in the world. According to the Center for Nonproliferation Studies at the Monterey Institute of International Studies, there are eleven states with suspected or confirmed offensive biological programs. Of these, six are in the Middle East.[29] Additionally, more weapons of mass destruction (WMD) attacks have occurred in the Middle East than in any other region. Although most of the examples in Table 10.2 are chemical warfare (CW) and not biological, chemical and biological warfare (CBW) use clearly indicates that this region of the world has an entirely different view about the use of weapons considered taboo by much of the rest of the world. Table 10.2 shows some regional highlights.

One adversary option might be to use a nonlethal BW agent, perhaps VEE (Venezuelan equine encephalitis), on a U.S. installation, making personnel sick, thereby incapacitating them, without killing them. This could be used as a "show of capability, resolve, and even compassion" by the adversary. The adversary could announce what he had done after people started recovering from the disease. This would allow time to ensure its effectiveness and that deaths were minimal. If the BW attack failed, then the adversary would not lose credibility by making premature claims. If there were many unexpected deaths, then the adversary could merely remain quiet and avoid potential retaliation by the United States.

With the announcement by the group that it was responsible, it could also announce it abhors killing and would only choose killing as a last resort. The adversary could state that he has lethal BW agents, but elected not to use those to avoid killing the sons and daughters of the United States and that he only wants them out of the region.

This likely would trigger great debates in Washington, DC, and eventually in Middle Eastern countries, and the U.S. Congress might pressure the president to withdraw U.S. forces. If the United States stayed in the region and a lethal attack did occur, then local populations around U.S. bases would die along with the targeted Americans. Thereafter, local governments would be under enormous pressure to ask the United States to withdraw rather than attract further BW attacks in their country.

Another adversary option would be to release a lethal agent just outside a U.S. base so that the wind would carry it away from the base. The downwind casualties would be blamed on the Americans, forming the local mistrust of the American government. This could be a particularly small attack aimed at killing as few as twenty to fifty of the local population. The responsible group would never claim credit but would inform the media and others that the United States had launched one of its own BW agents (even though the United States does not have any offensive BW agents). The regional media likely would have a "heyday" with this, causing a ground swell of anger against the United States. If, after several months, the United States had not elected to greatly downsize its presence in the region, another similar attack could be launched. Again, the United States would be blamed. Locals might start evacuating areas close to U.S. installations, and the U.S. presence in the region could become politically impossible to maintain. Such small scale events could be repeated over and over with lethal or nonlethal BW agents.

Another BW scenario to consider is an adversary's use of a lethal agent against a U.S. installation. The adversary would never claim credit, but might release an extremely small dose of BW agent, like anthrax or tularemia, trying to kill perhaps two to ten Americans. This could raise fear of future lethal attacks and cause U.S. officials and members of the U.S. Congress to debate if the United States should remain in the Middle East. If a few local citizens died, the host government might also begin to be more uncomfortable with the U.S. presence, fearing that it was a magnet for such BW strikes. A single attack might not cause the United States to "tuck tail and run," but if repeated often enough, the United States might reconsider and withdraw its forces from harm's way.

Scenario Three: A Bioterrorist Attack on a Large U.S. or Allied Population Center

The nation has learned to fear anthrax attacks since just after the September 11 attacks on the Pentagon and World Trade Center. Upon learning that

Table 10.1
States with Past and Present Agricultural BW Capabilities

State	Status	Dates	Disease	Comments
Canada	Former	1941–60s	anthrax, rinderpest	Exact date of project termination unclear
Egypt	Probable	1972–present	anthrax, brucellosis, glanders, psittacosis, Eastern equine encephalitis	
France	Former	1939–72	potato beetle, rinderpest	Exact date of project termination unclear
Germany	Former	1915–17, 1942–45	anthrax, foot-and-mouth disease, glanders, potato beetle, wheat fungus	In WWII experimented w/ turnip weevils, antler moths, potato stalk rot/tuber decay, & misc. anticrop weeds
Iraq	Known	1980s–? (CPC)	aflatoxin, anthrax, camelpox, foot-and-mouth disease, wheat stem rust (camel pox may have been surrogate for smallpox)	Occupation since OIF has failed to locate BW weapons (CPC)
Japan	Former	1937–45	anthrax, glanders	During WWII experimented with misc. anticrop fungi, bacteria, nematodes
North Korea	Probable	?–present	anthrax	

Rhodesia (Zimbabwe)	Uncertain/ Former	1978–80	anthrax	Suspicious epidemic of cattle anthrax resulted in 182 human deaths. Some scientists believe govt. forces infected livestock to impoverish rural blacks during last phase of civil war.
South Africa	Former	1980–93	anthrax	
Syria	Probable	?–present	anthrax	
United Kingdom	Former	1937–60s	anthrax	Exact date of project termination unclear
United States	Former	1943–69	anthrax, brucellosis, Eastern & Western equine encephalitis, foot-and-mouth disease, fowl plague, glanders, late blight of potato, Newcastle disease	psittacosis, rice blast, rice brown spot disease, rinderpest, Venezuelan equine encephalitis, wheat blast fungus, wheat stem rust
USSR (Russia, Khazakstan, Uzbekistan)	Formerly active; current status unclear	1935–92	African swine fever, anthrax, Avian influenza, brown grass mosaic, brucellosis, contagious bovine pleuropneunomia, contagious ecthyma (sheep), foot-and-mouth disease, glanders, maize rust, Newcastle disease virus, potato virus, psittacosis, rice blast, rinderpest	Additionally experimented with: rye blast, tobacco mosaic, Venezuelan equine encephalitis, vesicular stomatitis, wheat & barley mosaic streak, wheat stem rust, parasitic insects, and insect attractants

Source: Monterey Institute of International Studies, Center for Nonproliferation Studies. *Agro-terrorism: Agriculture Biowarfare: State Programs to Develop Offensive Capabilities*, created October 2000, on-line, Internet, September 12, 2001, available from http://cns.miis.edu/research/cbw/agprogs.htm. (Chart edited for space considerations; see complete chart and extensive footnotes on Web page.) Modified by USAF Counterproliferation Center (CPC) in aftermath of OIF.

Table 10.2
Example of CBW Uses in the Middle East

Date	Country	Specific CB Agent	Description
1917	Iraq	Glanders	In 1917, German agents infected over 4,500 British pack animals in Mesopotamia.
1920-30	Morocco	Mustard	Spain employed mustard shells and bombs against the Riff tribes.
1930	Libya	Mustard	Italy dropped 24 mustard gas bombs on an oasis in 1930 fighting Libyan rebels.
1935–36	Ethiopia	Mustard, tear gas, and various other agents	Benito Mussolini authorized use of chemical weapons on Dec. 16, 1935, with the first attack on Dec. 23 when Italian AF planes sprayed mustard gas and dropped bombs filled with mustard agent on Ethiopian soldiers and civilians. Italian forces repeatedly attacked Ethiopian soldiers and civilians with mustard gas and used tear gas, sneezing gas, and various asphyxiating agents. A letter from the Ethiopian delegate to the League of Nations, dated Apr. 13, 1936, alleges Italy made 20 "poison gas attacks," with mustard gas being used frequently.
1930s	Kurdistan	Lung Irr.	Soviet Union was accused of using lung irritants against Kurdistan tribesmen.
1944	Israel / Palestine	Unknown	Plot by Grand Mufti of Jerusalem and Germans to poison wells in Tel Aviv. Ten containers was discovered with enough poison to kill 10,000 people.
1957	Oman	BW	Britain was accused of using biological warfare agents in Oman.
1963–67	Yemen	Mustard, phosgene, and tear gas, possibly nerve gas	Egypt employed chemical weapons against royalist forces in the Yemen civil war. Egypt used Soviet-built aerial bombs to deliver phosgene and aerial bombs as well as artillery shells abandoned by British forces after World War II to deliver mustard gas. According to chemical weapons expert Milton Leitenberg, some of the nerve agent reportedly used by Egyptian forces may actually have consisted of hand grenades fitted with containers of organophosphate pesticides. This incident is sometimes referred to as the first use of nerve gases, but according to some reports this is unsubstantiated.

1965	Iraq	Unknown	In May 1965 at a press conference in London, a spokesman for the Kurdish Democratic Party stated that on at least two occasions during the previous six weeks, the Iraqi army had used gas against Kurdish forces.
1984–88	Iran /Iraq	Sarin, tabun, & sulfur mustard	During the 1980s Iran-Iraq War, Iraq repeatedly attacked Iranian troops with CW agents. The first allegation of Iraqi CW attacks was in Nov. 1980. In Nov. 1983, Iran made its first official complaint to the UN regarding Iraqi CW attacks. Iraq was confirmed to have used mustard/nerve agents against Iranian forces from 1983–1988. Iran is believed to have conducted initial CW attacks by firing captured Iraqi CW munitions at Iraqi forces in 1984 or 1985. By end of the war, Iran reportedly employed domestically produced CW munitions against Iraqi soldiers. First ever use of tabun (nerve agent) on battlefield was by Iraq in 1984.
1987	Chad	Unknown	Libya reportedly used Iranian-supplied chemical weapons against Chad troops.
1988	Iraq	Hydrogen cyanide, mustard, sarin, and tabun	Iraqi warplanes attacked the Kurdish city of Halabja, Iraq, with mustard and nerve agents, killing up to 5,000 people, mostly civilians. (Following Iraqi mustard gas attacks on Halabja, fleeing Kurds may have been mistaken for Iraqi troops and bombarded with hydrogen cyanide [AC] artillery shells by Iranian forces.)
1990	Sudan	Mustard	President Omar al-Bashir's Sudanese government had been accused of producing CW with Iranian and/or Iraqi assistance. The government was accused of initiating several mustard gas attacks on civilians and Sudanese People's Liberation Army forces in the Nuba mountains region. The allegations were not independently confirmed.
1997	Jordan	Toxic gas	Israeli agents used toxic gas in assassination attempt on Hamas official in Amman.

Source: USAF Counterproliferation Center, unclassified research 2001.

So how would the BW attack be deployed in the Middle East? Keep in mind the objective is the withdrawal of the United States from the region, so there are multiple options an adversary might select. There are many possibilities, but the three scenarios listed on page 193 are illustrative of the variety of problems we may face.

some of the Al Qaeda terrorists had explored renting crop dusters, these important agricultural aircraft were temporarily grounded, and the news media informed the public that a biological attack might occur.

Similar to the September 11 attacks, a BW attack might take place in several major U.S. cities. Anthrax has already been sent via the United States Postal Service to senators and various news agencies. Anthrax would probably be the agent of choice in a mass casualty attempt because it is not contagious and the perpetrators would not have to worry about the disease getting back to their country. Likewise, terrorists would not even have to die because they could be vaccinated and treated with antibiotics prior to delivering the agents to protect them even if they personally got exposed. They could also easily depart the country before the first symptoms appeared, defeating the ability of federal authorities to arrest them. Five 100-pound bags of anthrax could easily be smuggled in grain sacks on one of many shipments that arrive in U.S. ports everyday. These bags could be lined with plastic so no powder was prematurely released. Three to five major cities, on the order of Houston or Los Angeles, would be targeted, each requiring only a 100-pound bag. Appropriate aerosolizing devices could be easily procured in the United States to mount on an automobile, airplane, or boat.

If the correct climatic conditions were present, and if the agent were correctly manufactured and employed, hundreds of thousands would potentially become infected and die. Such a mass casualty attack would overwhelm the U.S. medical system, and a human, economic, and political catastrophe would be the result.

SUMMARY

Despite the anthrax attacks that followed the September 11 events, many of our national leaders still do not believe that a mass casualty BW event will happen in the next ten years. This view is based on one of the several myths discussed, and such myths inhibit adequate funding of U.S. and allied biodefense programs.

United States national security leaders, programs, and budgets need to focus on three scenarios outlined and on other BW possibilities, and respond with a concerted biodefense effort fueled by urgency. The counteragroterrorism effort is woefully underfunded. This program is of extreme importance, and it needs billions of additional dollars to upgrade the protection of our agricultural industry.

United States military forces in the Middle East must be well prepared for a BW attack, but all countries in the region have a long way to go before their biodefenses are adequate against the threat. CENTCOM and OSD have an aggressive Cooperative Defense Initiative (CDI) with allies and friends in the region designed to overcome the threat of weapons of mass destruction. Huge steps forward have already been made in preparation for a BW attack, but there is still much work ahead. Detection capabilities in the region have improved, but it still requires several hours to ascertain laboratory results, and these are limited to just a few of the possible BW agents. Detection capabilities are only in place on U.S. installations and not in local areas. Although there is a correct emphasis on the concern for ballistic missiles within the CDI, the threat of biocruise missiles in chapter 8, "Assessment of the Emerging Biocruise Threat," by Rex R. Kiziah may be an even more likely threat and should be addressed with equal effort.[30]

One of the most horrifying possibilities would be a coordinated simultaneous BW attack against several major U.S. or allied cities. Those attacks could occur today, and we might be unaware of them until days after the attack. The results, as have been documented in a series of major exercises, would be frightening. Many hundreds of thousands could die and U.S. and allied societies would be thrown into chaos and panic. The United States will have to take up the yoke of preventing attacks and preparing for consequence management, managing the aftermath of such attacks, with the same vigor our nation used during the Cold War. Otherwise, our national security will be jeopardized.

Myths to the contrary, the biological warfare and bioterrorist threats are real and require the full commitment of the United States and its allies to have a well-funded biodefense effort.

Notes

CHAPTER 1

1. Of course, some small percentage of the 320,000 troops had already received anthrax vaccinations and were somewhat protected. The OSD calculated that had all 320,000 received such shots, that an Iraqi anthrax attack would have killed just 122 as compared to the 76,300 in the worst case scenario.

2. U.S. Army Medical Research Institution of Infectious Diseases, *USAMRIID's Medical Management of Biological Casualties Handbook*, 4th ed. (Fort Detrick, Frederick, MD: USAMRIID, February 2001), D-1 to D-2.

CHAPTER 2

1. "New cases of foot-and-mouth disease confirmed," *Montgomery (AL) Advertiser*, 26 February 2001, 8; "Foot-and-mouth outbreak starts panic," *Montgomery (AL) Advertiser*, 27 February 2001, 8A; "Fears over foot-and-mouth spark riots in Brussels," *Financial Times.com*, 26 February 2001, n.p.; on-line, Internet, 27 February 2001, available from http://news.ft.com/news/worldnews/uk; David Evans, "Fears mount in Europe over foot-and-mouth disease," Reuters, 26 February 2001, n.p.; on-line, Internet, 27 February 2001, available from http://dailynews.yahoo.com/htx/wl/nm/?4; Martin Fletcher, "Germany confiscates Britons' sandwiches," *Times* (London), 27 February 2001, n.p.; on-line, Internet, 27 February 2001, available from http://www.thetimes.co.uk/section/0,2,0.html; Kevin Connolly, "Ireland battens down the hatches," *BBC News*, 1 March 2001, n.p.; on-line, Internet, 1 March 2001, available from http://news.bbc.co.uk/hi/english/world/europe/newsid_1196000/1196950.stm; Jorn Madslien, "Rising cost of farm crisis," *BBC News*, 1 March 2001, n.p.; on-line, Internet, 1 March 2001, available from http://news.bbc.co.uk/hi/english/business/newsid_1196000/1196039.stm; "Europe-wide alert over farm virus," *BBC News*, 1 March 2001, n.p.; on-line, Internet, 1 March 2001, available from http://news.bbc.co.uk/hi/english/world/europe/newsid_1195000/1195989.stm.

2. David Brown, "Ministry vets trace trail of infection," *Telegraph* (London), 27 February 2001, n.p.; on-line, Internet, 27 February 2001, available from http://www.telegraph.co.uk/et.

3. U.S. Senate, *Agricultural Biological Weapons Threat to the U.S.: Hearing before the Subcommittee on Emerging Threats and Capabilities of the Committee on Armed Services*, 106th Cong., 1st sess., 1999, 36.

4. Corrie Brown, "Emerging Infectious Diseases of Animals: An Overview," in *Emerging Diseases of Animals*, eds. Corrie Brown and Carole Bolin (Washington, DC: ASM Press, 2000), 2.

5. Office International Des Epizooties, "Definition for Lists A and B Diseases," on-line, Internet, 13 February 2001, available from http://www.oie.int/eng/maladies/en_classification.htm.

6. Office International Des Epizooties, "Foot and Mouth Disease," on-line, Internet, 13 February 2001, available from http://www.oie.int/eng/maladies/fiches/a_a010.htm; USDA Animal and Plant Health Inspection Service, "Foot and Mouth Disease," on-line, Internet, 12 February 2001, available from http://www.aphis.usda.gov/oa/pubs/fsfmd.html; Office International Des Epizooties, "Disease Information," on-line, Internet, 28 February 2001, available from http://www.oie.int/eng/info/hebdo/a_dsum.htm; Clarence M. Fraser, ed., *The Merck Veterinary Manual* (Rahway, NJ: Merck & Co., Inc, 1991), 338–40; Corrie Brown, "Economic Considerations of Agricultural Diseases," *Annals of the New York Academy of Sciences* 894 (1999), 93; Floyd P. Horn and Roger G. Breeze, "Agriculture and Food Security," *Annals of the New York Academy of Sciences*, 894 (1999), 13; Peter L. Nara, "The Status and Role of Vaccines in the U.S. Food Animal Industry: Implications for Biological Terrorism," *Annals of the New York Academy of Sciences*, 894 (1999), 212.

7. Stockholm International Peace Research Institute, *The Problem of Chemical and Biological Warfare*, vol. I, *The Rise of CB Weapons* (New York: Humanities Press, 1971), 216.

8. Erhard Geissler and John Ellis van Courtland Moon, eds., *Biological and Toxin Weapons: Research, Development and Use from the Middle Ages to 1945* (New York: Oxford University Press, 1999), 114.

9. Ken Alibek, *Biohazard* (New York: Random House, 1999), 37–38.

10. Ibid., 38.

11. Lt. Col. Robert P. Kadlec, "Biological Weapons for Waging Economic Warfare," *Battlefield of the Future*, on-line, Internet, 2 February 2001, available from http://www.airpower.maxwell.af.mil/airchronicles/battle/chp10.html.

12. Rocco Casagrande, "Biological Terrorism Targeted at Agriculture: The Threat to U.S. National Security," *The Nonproliferation Review* (Fall/Winter 2000), 93.

13. Ibid., 94. Plum Island Animal Disease Center, "ARS Research Units at Plum Island," on-line, Internet, 13 February 2001, available from http://www.ars.usda.gov/plum/ars.htm.

14. Casagrande, 94. Corrie Brown, "Economic Considerations of Agricultural Diseases," *Annals of the New York Academy of Sciences* 894 (1999), 93.

15. Office International Des Epizooties, "Foot and Mouth Disease," on-line, Internet, 13 February 2001, available from http://www.oie.int/eng/maladies/fiches/a_a010.htm.

16. U.S. Senate, 35.

17. Ibid., 35.

18. Steve Goldstein, "U.S. officials awakening to threat of agroterror," *The Dallas Morning News*, 27 June 1999, n.p.; on-line, Internet, 13 February 2001, available from http://www.dallasnews.com/national/0627natagroterror.htm.

19. Michael V. Dunn, "The Threat of Bioterrorism to U.S. Agriculture," *Annals of the New York Academy of Sciences*, 894 (1999), 186. Dr. Jimmy Villard, "The Threat of Intentional Introduction of Foreign Animal Diseases into the United States," on-line, Internet, 28 February 2001, available from http://aphis.usda.gov/vs/ep/avma/avma-sym.html.

20. Patrick E. Tyler, "Pig Plague Ravages Taiwan and Many Blame China," *New York Times*, 19 April 1997, n.p.; on-line, Internet, 22 February 2001, available from http://www.tibet.ca/wtnarchive/1997/4/20_2.html.

21. Casagrande, 100.

22. Ibid., 99. Mark Wheelis, "Agricultural Biowarfare and Bioterrorism," *Chemical and Biological Arms Control Program*, 1 February 2001, 5; on-line, Internet, 5 February 2001, available from http://www.fas.org/bwc/agr/attack.htm.

23. Wheelis, 5; Judith Miller, "U.S. Would Use Long Island Lab to Study Food Terrorism," *New York Times*, 22 September 1999, 4; on-line, Internet, 13 February 2001, available from http://www.fas.org/nuke/guide/usa/facility/docs/e19990922long.htm.

24. Peter S. Probst, "Terrorism Overview," *Annals of the New York Academy of Sciences*, 894 (1999), 154.

25. Wheelis, 6.

26. Ibid., 9. Terrance M. Wilson, et al., "Agroterrorism, Biological Crimes, and Biological Warfare Targeting Animal Agriculture," in *Emerging Diseases of Animals*, ed. Corrie Brown and Carole Bolin (Washington, DC: ASM Press, 2000), 33.

27. U.S. Senate, 29. Wilson, et al., 33.

28. Casagrande, 98.

29. Wheelis, 10.

30. U.S. Senate, 25, 29. Wheelis, 9.

31. Wheelis, 10.

32. U.S. Senate, 29.

33. Jessica Stern, "Apocalypse Never, but the Threat Is Real," *Survival* 40, no. 4 (Winter 1998–99), 177.

34. Wheelis, 9.

35. "Brown: Outbreak 'under control'," *BBC News*, 1 April 2001, n.p.; on-line, Internet, 1 April 2001, available from http://news.bbc.co.uk/hi/english/uk/newsid_1254000/1254262.stm.

36. Casagrande, 97.

37. Horn and Breeze, 14.

38. Linda Rothstein, "Oh no, not *another* weapon of mass destruction," *The Bulletin of the Atomic Scientists*, November/December 1999, n.p.; on-line, Internet, 13 February 2001, available from http://www.bullatomsci.org/issues/1999nd99/nd99rothstein.html.

39. Casagrande, 92.

40. Ibid., 93. U.S. Senate, 38. "APHIS recruiting veterinarians for deployment during a foreign animal disease outbreak," *Journal of the American Veterinary*

Medical Association, 1 January 2001, n.p.; on-line, Internet, 1 March 2001, available from http://www.avma.org/onlnews/javma/jan01/s010101f.asp.

41. USDA Animal and Plant Health Inspection Service, 3.

42. U.S. Senate, 38.

43. Lonnie King, "Roundtable Summary: A Domestic Legislative Agenda for Improving Food Safety and Safeguards from Terrorist Attacks on the U.S. Food Supplies and U.S. Agricultural Interests," *Annals of the New York Academy of Sciences*, 894 (1999), 229.

44. Wilson, et al., 42; Brad Roberts, ed., *Hype or Reality: The "New Terrorism" and Mass Casualty Attacks* (Alexandria, VA: The Chemical and Biological Arms Control Institute, 2000), 111.

45. Wilson, et al., 41, 43; Peter L. Nara, 207.

46. U.S. Senate, 24–25.

47. Ibid., 24.

48. Probst, 158.

49. U.S. Senate, 35, 38; Wilson, et al., 40; Horn and Breeze, 13.

50. U.S. Senate, 48.

51. Brown, "Emerging Infectious Diseases of Animals: An Overview," 2; U.S. Senate, 37.

52. Michael Mann, et al., "Lives and livelihoods laid waste by disease," *Financial Times.com*, 2 March 2001, n.p.; on-line, Internet, 5 March 2001, available from http://news.ft.com/ft/gx.cgi/ftc?pagename=View&c=Article&cid=FT3TW3E8UJC&live=true; Felicity Spector, "Britain, the Isle of Contagion," *New York Times*, 3 March 2001, n.p.

53. Corrie Brown, "Emerging Infectious Diseases of Animals: An Overview," 3; U.S. Senate, 37; Horn and Breeze, 14.

54. "V.E.T.T. to the rescue of animal health in Oregon," 11 August 1999, n.p.; on-line, Internet, 13 February 2001, available from http://www.oad.state.or.us/Information/sow/VETT.html.

55. David R. Franz, "Foreign Animal Disease Agents as Weapons in Biological Warfare," *Annals of the New York Academy of Sciences*, 894 (1999), 103.

56. Department of Defense, *Proliferation: Threat and Response* (Washington, DC: Office of the Secretary of Defense, January 2001), 65; Wilson, et al., 36–37; Dunn, 187; "Veterinary Services Emergency Programs," n.p.; on-line, Internet, 1 March 2001, available from http://www.aphis.usda.gov/vs/ep; Anne Kohnen, "Responding to the Threat of Agroterrorism: Specific Recommendations for the United States Department of Agriculture," October 2000, 29–30; on-line, Internet, 18 February 2001, available from http://ksgnotes1.harvard.edu/BCSIA/Library.nsf/pubs/ESDP4Kohnen.

57. Kohnen, 30; Wilson, et al., 37; "Veterinary Services Emergency Programs," n.p.

58. John B. Adams, "The Role of National Animal Health Emergency Planning," *Annals of the New York Academy of Sciences*, 894 (1999), 74.

59. Casagrande, 93; Nara, 208.

60. "V.E.T.T. to the rescue of animal health in Oregon," n.p.

61. Casagrande, 93; Wilson, et al., 49; Horn and Breeze, 11; Rothstein, n.p., U.S. Senate, 49; Gilmore Commission, "Second Annual Report of the Advisory Panel to Assess Domestic Response Capabilities for Terrorism Involving Weapons of Mass

Destruction," 15 December 2000, 39, on-line; Internet, 7 March 2001, available from http://rand.org/nsrd/terrpanel/terror2.pdf.

62. Casagrande, 101; Horn and Breeze, 14; Senate, 2, 17.

63. Thomas Frazier, "Natural and Bioterrorist/Biocriminal Threats to Food and Agriculture," *Annals of the New York Academy of Sciences*, 894 (1999), 5.

64. "APHIS recruiting veterinarians for deployment during a foreign animal disease outbreak," n.p.

65. "Special issue of *Businessweek* foretells of catastrophic animal disease outbreak," *Vet Network Newsletter*, 9 March 2001, n.p.; on-line, Internet, 9 March 2001, available from http://www.vetnetwork.com/vetnews/news/bio_invasion.html.

66. Casagrande, 103.

67. Nara, 208–9; Roberts, 112–13; Kohnen, 16; Plum Island Animal Disease Center, "Selected Scientific Accomplishments," 1–2, on-line, Internet, 11 March 2001, available from http://www.ars.usda.gov/plum/accomplish.htm.

68. U.S. Senate, 16. Colonel William Inskeep, Department of Veterinary Pathology, Armed Forces Institute of Pathology, phone interview by author, 12 March 2001.

69. U.S. Senate, 20. "National Guard Anti-Terrorism Teams at Risk," *Washington Post*, 26 February 2001, n.p.; on-line, Internet, 1 March 2001, available from http://ebird.dtic.mil/Feb2001/e20010226anti.htm.

70. U.S. Senate, 51.

71. Wilson, et al., 43; Casagrande, 102.

72. Horn and Breeze, 11.

73. U.S. Senate, 30.

CHAPTER 3

1. Donald A. Henderson, "The Looming Threat of Bioterrorism," *Science* 283 (26 February 1999), 1279–82.

2. Jonathan B. Tucker and Amy Sands, "An Unlikely Threat," *Bulletin of the Atomic Scientists* 55, no. 4 (July/August 1999), 46–48.

3. Jeffrey D. Simon, Ph.D., "Biological Terrorism—Preparing to Meet the Threat," *Journal of American Medication Association* 278, no.5 (6 August 1997), 428–30.

4. Donna E. Shalala, Secretary of Health and Human Services, "How Prepared Are We?" *Emerging Infectious Diseases* 5, no. 4 (July/August 1999), 492–93.

5. Jonathan B. Tucker, "The Biological Weapons Threat," *Current History* (April 1997), 170.

6. Ibid., 171–2.

7. William S. Cohen, "Defending Against Biological Warfare," *Public Broadcasting System: Frontline* 1998, n.p.; on-line, Internet, 9 February 2001, available from http://www.pbs.com/frontline.htm.

8. Henderson, "The Looming Threat of Bioterrorism."

9. "Response to Terrorism," *United States Information Agency*, 15 March 1999, n.p.; on-line, Internet, 9 February 2001, available from http://usinfo.state.gov/topical/pol/terror/99031501.htm.

10. "White House Fact Sheet: President Clinton Unveils New Efforts to Combat Terrorism in an Address to the International Association of Firefighters," *United*

States Information Agency, 15 March 1999, n.p.; on-line, Internet, 9 February 2001, available from http://usinfo.state.gov/topical/pol/terror/99031501.htm.

11. Shalala, "Bioterrorism: How Prepared Are We?"

12. Henderson, "The Looming Threat of Bioterrorism."

13. David W. Siegrist, "The Threat of Biological Attack: Why Concern Now?" *Emerging Infectious Diseases* 5, no. 4 (July/August 1999), n.p.; on-line, Internet, 9 February 2001, available from http://www.cdc.gov/ncidod/EID/vol5no4/siegrist.htm.

14. Melissa Hendricks, "Rx Against Terror," *Johns Hopkins Magazine* (February 1999), n.p.; on-line, Internet, 9 February 2001, available from http://www.johnshopkins.com.

15. Amy E. Smithson, "Ataxia: The Chemical and Biological Terrorism Threat and the US Response," 319, on-line, Internet, 9 February 2001, available from http://www.stimson.org/cwc/ataxia.htm.

16. John G. Bartlett, "Applying Lessons Learned from Anthrax Case History to Other Scenarios," *Emerging Infectious Diseases* 5, no. 4 (July/August 1999), 561–3.

17. Ibid.

18. Donald A. Henderson, "Bioterrorism as a Public Health Threat," *Emerging Infectious Diseases* 4, no. 3 (July/September 1998), n.p.; on-line, Internet, 9 February 2001, available from http://www.cdc.gov/ncidod/EID/vol5no4/hendrsn.htm.

19. Jonathan D. Silver, "Local Doctors Fail Their Test on Diagnosing Germ Terrorism," *Pittsburgh (PA) Post-Gazette*, 13 February 2000.

20. Bartlett, "Applying Lessons Learned from Anthrax Case History to Other Scenarios."

21. Smithson, "Ataxia," 252.

22. Bartlett, "Applying Lessons Learned from Anthrax Case History to Other Scenarios."

23. Julie A. Pavlin, "Epidemiology of Bioterrorism," *Emerging Infectious Diseases* 5, no. 4 (July/August 1999), 529.

24. Bartlett, "Applying Lessons Learned from Anthrax Case History to Other Scenarios."

25. Henderson, "Bioterrorism as a Public Health Threat."

26. Laurie Garrett, *The Coming Plague: Newly Emerging Diseases in a World Out of Balance* (New York: Farrar, Straus and Giroux, 1994), 174–91.

27. David R. Franz et al., "Clinical Recognition and Management of Patients Exposed to Biological Warfare Agent," *Journal of the American Medical Association* 278, no. 5 (6 August 1997), 400–401.

28. Bartlett, "Applying Lessons Learned from Anthrax Case History to Other Scenarios."

29. Henderson, "The Looming Threat of Bioterrorism."

30. Smithson, "Ataxia," 251.

31. Henderson, "The Looming Threat of Bioterrorism."

32. "Chemical and Biological Terrorism: Research and Development to Improve Civilian Medical Response," Committee on Research and Development Needs for Improving Civilian Medical Response to Chemical and Biological Terrorism Inci-

dents, *National Research Council*, n.p.; on-line, Internet, 9 February 2001, available from http://www.nap.edu/readingroom/books/terrorism.html.

33. "Emerging Infectious Diseases: Concerns on Needed Laboratory Capacity Could Strengthen Surveillance," *General Accounting Office*, GAO-HEHS-99-26, 5 February 1999, n.p.; on-line, Internet, 9 February 2001, available from frevebgate.access.gpo.gov/cgi-bin/multidb.cgi.

34. "Chemical and Biological Terrorism: Research and Development to Improve Civilian Medical Response," *National Research Council.*

35. Ibid.

36. Ibid.

37. Garrett, *The Coming Plague*, 605.

38. "Emerging Infectious Diseases: Concerns on Needed Laboratory Capacity Could Strengthen Surveillance," *General Accounting Office*, GAO-HEHS-99-26.

39. Hendricks, "Rx Against Terror."

40. Garrett, *The Coming Plague*, 605–6.

41. "Chemical and Biological Terrorism: Research and Development to Improve Civilian Medical Response," *National Research Council.*

42. Smithson, "Ataxia," 254–58.

43. Ibid.

44. Ibid.

45. "Preventing Emerging Infectious Diseases: A Strategy for the 21st Century," *Centers for Disease Control and Prevention*, 28 September 1999, n.p.; on-line Internet, 9 February 2001, available from http://www.cdc.gov/ncidod/emergplan/9obj11.htm.

46. Jonathan B. Tucker, "National Health and Medical Services Response to Incidents of Chemical and Biological Terrorism," *Journal of the American Medical Association* 278, no. 5 (6 August 1997), 362–68.

47. Smithson, "Ataxia," 254–58.

48. Ibid.

49. "Chemical and Biological Terrorism: Research and Development to Improve Civilian Medical Response," *National Research Council.*

50. Ibid.

51. James M. Hughes, "The Emerging Threat of Bioterrorism," *Emerging Infectious Diseases* 5, no. 4 (July/August 1999), n.p.; on-line, Internet, 9 February 2001, available from http://www.cdc.gov/ncidod/EID/vol5no4/hughes.htm.

52. Smithson, "Ataxia," 300.

53. Ibid.

54. Ibid., 301.

55. Ibid., 302.

56. "Chemical and Biological Terrorism: Research and Development to Improve Civilian Medical Response," *National Research Council.*

57. Ibid.

58. Garrett, *The Coming Plague*, 602.

59. "Chemical and Biological Terrorism: Research and Development to Improve Civilian Medical Response," *National Research Council.*

60. Ibid.

61. Tucker, "National Health and Medical Services Responses to Incidents of Chemical and Biological Terrorism."

62. Joseph E. McDade, "Addressing the Potential Threat of Bioterrorism—Value Added to an Improved Public Health Infrastructure," *Emerging Infectious Diseases* 5, no. 4 (July/August 1999), n.p.; on-line, Internet, 9 February 2001, available from http://www.cdc.gov/ncidod/EID/vol5no4/mcdade.htm.

63. Hughes, "The Emerging Threat of Bioterrorism."

64. William J. Clinton, "Keeping America Secure for the 21st Century," National Academy of Sciences, Washington, DC, 2 January 1998.

CHAPTER 4

1. Stephen M. Block, "Living Nightmares: Biological Threats Enabled by Molecular Biology," *The New Terror: Facing the Threat of Biological and Chemical Weapons*, ed. Sidney Drell, Abraham D. Sofaer, and George D. Wilson (Stanford, CA: Hoover Institution Press, 1999), 42.

2. William S. Cohen, "The Anthrax Threat," *Washington (DC) Post*, 6 February 2000, B6; Department of Defense, "Information about the Anthrax Vaccine and the Anthrax Vaccine Immunization Program (AVA) Agency," 28 October 1999, 26; on-line, Internet, 10 January 2000, available from http://www.anthrax. osd.mil, 3; U.S. Department of State (distributed by the Office of International Information Programs), transcript, "Pentagon Spokesman's Regular Briefing," 17 February 2000, n.p.; on-line, Internet, 21 February 2000, available from http://pdq.state.gov/scripts/cqcgi.exe/@pdqtest1.env; Department of Defense, "DoD Response to the Staff Report of the House Government Reform's Subcommittee on National Security, Veterans Affairs, and International Relations entitled, 'The Department of Defense Anthrax Vaccine Immunization Program: Unproven Force Protection,'" 29 February 2000, 76; on-line, Internet, 10 May 2000, available from http://www.anthrax.osd.mil/anthraxfacts.pdf, 1, 39.

3. Jonathan B. Tucker, "From Arms Race to Abolition: The Evolving Norm against Biological and Chemical Warfare," *The New Terror: Facing the Threat of Biological and Chemical Weapons,* 158–224; and W. Seth Carus, "Biological Warfare Threats in Perspective," *Critical Issues in Microbiology* 24, no. 3 (1998): 149–55.

4. James E. Gibson, *Dr. Bodo Otto and the Medical Background of the American Revolution* (Baltimore: George Banta Publishing Company, 1937), 88–99.

5. Inoculation, or variolation, was introduced into the colonies on 26 June 1721, when Zabdie Boylston inserted material from a fresh smallpox lesion into the skin of his son and two of his slaves. After they recovered from the inoculation, they were immune to smallpox. The practice of variolation was an ancient Chinese technique that Africans had used for many centuries. It began to be accepted in Europe in the 1700s. British military forces before the American Revolutionary War increasingly used variolation.

6. Dr. Stanhope Bayne-Jones, *The Evolution of Preventive Medicine in the United States Army, 1607–1939* (Washington, DC: Office of the Surgeon General, Department of the Army, 1968), 15–53.

7. Glanders is a disease that normally infects horses and is caused by *Burkholderia mallei*. The disease produces a high mortality rate and renders any surviving animals useless for service for long periods if not permanently; references to the German

attacks in Mesopotamia include the following: Stockholm International Peace Research Institute, *The Problem of Chemical and Biological Warfare*, vol. 1, *The Rise of CB Weapons* (New York: Humanities Press, 1971), 216; and Frederick R. Sidell, Ernest T. Takafuji, and David R. Franz, eds., *Textbook of Military Medicine: Medical Aspects of Chemical and Biological Warfare* (Washington, DC: Office of the Surgeon General, U.S. Army, 1997), 16.

8. Sidell, 16; Rise of CB Weapons, 216; Capt Henry Landau, *The Enemy Within* (New York: G. P. Putnam's Sons, 1937), 72–73, 169, 218; and Mark Wheelis, "Biological Sabotage in the First World War," in *Biological and Toxin Weapons: Research, Development and Use from the Middle Ages to 1945,* ed. Erhardt Geissler and J. E. V. C. Moon (New York: Oxford Press, 1999).

9. SIPRI, *The Problem of Chemical and Biological Warfare, Vol. I, Rise of CB Weapons,* 216.

10. Thomas W. McGovern and George W. Christopher, "Biological Warfare and Its Cutaneous Manifestations," Dr. Rhett Drugge and Heather A. Dunn, eds., *The Electronic Textbook of Dermatology,* n.p.; on-line, Internet, 4 May 2000, available from http://www.telemedicine.org/BioWar/biologic.htm; and Sheldon H. Harris, *Factories of Death: Japanese Biological Warfare, 1932–1945, and the American Cover-Up* (New York: Routledge, 1994), 1–147.

11. Sidell, 418, 427; and Harris, 1–147.

12. David Hoffman, "Russia Challenged to Disclose Status of Biological Weapons," *Washington Post Foreign Service,* 26 February 1998, A17.

13. Ken Alibek with Stephen Handelman, *Biohazard* (New York: Random House, 1999), 29–31.

14. Sidell, 656.

15. Alibek, 1–18.

16. Dean A. Wilkening, "BCW in Attack Scenario," *The New Terror: Facing the Threat of Biological and Chemical Weapons,* 91–3; and David E. Kaplan and Andrew Marshall, *The Cult at the End of the World* (New York: Crown Publishers, 1996), 1–283.

17. Wilkening, 91; and W. Seth Carus, *Bioterrorism and Biocrimes: The Illicit Use of Biological Agents in the 20th Century,* rev. ed. (Washington, DC: National Defense University, Center for Counterproliferation Research, 1998), 58.

18. U.S. State Department, "Overview of State-Sponsored Terrorism," *Patterns of Global Terrorism: 1999 Report,* 1 May 2000, n.p.; on-line, Internet, 2 June 2000, available from http://www.state. gov/www/global/terrorism/1999report/sponsor.html.

19. Barry R. Schneider, *Future War and Counterproliferation: U.S. Military Responses to NBC Proliferation Threats* (Westport, CT: Praeger Publishers, 1999), 1–43.

20. Carus, "Biological Warfare Threats in Perspective," 149–55.

21. Wilkening, 95; and Jonathan B. Tucker, "Historical Trends Related to Bioterrorism: An Empirical Approach," *Emerging Infectious Diseases* 5, no. 4 (1999), 503.

22. Block, 49; and Hoffman, A17.

23. Judith Miller, "Russia Opens Door to Lab That Created Deadly Germs," *New York Times,* 24 May 2000, n.p.; on-line, Internet, 26 May 2000, available from http://ebird.dtic.mil/May2000/e20000524russia.htm.

24. Dr. Brad Roberts, "Remarks of Brad Roberts, Institute for Defense Analyses for the Conference Panel 'State Biological Weapons Terrorism' Carnegie International Non-Proliferation Conference, March 16, 2000," Carnegie Endowment for International Peace Non-Proliferation Conference 2000, n.p.; on-line, Internet, 17 May 2000, available from http://www.ceip.org/programs/npp/roberts2000.htm; and "Plague War: What Happened in South Africa?" *PBS Frontline*, 13 October 1998.

25. Carus, *Bioterrorism and Biocrimes,* 5, 11, 12.

26. Ibid., 5; and Wilkening, 103.

27. Jeff Jacoby, "The Real Terrorist Threat," *Boston Globe,* 18 May 2000, 23.

28. "Remarks of Dr. Brad Roberts."

29. Sidell, 468; Daniel C. Dragon and Robert P. Rennie, "The ecology of anthrax spores: tough but not invincible," *Canadian Veterinarian Journal* 36 (1995): 295; and Theodore J. Cieslak and Edward M. Eitzen, "Clinical and Epidemiologic Principles of Anthrax," *Emerging Infectious Diseases* 5, no. 4 (1999), 552–55.

30. Cieslak and Eitzen, 552–55.

31. Sidell, 468.

32. Ibid., 548.

33. Ibid., 468; and also found in Cieslak and Eitzen, 552–55, which referenced the original work of Louis Pasteur, C-E Chamberlain, and E. Roux, "Compte rendu sommarie des experiences faites a Pouilly-le-Fort, pres Melun, sur la vaccination charbonneuse," in *Competes Rendus des seances De L'Academie des Sciences* 92 (1881), 1378–83.

34. Sidell, 469; "DoD Response to the Staff Report of the House Government Reform's Subcommittee on National Security," 5; and Annual report of the Surgeon General of the Public Health Service of the United States, *Anthrax in Man* (Washington, DC: Government Printing Office, 1917), 259–60.

35. P. S. Brachman, "Inhalation Anthrax," *Annual of the New York Academy of Science* 353 (1980), 83–93.

36. "DoD Response to the Staff Report of the House Government Reform's Subcommittee on National Security," 5.

37. Cieslak and Eitzen, 552; J. C. A. Davies, "A Major Epidemic of Anthrax in Zimbabwe," *Central Africa Journal of Medicine* (Zimbabwe), pt. 1, 28, no. 12 (December 1982), 291–98, and pt. 2, 29, no. 1 (January 1983), 8–12, and pt. 3, 31, no. 9 (September 1985), 176–80; and Sidell, 469.

38. Sidell, 467–78; Cieslak and Eitzen, 552–55; Dragon, 295–301; Philip S. Brachman and Arthur M. Friedlander, "Anthrax," in Stanley A. Plotkin and Walter A. Orenstein, *Vaccines,* 3d ed. (Philadelphia: W. B. Saunders, 1999), 629–38; and A. Watson and D. Keir, "Information on which to base assessments of risk from environments contaminated with anthrax spores," *Epidemiologic Infections* 113 (1994), 479–90.

39. Brachman and Friedlander, 629–38.

40. Terry C. Dixon et al., "Anthrax," *New England Journal of Medicine* 341, no. 11 (September 1999), 818.

41. Ibid., 815.

42. Ibid.; Wilkening, 76–114; "Pentagon Spokesman's Regular Briefing"; "DoD Response to the Staff Report of the House Government Reform's Subcommittee on National Security," 39; J. F. Mazzuchi et al., "Protecting the Health of U.S.

Military Forces: A National Obligation," *Aviation, Space, and Environmental Medicine* 71, no. 3 (March 2000), 260–65; and Ronal M. Atlas, "The Medical Threat of Biological Weapons," *Critical Issues in Microbiology* 24, no. 3 (1998), 157–67.

43. Cieslak and Eitzen, 552–55.

44. Ibid.

45. Ibid.; and Brachman and Friedlander, 629–38.

46. Dragon, 295.

47. Watson, 479–90; and Thomas V. Inglesby et al., "Anthrax as a Biological Weapon: Medical and Public Health Management," *Journal of the American Medical Association* 281 (May 1999), 1735–45.

48. Watson, 479–90; Inglesby, 1735–45; and Brachman and Friedlander, 629–38.

49. Cieslak and Eitzen, 553; and Dixon et al., 818.

50. "Information about the Anthrax Vaccine," 18.

51. Kenneth Berns et al., "Preventing the Misuse of Microorganisms: The Role of the American Society for Microbiology in Protecting against Biological Weapons," *Critical Issues in Microbiology* 24, no. 3 (1998), 274.

52. Hoffman, A17; and Lt. Col. George W. Christopher et al., "Biological Warfare: A Historical Perspective," *Journal of the American Medical Association* 278, no. 5 (August 1997), 416.

53. Alibek and Handelman, 75; Christopher, 416; Hoffman, A17; and Jeanne Guillemin, *Anthrax: The Investigation of a Deadly Outbreak* (Berkeley, CA: University of California Press, 1999).

54. Christopher, 414.

55. "Pentagon Spokesman's Regular Briefing."

56. Briefing, Jerry Brubaker, Defense Threat Reduction Agency, Air War College, Maxwell AFB, Ala., 1994.

57. Carus, *Bioterrorism and Biocrimes,* 57–58.

58. Atlas, 157–67.

59. Jane M. Orient, "Chemical and Biological Warfare: Should Defenses Be Researched and Deployed?" *Journal of the American Medical Association* 262 (August 1989), 644–48.

60. Atlas, 157–67; and John C. Gannon, "The U.S. Intelligence Community and the Challenge of BCW," in *The New Terror: Facing the Threat of Biological and Chemical Weapons,* 129.

61. Berns, 275.

62. "Information about the Anthrax Vaccine," 3.

63. "DoD Response to the Staff Report of the House Government Reform's Subcommittee on National Security," 3; and "Pentagon Spokesman's Regular Briefing."

64. Atlas, 161.

65. "Pentagon Spokesman's Regular Briefing"; and "DoD Response to the Staff Report of the House Government Reform's Subcommittee on National Security," 2.

66. Atlas, 157–56.

67. "Pentagon Spokesman's Regular Briefing."

68. Ibid.; and "Information about the Anthrax Vaccine," 3.

69. Dragon, 296.

70. Ibid.; Watson 479–90; and Dixon, 815.

71. Brad Roberts, "Export Controls and Biological Weapons: New Roles, New Challenges," *Critical Issues in Microbiology*, 24, no. 3 (1998), 239.

72. "Information about the Anthrax Vaccine," 3; and "DoD Response to the Staff Report of the House Government Reform's Subcommittee on National Security," 2.

73. Mazzuchi, 261; and Atlas, 157–67.

74. Sidell, 441; and Raymond A. Zilinskas, "Iraq's Biological Weapons: The Past as Future?" *Journal of the American Medical Association* 278, no. 5 (August 1997), 418–24.

75. Office of Technology Assessment, U.S. Congress, *Proliferation of Weapons of Mass Destruction*, Publication OTA-ISC-559 (Washington, DC: Government Printing Office, 1993), 53–55; and "Information about the Anthrax Vaccine," 3.

76. Robert H. Kupperman and Darrell M. Trent, *Terrorism: Threat, Reality, Response* (Stanford, CA: Hoover Institution Press, 1979), 57; "Information about the Anthrax Vaccine," 3; and Atlas, 157–67.

77. Carus, "Biological Warfare Threats in Perspective," 149–55.

78. Atlas, 160.

79. "Pentagon Spokesman's Regular Briefing."

80. Carus, "Biological Warfare Threats in Perspective," 154.

81. "DoD Response to the Staff Report of the House Government Reform's Subcommittee on National Security," 1, 2; and "Information about the Anthrax Vaccine," 2.

82. Peter Grier, "Up in the Air about Anthrax," *Air Force Magazine* 82, no. 10 (October 1999), 68–71.

83. Atlas, 160; and Raymond A. Zilinskas, "Verifying Compliance to the Biological and Toxin Weapons Convention," *Critical Issues in Microbiology* 24, no. 3 (1998), 195–218.

84. Hoffman, A-17.

85. Zilinskas, "Verifying Compliance," 195–218; and "Remarks of Dr. Brad Roberts."

86. Zilinskas, "Verifying Compliance," 195–218; and Rolf Ekéus, "UN biological Inspections in Iraq," in *The New Terror: Facing the Threat of Biological and Chemical Weapons*, 246–47.

87. Ekéus, 237–54.

88. Tom Mangold and Jeff Goldberg, *Plague War: The Terrifying Reality of Biological Warfare* (New York: St. Martin's Press, 1999), ch. 24, 234–245.

89. Mangold and Goldberg.

90. Arthur M. Friedlander et al., "Postexposure Prophylaxis against Experimental Inhalation Anthrax," *Journal of Infectious Diseases* 167 (May 1993), 1239–43.

91. Philip S. Brachman et al., "Field Evaluation of Human Anthrax Vaccine," *American Journal of Public Health* 52 (April 1962), 632–45.

92. P. Hambleton, J. A. Carmen, and J. Melling, "Anthrax: The disease in relation to vaccines," *Vaccine* 2 (1984), 125–32.

93. B. E. Ivins et al., "Efficacy of a standard human anthrax vaccine against *Bacillus anthracis* aerosol spore challenge in rhesus monkeys," *Salisbury Medical Bulletin* 87, supplement (1996), 125–26.

94. Arthur M. Friedlander, Phillip R. Pittman, and Gerald W. Parker, "Anthrax Vaccine: Evidence for Safety and Efficacy against Inhalational Anthrax," *Journal of the American Medical Association* 282, no. 22 (December 1999), 2104–6.

95. G. G. Wright, T. W. Green, and R. G. Kanode Jr., "Studies on Immunity in Anthrax, v: Immunizing Activity of Alum-Precipitated Protective Antigen," *Journal of Immunology* 73 (1954), 387–91.

CHAPTER 5

1. This is the approach used in an article recently published by Mazzuchi, et al. In this article the authors emphasize that the decision to immunize is a command policy decision even though maintaining the health of the service members is the primary objective. (John F. Mazzuchi, Robert G. Claypool, Kenneth C. Hyams, David Trump, James Riddle, Relford E. Patterson, Sue Bailey, "Protecting the Health of U.S. Military Forces: A National Obligation," *Aviation, Space, and Environmental Medicine* 71, no. 3 (March 2000), 260–65.)

2. "Peer-reviewed" refers to the process major medical journals use to decide if submissions are worthy of publication. Normally, the lead investigator submits a manuscript for consideration to the editorial board. The editorial board then selects members of the board (unknown to the author of the manuscript) to review the article to see if it meets stringent criteria such as scientific process, experimental design, analysis of the data, discussion, and conclusions. Some journal editorial boards "blind" the editorial reviewers and authors from each other so the reviewers and authors do not know each other to make the review process more objective. The peer-review process is considered to be the most effective means of assuring quality publications in the medical literature. It should be noted that medical textbooks are not peer-reviewed although there is an editor to whom writers of the individual book chapters submit their manuscripts. Therefore, publishing in a textbook is not considered to be as significant as publication in a peer-reviewed journal.

3. For more detailed information, the reader is referred to the Defense Department's informational world-wide-web site addressing anthrax vaccination at http://www.anthrax.osd.mil/. This site includes several links to papers, covering a variety of issues related to the anthrax vaccine. There are also several web sites outlining the reasons against the Defense Department's anthrax vaccination program. The most prominent and complete with numerous links to other sites is http://www.dallasnw.quik.com/cyberella/index.htm. It is important to note that these sites present nearly identical historical, clinical, and factual information. Where these sites differ is how they interpret the information and what conclusions they draw.

4. Numerous extensive reviews of the disease process of anthrax, the vaccine, and the threat weaponized anthrax poses to United States military personnel already exist in the literature. Many are cited in this chapter.

5. Numerous countries, including those who are signatories of the Biological Weapons and Toxins Convention (including the former Soviet Union and Iraq) are known to have offensive biological weapons development programs, including development of weapons using anthrax as the agent. Major D. L. Clement, in an interesting study, concludes that overt use of tactical biological agents on the battlefield is unlikely due to difficulty in hiding the identity of the attacker and the risk of overwhelming response. Biological attacks against United States forces overseas are more likely to be on a small scale by terrorist groups. He identifies anthrax as the ideal biological warfare agent and concludes its use by terrorists or covert operators (such as special forces) against U.S. forces either in the U.S. or overseas is highly

plausible, especially during deployments. (Major David Lee Clement, "A Determination of the Military Significance of Modern Biological Warfare," Master's Thesis, U.S. Army Command and General Staff College, Ft. Leavenworth, KS, (1993), 70, 79.) Inglesby, in his article published in the *Journal of the American Medical Association* (Thomas V. Inglesby, et al., "Anthrax as a Biological Weapon," *Journal of the American Medical Association* 281, no. 18 [12 May, 1999], 1735–45), states anthrax is one of the most serious agents that could be used as a biological weapon, presenting a clinical discussion of anthrax to demonstrate why it would make such an effective weapon. (See also Mazzuchi, et al., 261.) For more information related to the threat anthrax poses as a potential biological weapon, the reader is referred to the United States Air Force Counterproliferation Center's world-wide-web site at http://www.au.af.mil/au/awc/awcgate/awc-cps.htm, which is updated regularly and contains numerous links to other important sites on this topic.

6. The Gram stain is a special stain invented by and named for Christian Gram. (Bob A. Freeman, "The Physical and Chemical Structure of Bacteria," *Burrows Textbook of Microbiology* 21st Edition, (Philadelphia: W. B. Saunders Company, 1979), 25.) It is used to classify bacteria when looking through a microscope. Gram positive bacteria absorb a crystal violet stain, turning them deep violet in color, whereas Gram negative bacteria do not.

7. Terry C. Dixon, et al., "Anthrax," *The New England Journal of Medicine* 341, no. 11 (9 September 1999), 815–26.

8. R. K. Holmes, "Diphtheria, Other Cornybacterial Infections, and Anthrax," in *Harrison's Principles of Internal Medicine,* 14th ed., eds. Anthony S Fauci, M.D., et al. (New York: McGraw-Hill, 1998), 892–99. See also, Phillip S. Brachman, "Anthrax," in *Infectious Diseases* 3rd ed., ed. Paul D. Hoeprich, M.D. (Philadelphia: Harper & Row, Publishers, 1983), 939–44.

9. Thomas V. Inglesby, et al., "Anthrax as a Biological Weapon," *Journal of the American Medical Association* 281, no. 18 (12 May, 1999), 1735–45.

10. "Anthrax History: What You Need to Know," (no date), n.p., on-line, Internet, 11 February 2000, available from http://www.anthrax.osd.mil/.

11. Daniel Lew, "Bacillus Anthracis," in *Principles and Practice of Infectious Diseases,* 4th ed., vol. 2, eds. Gerald l. Mandell, John E. Bennett, and Raphael Dolin (New York: Churchill Livingstone, 1995), 1885–89.

12. Kenneth W. Hedlund, "Anthrax Toxin: History and Recent Advances and Perspectives," *Journal of Toxicology* 11, no. 1, (1992), 41–88.

13. Holmes, 897.

14. Brachman, 944.

15. Inglesby, 1736.

16. Brachman, 940.

17. Ibid., 943.

18. Ibid., 942.

19. Inglesby, 1737.

20. Dixon, 819.

21. Inglesby, 1737.

22. Ibid., 1744.

23. Ibid., 1736–37.

24. Special Committee on Aging, U.S. Senate, *The CDC and Emergency Pre-*

paredness for the Elderly and Disabled, 11 February 2002, n.p.; on-line Internet, 4 Mar 2002, available from http://www.cdc.gov/washington/legislative/02112002.htm.

25. Ibid., 1743–1744. See also a paper written as part of a series entitled "The Military Readiness Project," sponsored by the Family Research Council. (George T. Havrilak, "The Pentagon's Anthrax Vaccination Immunization Program," [no date], n.p.; on-line, Internet, 9 September 2000, available from http://www.frc.org/military/mp99k1mf.html.)

26. Dixon, 818.

27. "Hemorrhagic meningitis" refers to inflammation of the protective coverings of the brain and spinal cord with associated bleeding.

28. Ibid., 819.

29. There are two different types of anthrax vaccine in existence today for human use. ("An Assessment of the Safety of the Anthrax Vaccine: A Letter Report" [30 March 2000], n.p.; on-line, Internet, 12 August 2000, available from http://www.nap.edu/html/anthrax_vaccine/.) Vaccines manufactured by filtering and purifying protective antigen (such as Anthrax Vaccine Adsorbed) are used in the West, primarily by the U.S. and the United Kingdom. The former Soviet Union manufactured an anthrax vaccine using live attenuated (weakened) anthrax spores. This type of vaccine is not available in the West. Although the efficacy of the live, attenuated spore vaccine has been reported to be higher than protective antigen-based vaccines (Hedlund, 64, and Meryl Nass, "Anthrax Vaccine," *New Vaccines and New Vaccine Technology* 13, no. 1 [March 1999], 187–208), an obvious concern related to using this type of vaccine is that the live spores, although weakened, could still cause anthrax. (Inglesby, 1740.)

30. In addition to Anthrax Vaccine Adsorbed, there have been a number of experimental anti-anthrax vaccines developed but not necessarily tested or released for use in humans. All anti-anthrax vaccines developed in some way center on provoking an immunogenic response to protective antigen. (Hedlund, 64–68.)

31. Ibid., 67, 76.

32. Arthur M. Friedlander, Phillip R. Pittman, and Gerald W. Parker, "Anthrax Vaccine: Evidence for Safety and Efficacy Against Inhalation Anthrax," *Journal of the American Medical Association* 282, no. 22 (8 December 1999), 2104–6.

33. In large doses and with repeated exposure formaldehyde may cause cancer. But there is no evidence that repeated doses of trace amounts of formaldehyde when used as a preservative in vaccines is harmful.

34. "Anthrax Vaccine—Ingredients," (no date), n.p.; on-line, Internet, 11 February 2000, available from http://www.anthrax.osd.mil/.

35. "Accusations—Squalene," (no date), n.p.; on-line, Internet, 11 February 2000, available from http://www.anthrax.osd.mil/oldavip/qna/SQUALENE.htm.

36. Albert L. Lehninger, "The Biosynthesis of Lipids," *Biochemistry*, 2nd Edition (New York: Worth Publishers, Inc., 1975), 679–83.

37. For more information see http://www.takari.com/prima.html and http://www.squalene.net/history.htm.

38. Karen Jowers, Únusual Compound Detected in Samples of Anthrax Vaccine," *Air Force Times* 61, Issue 11 (9 October 2000), 28.

39. "Information About the Anthrax Vaccine and the Anthrax Vaccine Immu-

nization Program (AVIP)," (15 October 2000), n.p.; on-line, Internet, 2 November 2000, available from http://www.anthrax.osd.mil/HTML_interface/default.html.

40. A study reported by Asa, et al., claims to have found that squalene antibodies are only found in the blood of people suffering from Gulf War Syndrome. This claim forms the basis of several press reports in the mainstream media accusing that the Department of Defense secretly added squalene to Anthrax Vaccine Adsorbed. (Pamala B. Asa, Yon Cao, Robert F. Garry, "Antibodies to Squalene in Gulf War Syndrome," *Experimental and Molecular Pathology* 68, no. 1 [February 2000], 55–64.) It is very important to note that this study is poorly constructed and has been refuted due to insufficient numbers of subjects in the study population and lack of sufficient control groups. In addition, the authors themselves caution in the article that the results of their study do not establish that squalene was used in Anthrax Vaccine Adsorbed or any other vaccine during the Persian Gulf War.

41. Meryl Nass, "Anthrax Vaccine Safety and Efficacy: Response to the Army Surgeon General Ronald Blanck's Posting," (4 May 1998), n.p.; on-line, Internet, 15 February 2000, available from http://www.dallasnw.quik.com/cyberella/Anthrax/safety4.html.

42. The first anthrax vaccine was produced in the 1800's by Louis Pasteur for use in animals. It was the first vaccine ever developed to protect against bacterial infection, making anthrax the first disease for which a vaccine was ever produced. Anthrax is probably the most studied and scrutinized of any bacterial infectious disease process. "Anthrax Vaccine Immunization Program," n.p., on-line, Internet, 11 February 2000, available from http://www.anthrax.osd.mil/.

43. PS Brachman, et al., "Field Evaluation of a Human Anthrax Vaccine," *American Journal of Public Health* 62 (1962), 632–645.

44. *Federal Register* 50, no. 240 (13 December 1985, Part II), 51002-51117; on-line, Internet, available from http://www.anthrax.osd.mil/oldavip/FedReg1.htm. See also, Friedlander, "Anthrax Vaccine: Evidence for Safety and Efficacy Against Inhalation Anthrax," 2104. See also, Meryl Nass, "Anthrax Vaccine," *New Vaccines and New Vaccine Technology* 13, no. 1 (March 1999), 187–208.

45. "Anthrax Vaccine—Overview," n.p., on-line, Internet, 11 February 2000, available from http://www.anthrax.osd.mil/oldavip/qna/OVERVIEW.HTM.

46. Friedlander, "Anthrax Vaccine: Evidence for Safety and Efficacy Against Inhalation Anthrax," 2104.

47. Dr. Robert C. Myers, Statement Presented to the Subcommittee on National Security, Veterans Affairs, and International Relations, 29 April 1999, n.p.; on-line, Internet, 11 February 2000, available from http://www.bioportcorp.com/testimony_of_drmyers.htm.

48. Ibid.

49. "Anthrax Vaccine Adsorbed Stockpile Analysis—Supplemental Testing Needed and/or Resolvable Food and Drug Administration Issues, " (13 November 1998), n.p.; on-line, Internet, 15 February 2000, available from http://www.anthraxvaccine.org/suppdocs/doc14.htm.

50. Myers, n.p.

51. Department of Defense Press Release (14 December 1999), n.p.; on-line, Internet, 11 February 2000, available from http://www.bioport.com/release12-14-99.htm.

52. Fuad El-Hibri, CEO of BioPort Corporation, Statement Presented to the Subcommittee on National Security, Veterans Affairs, and International Relations, (30 June 1999), n.p.; on-line, Internet, 11 February 2000, available from http://www.bioportcorp.com/El-HibriOral_Test_6-30.htm.

53. Department of Defense Press Release: 14 December 1999.

54. Rudi Williams, "Short Supply Forces Anthrax Vaccination Slowdown," *American Forces Press Service* (12 July, 2000), n.p.; on-line, Internet, 26 August 2000, available from http://www.defenselink.mil/news/Jul2000/n07122000_20007124. html.

55. Myers, n.p.

56. Department of Defense Press Release (14 December 1999), n.p.

57. "Accusations—Squalene," n.p.

58. "Department of Defense Information About the Anthrax Vaccine and the Anthrax Vaccine Immunization Program (AVIP)," (23 June 2000), n.p.; on-line, Internet, 26 August 2000, available from http://www.anthrax.osd.mil/Site_Files/Ed_products/Infopaper/Infopaper.htm.

59. William S. Cohen, "Anthrax Vaccination Slowdown," (10 July 2000), n.p.; on-line, Internet, 26 August 2000, available from http://www.anthrax.osd.mil/Site_Files/Anthrax Vaccine Immunization Programslowdown/video_text.htm.

60. Todd Silver, "Federal Vaccine Manufacture Weighed: Pending Shortage of Anthrax Preparation Finds Congress Dissatisfied with the Status Quo," *U.S. Medicine* 36, no. 8 (August 2000), 47, 49–50.

61. "Frequently Asked Questions About Bioport and the Anthrax Vaccine," n.p.; on-line, Internet, 28 January 2004, available from http://www.bioport.com/NewsRoom/FAQs/QA_BioPort-AVA.asp.

62. Brachman, "Field Evaluation of a Human Anthrax Vaccine, 632."

63. Nass, "Anthrax Vaccine," 189.

64. Myers, n.p.

65. Ibid.

66. *Federal Register*, n.p.

67. Susan S. Ellenberg, Director, Division of Biostatistics and Epidemiology, Center for Biologics Evaluation and Research, Food and Drug Administration, Statement to Subcommittee on National Security, Veterans Affairs, and International Relations, (21 July 1999), n.p.; on-line, Internet, 19 February 2000, available from http://www.hhs.gov/progorg/asl/testify/t990721b.html.

68. Friedlander, "Anthrax Vaccine: Evidence for Safety and Efficacy Against Inhalation Anthrax," 2104.

69. "Anthrax Vaccine—Safety," (no date), n.p.; on-line, Internet, 11 February 2000, available from http://www.anthrax.osd.mil/oldavip/qna/SAFETY.HTM.

70. "Anthrax Vaccine Adsorbed," Food and Drug Administration Required Product Insert, (no date), n.p.; on-line, Internet, 11 February 2000, available from http://bioportcorp.com/AnthraxIns.htm. See also, Myers, n.p.

71. Phillip S. Brachman, "Inhalation Anthrax," a public domain document originally published in *Annals of the New York Academy of Sciences* 353 (no date), pages 83–93.

72. F. Marc LaForce, "Anthrax," *Clinical Infectious Diseases* 19 (December 1994), 1009–14. See also, "Vaccine Safety," (no date), n.p.; on-line, Internet,

4 September 2000, available from http://www.anthrax.osd.mil/Site_Files/safety/safety_info.htm. See also, Hedlund, 72–73.

73. *Federal Register*. See also, Lew, 1886. See also, LaForce, 1010.

74. Friedlander, "Anthrax Vaccine: Evidence for Safety and Efficacy Against Inhalation Anthrax," 2105–6.

75. The Food and Drug Administration has not approved Anthrax Vaccine Adsorbed for use to protect against inhalation anthrax. But, lack of Food and Drug Administration approval for a specific indication does not prohibit the use of a medication for that indication if clinical evidence exists to support it. Food and Drug Administration licensure means that the medical product may be sold commercially in the U.S. Food and Drug Administration approval means testing for that indication has been completed according to Food and Drug Administration specifications in connection with the licensing process. Lack of Food and Drug Administration approval only means that the rigorous testing required by the Food and Drug Administration (paid for by the manufacturer) before it will grant its endorsement has not been completed. If there is reasonable clinical evidence to support using a medication for an indication not approved by the Food and Drug Administration, a physician may prescribe that medication for that use based on the physician's clinical judgment. Such use is also not considered experimental since the medication is already licensed. In a letter to the Honorable Dan Burton dated 26 November 1999, Melinda K. Plaisier, the Associate Commissioner for Legislation for the Food and Drug Administration discusses the procedures by which lots are released by the Food and Drug Administration for sale and distribution. Regarding indications for use, she states, "The labeling for Anthrax Vaccine Adsorbed does not mention route of exposure (e.g., cutaneous) per se. Use of the vaccine for protection against both cutaneous and inhalation anthrax exposure is not inconsistent with the labeling for Anthrax Vaccine Adsorbed." She adds that there is no reason for Anthrax Vaccine Adsorbed to be returned to an investigational new drug status when used to vaccinate against inhalation anthrax, especially since the rarity and risk of human inhalation anthrax precludes gathering additional clinical data.

76. "FDA Statement: FDA Issues Final Rule and Final Order Regarding Safety and Efficacy of Certain Liscensed Biological Products Including Anthrax Vaccine," (30 December 2003), n.p., on-line, Internet, 28 January 2004, available from http://www.fda.gov/bbs/topics/NEWS/2003/NEW01001.html.

77. Myers, n.p. See also, "Medical Readiness: Issues Concerning the Anthrax Vaccine," Government Accounting Office Testimony before The Subcommittee on National Security, Veterans Affairs, and International Relations, 21 July 1999, Government Accounting Office/T-NSIAD-99-226, 7–9.

78. "Anthrax Vaccine Adsorbed," Food and Drug Administration Required Product Insert, n.p.

79. "Anthrax Vaccine—Safety," n.p.

80. Agency Group 09, "Surgeon General Testifies on Anthrax Vaccine," *FDCH Regulatory IntelligenceDatabase,* 3 November 1999.

81. Friedlander, "Anthrax Vaccine: Evidence for Safety and Efficacy Against Inhalation Anthrax," 2104. See also, "Anthrax Vaccine Adsorbed," Food and Drug Administration Required Product Insert.

82. Friedlander, "Anthrax Vaccine: Evidence for Safety and Efficacy Against Inhalation Anthrax," 2104.

83. Ellenberg, n.p.

84. *Federal Register*, n.p.

85. "Anthrax Vaccine—Safety," n.p. See also, Mazzuchi, et al., 261.

86. Friedlander, "Anthrax Vaccine: Evidence for Safety and Efficacy Against Inhalation Anthrax," 2105. See also, Mazzuchi, et al., 261.

87. Friedlander, "Anthrax Vaccine: Evidence for Safety and Efficacy Against Inhalation Anthrax," 2105.

88. "Medical Readiness: Safety and Efficacy of the Anthrax Vaccine," Government Accounting Office Testimony before The Subcommittee on National Security, Veterans Affairs, and International Relations, 29 April 1999, GAO/T-NSIAD-99-148, 4–5.

89. Ibid., 4.

90. "Anaphylaxis in Relation to Anthrax Vaccination: Analysis by Anthrax Vaccine Immunization Program Agency," (2 December 1999), n.p.; on-line, Internet, 12 August 2000, available from http://www.anthrax.osd.mil/SCANNED/ARTICLES/grabedocs/anaphylaxis.htm.

91. Inglesby, 1735–1736, 1740, 1744.

92. "Anthrax Vaccine—Safety," n.p.

93. "Form VAERS-1 Reports," (October 1, 2002), n.p.; on-line, Internet, 28 January 2004, available at http://www.anthrax.osd.mil/media/pdf/vaerschart.pdf.

94. Friedlander, "Anthrax Vaccine: Evidence for Safety and Efficacy Against Inhalation Anthrax," 2105.

95. "Surveillance for Adverse Events Associated with Anthrax Vaccination—U.S. Department of Defense, 1998–2000," *Morbidity and Mortality Weekly Report* 49, no. 16 (28 April 2000), 341–45; on-line, Internet, 12 August 2000, available from http://www.cdc.gov/epo/mmwr/preview/mmwrhtml/mm4916a1.htm.

96. "Safety Review of Anthrax Vaccine (24 April 2000)," n.p.; on-line, Internet, 12 August 2000, available from http://www.anthrax.osd.mil/SCANNED/ARTICLES/grabedocs/safetyReview-Anthrax Vaccine Adsorbed.htm.

97. Charles L. Cragin, Acting Secretary of Defense for Reserve Affairs, "The Anthrax Vaccine: Safe, Effective, and Necessary," *Defense Link* (August 1999), n.p.; on-line, Internet, 11 February 2000, available from http://www.defenselink.mil/news/Aug1999?n08171999_9908176.html. See also Myers, n.p.

98. Friedlander, "Anthrax Vaccine: Evidence for Safety and Efficacy Against Inhalation Anthrax," 2105.

99. "DoD News: Panels Find Vaccines May Relate to Reservists Illness, Death," (November 19, 2003), n.p.; on-line, Internet, 28 January 2004, available from http://www.dod.mil/releases/2003/nr20031119-0656.html.

100. "Safety Review of Anthrax Vaccine, 24 April 2000."

101. Myers, n.p.

102. Anthrax Vaccine Adsorbed has been administered to thousands of veterinary and laboratory workers, livestock handlers, and workers in the wool sorter and animal hide industry since 1970. In addition, there have been at least four major independent reviews by civilian panels on the safety and efficacy of Anthrax Vaccine Adsorbed. ("Vaccine Safety," (no-date), n.p.; on-line, Internet, 4 September 2000, available from http://www.anthrax.osd.mil/Site_Files/safety/safety_info.htm.)

103. It should be noted that the strength of clinical evidence would be enhanced if more data were published in the peer-reviewed literature and researchers should be encouraged to submit their data to the peer-review process. ("An Assessment of the Safety of the Anthrax Vaccine: A Letter Report," n.p.)

104. Ibid.

105. Nass, "Anthrax Vaccine," 203. See also, Nass, "Anthrax Vaccine Safety and Efficacy: Response to the Army Surgeon General Ronald Blanck's Posting."

106. Ken Alibek, *Biohazard,* (New York: Random House, 1999), 261, 281. See also, Inglesby, 1744.

107. Dr. Nass cites a study in which different strains of anthrax were tested in guinea pigs vaccinated with Anthrax Vaccine Adsorbed. In the study, nine of twenty-seven strains appeared to be resistant to vaccination. (Nass, "Anthrax Vaccine Safety and Efficacy: Response to the Army Surgeon General Ronald Blanck's Posting.") Friedlander, "Anthrax Vaccine: Evidence for Safety and Efficacy Against Inhalation Anthrax," however, provides a thorough review of several animal studies, including the study cited by Dr. Nass, in which Anthrax Vaccine Adsorbed is tested against various strains of anthrax in several different animal species. He demonstrates that, while Anthrax Vaccine Adsorbed provided variable protection against certain strains of anthrax in guinea pigs, Anthrax Vaccine Adsorbed provided excellent protection against even the most virulent and seemingly resistant strains (such as the Ames strain) in non-human primates and rabbits, even after just two doses of Anthrax Vaccine Adsorbed. This most likely reflects species-specific differences with the guinea pig's immune system, making it more difficult to immunize the guinea pig against anthrax compared to other animal species, and is not due to any strain of anthrax developing resistance to the anthrax vaccine. (Friedlander, "Anthrax Vaccine: Evidence for Safety and Efficacy Against Inhalation Anthrax," 2105–6.)

108. "Anthrax Vaccine Casualties at One Military Installation," (no date), n.p.; online, Internet, 2 September 2000, available from http://www.dallasnw.quik.com/cyberella/Anthrax/dover4-1.html.

109. Friedlander, "Anthrax Vaccine: Evidence for Safety and Efficacy Against Inhalation Anthrax," 2104.

110. Dr. Nass reports the results of a survey sent out to members of the 9th Airlift Squadron at Dover Air Force Base. In this report, she admits that the survey results cannot be used to establish that Anthrax Vaccine Adsorbed actually caused the symptoms due to the lack of a control group. Overall 252 surveys were sent out and 139 were completed and returned. She interprets 81 as probably having a systemic reaction due to Anthrax Vaccine Adsorbed. At least six indicated they felt Anthrax Vaccine Adsorbed did not cause their symptoms. Even though she admits there can be no statistical analysis of this data and it is not possible to prove causality, Dr. Nass concludes something must be wrong at Dover because it is just not normal for so many otherwise healthy people at one location to be having symptoms or strange illnesses of one sort or another. A useful analysis would be to compare the rate of occurrence of symptoms and diseases in 9th Airlift Squadron personnel against the rate of occurrence in all unvaccinated personnel at Dover and the U.S. population in general, but this is not provided. Nor is there an attempt to look for recurring patterns of symptoms. Indeed, it appears from the survey results that the patterns of symptoms vary widely, with no two individuals' symptom patterns matching.

(Meryl Nass, "Survey Results of the 9th Airlift Squadron," [no date], n.p.: on-line, Internet, 27 August 2000, available from http://www.anthraxvaccine.org.)

111. Lieutenant General Paul K. Carlton, Jr., "Anthrax," (no date), n.p.; on-line, Internet, 4 September 2000, available from http://sg-www.satx.disa.mil/af/sg/presentations/Anthrax_Threat.ppt.

112. Havrilak, n.p.

113. Hedlund, 76.

114. Ellenberg, n.p.

115. Gina Terracciano, Robert Chen, Jenifer Lloyd, "Surveillance for Adverse Events Following Vaccination" (September 1997), n.p.; on-line, Internet, 15 February 2000, available from http://www.cdc.gov/nip/vacsafe/vaccinesafety/publications/aesurveillance.htm.

116. Ellenberg, n.p.

117. Nass, "Ádverse Effects: Anthrax Vaccine."

118. Friedlander, "Anthrax Vaccine: Evidence for Safety and Efficacy Against Inhalation Anthrax," 2105.

119. Lieutenant General Hal M. Hornberg, "Vaccine is Safe, Effective," *Air Force Times* 60, Issue 16 (22 November 1999), 55.

120. Laura Laughlin, "Shot to Hell," *Phoenixnewtimes.com* (27 January 2000), n.p.; on-line, Internet, 14 February 2000, available from http://www.phoenixnewtimes.com/issues/2000-01-27/feature.html.

121. "Food and Drug Administration Inspection Cites Problems in Anthrax Vaccine Production," *Associated Press* (15 December 1999), n.p., on-line, Internet, 14 February 2000, available from http://AppLogic+FTContentServer?section=archieve&pagename=story&storyid=115019020857.

122. Thomas L. Rempfer, "Why Am I Resisting the Vaccine? The Military Trained Me To," *Washingtonpost.com* (30 January, 2000), n.p.; on-line, Internet, 5 February 2000, available from http://www.washingtonpost.com/wp-srv/Wplate/2000-01/30/1531-013000-idx.html. See also, "Anthrax Vaccine Protestors Gather Outside Air Force Base," *Miami (FL) Herald* (29 January 2000), n.p.; on-line, Internet, 5 February 2000, available from http://www.herald.com/content/today/digdocs/026528.htm.

123. "Anthrax Vaccine Immunization Program" (no date), n.p.; on-line, Internet, 11 February 2000, available from http://www.anthrax.osd.mil/.

124. "Anthrax Vaccine Links and Information" (no date), n.p.; on-line, Internet, 27 August 2000, available from http://www.dallasnw.quik.com/cyberella/index.htm.

125. Kathryn C. Zoon, letter (28 April 1998), n.p.; on-line, Internet, 4 September 2000, available from http://www.dallasnw.quik.com/cyberella/Anthrax/Zoon4_98.html.

126. John Davidson, "Anti bio-weapon vaccine for troops fails safety tests," *Independent* (6 December 1999), n.p.; on-line, Internet, 2 September 2000, available from http://www.dallasnw.quik.com/cyberella/Anthrax/UKHealth.html.

127. Ibid.

128. Several independent nationally renowned scientific groups have addressed this issue and have found no evidence to link anthrax vaccine with illnesses among

Gulf War veterans. There have been several unsubstantiated allegations in the media and elsewhere about experimental vaccines that may have contained non-Food and Drug Administration-licensed substances such as squalene. Only the Food and Drug Administration-licensed anthrax vaccines have been used. ("Anthrax Vaccine and the Persian Gulf War," [no date], n.p.; on-line, Internet, 15 February 2000, available from http://www.anthrax.osd.mil/oldavip/qna/GULFWAR.HTM.)

129. "Anthrax Vaccine Home Page," (no date), n.p.; on-line, Internet, 11 February 2000, available from http://www.anthraxvaccine.org/.

130. "Dr. Meryl Nass," (no date), n.p.; on-line, Internet, 27 August 2000, available from http://www.dallasnw.quik.com/cyberella/Anthrax/credentials.html.

131. Laughlin, n.p.

132. Nass, "Anthrax Vaccine," 187–208.

133. Ibid., 199.

134. Ibid., 203.

135. "FDA Statement: FDA Issues Final Rule and Final Order Regarding Safety and Efficacy of Certain Liscensed Biological Products Including Anthrax Vaccine," n.p.

136. Nass, "Anthrax Vaccine," 189. See also, Inglesby, 1744.

137. New anthrax vaccines have been developed and are ready for clinical testing. But, so far, lack of funding has prevented the performance of clinical trial studies. (LaForce, 1013.)

138. Meryl Nass, "Alibek on Anthrax," (30 June 1999), n.p.; on-line, Internet, 15 February 2000, available from http://www.anthraxvaccine.org/email/email9.htm.

139. Jamie McIntyre, "All U.S. Troops to get Anthrax Vaccine," *CNN Interactive* (15 December 1997), n.p.; on-line, Internet, 17 February 2000, available from http://cnn.com?U.S./9712/15/military.anthrax/. See also, Cragin, n.p., and Mazzuchi, et al., 261. See also Inglesby, 1735, and Clement, 53–54, 79.

140. Scott, n.p.

141. Ibid.

142. Ibid.

143. "An Assessment of the Safety of the Anthrax Vaccine: A Letter Report," n.p.

144. "FDA Statement: FDA Issues Final Rule and Final Order Regarding Safety and Efficacy of Certain Liscensed Biological Products Including Anthrax Vaccine," n.p.

145. The letter dated 30 March 2000 is the result of a request the Secretary of Defense sent to the Institute of Medicine to assess the safety of Anthrax Vaccine Adsorbed. The Institute of Medicine commented that its assessment is an early step in sorting out the complex issues surrounding Anthrax Vaccine Adsorbed and has started a two-year in-depth study which will include a review of all available data from the Department of Defense. ("A Letter Report from the Institute of Medicine [IOM), 30 March 2000" (no date), n.p.; on-line, Internet, 12 August 2000, available from http://www.anthrax.osd.mil/SCANNED/ARTICLES/ltrReportINtro.htm.)

CHAPTER 6

1. Nicolau Barquet, and Pere Domingo, "Smallpox: The Triumph over the Most Terrible of the Ministers of Death," *Annals of Internal Medicine,* 15 October 1997,

n.p.; on-line, Internet, 16 February 2000, available from http://38.232.17.254/journal/annals/15oct97/smallpox.htm.

2. Frederick R. Sidell, Ernest T. Takafuji, and David R. Franz, eds., *Medical Aspects of Chemical and Biological Warfare* (Washington, DC: Office of the Surgeon General, United States Army 1997), 12.

3. Lawrence K. Altman, William J. Broad, and Judith Miller, "Smallpox: The Once and Future Scourge," *New York Times,* 15 June 1999, n.p.; on-line, Internet, 4 February 2000, available from http://search.nytimes.com/daily.

4. Barquet and Domingo, n.p.

5. Ibid.

6. Ibid.

7. Ibid.

8. Ibid.

9. Altman, Broad, and Miller, n.p.

10. "Smallpox as a Biological Weapon: Medical and Public Management," *Journal of the American Medical Association*, 9 June 1999, n.p.; on-line, Internet, 8 January 1999, available from http://jama-ama.org/issues/v28ln22/full/jst90000.html.

11. Ibid.

12. Ibid.

13. D. A. Henderson, "Smallpox: Clinical and Epidemiologic Features," *Emerging Infectious Diseases* 5, no. 5 (July–August 1999), 537.

14. Sidell, Takafuji, and Franz, 543.

15. Hervé Bazin, *The Eradication of Smallpox*, trans. Andrew Morgan and Genise Morgan (New York: Academic Press, 2000), 9.

16. Robert Temple, *The Genius of China: 3000 Years of Science, Discoveries and Inventions* (New York: Simon and Schuster, 1986), 135–7.

17. Bazin, 9.

18. Ibid., 12.

19. Barquet and Domingo, n.p.

20. Quoted in Hervé Bazin, *The Eradication of Smallpox*, trans. Andrew Morgan and Genise Morgan (New York: Academic Press, 2000), 14.

21. Bazin, 14, 15.

22. *Desk Reference on Vaccines & Immunity (Emphasizing Military Vaccination Programs)*, 12 November 1999, n.p., on-line, Internet, 16 February 2000, available from http://www.anthrax.osd.mil/SCANNED/ARTICLES/Sesk_Ref/mvp-guide.htm.

23. Altman, Broad, and Miller, n.p.

24. Barquet and Domingo, n.p.

25. Sidell, Takafuji, and Franz, 548.

26. Barquet and Domingo, n.p.

27. Sidell, Takafuji, and Franz, 548.

28. Ibid.

29. Arthur Kent, *History's Mysteries: The History of Smallpox*, The History Channel Video, 45 min., 1999, videocassette.

30. Altman, Broad, and Miller, n.p.

31. *Disease Eradication/Elimination Goals*, The World Health Organization, 1998, n.p.; on-line, Internet, 3 February 2000, available from http://www.who.int/aboutwho/en/disease_er.htm.

32. Ibid.

33. "International Notes Smallpox Surveillance—World Wide," *Weekly Epidemiologic Record* 50, no. 52 (24 December 1977), 390.
34. Ibid.
35. Ibid.
36. Altman, Broad, and Miller, n.p.
37. "Smallpox as Biological Weapon," n.p.
38. D.A. Henderson, "Smallpox: Clinical and Epidemiologic Features," *Emerging Infectious Diseases* 5, no. 5 (July–August 1999), 538.
39. Ibid., 538.
40. "Smallpox Surveillance—Worldwide," *Mobility and Mortality Weekly Report*, 24 October 1997, n.p.; on-line, Internet, 4 February 2000, available from http://www.cdc.gov/epo/mmwr/preview/mmwrhtml/00049694.htm.
41. "*Vaccinia* (Smallpox) Vaccine Recommendations of the Immunization Practices Advisory Council (ACIP)," *Mobility and Mortality Recommendations and Reports*, 13 December 1991, n.p.; on-line, Internet, 4 February 2000, available from http://www.cdc.gov/epo/mmwr/preview/mmwrhtml/00042032.htm.
42. Ibid.
43. *Medical Management of Biological Casualties Handbook*, 3rd ed. (Fort Detrick, MD: U.S. Army Medical Research Institute of Infectious Diseases, 1998), 59.
44. "*Vaccinia* (Smallpox) Vaccine Recommendations," n.p.
45. "Smallpox as Biological Weapon," n.p.
46. Plotkin, S., W. Orenstien. "Smallpox and vaccinia," in Zorab R, ed. *Vaccines.* 3rd ed. Philadelphia: Harcourt Brace & Company, 1999: 1230.
47. Ken Alibek with Stephen Handelman, *Biohazard* (New York: Random House, 1999), 114.
48. "Smallpox as Biological Weapon," n.p.
49. Ibid.
50. August Gribbin, "Scientists Test New Defense for Old Enemy—Smallpox," *Washington (DC) Times*, 19 August 1999.
51. Terence Chea, "Hunting for a Safer Smallpox Vaccine: Terrorist Attacks Spur Novavax to Seek a Treatment Without Serious Side Effects," *Washington (DC) Post*, 15 February 2002, E05.
52. Rick Weiss, "Smallpox Vaccine Turns Up: Discovered Doses Buy Time for U.S.," *Washington (DC) Post*, 28 March 2002, 1.
53. Warren King, "Smallpox Vaccine Plan Gets Officials' Attention," *Seattle (WA) Times*, 8 April 2002.
54. Altman, Broad, and Miller, n.p.
55. National Institute of Allergy and Infectious Disease, *RFA: AI-00-002: Anti-orthopoxvirus Drug Discovery and Development*, 20 October 1999.
56. National Institute of Allergy and Infectious Disease, *RFA: AI-00-003: Orthopoxvirus Genomics and Bioinformatics Resource Center*, 20 October 1999.
57. National Institute of Allergy and Infectious Disease, *RFA: AI-00-001: New Treatment for Complications from* Vaccinia *Immunization*, 20 October 1999.
58. John Bartlett, "Smallpox Vaccination in 2003: Key Information for Clinicians," *Clinical Infections Diseases*, 18 March 2003, n.p., on-line, Internet, 27 January 2004, available from http://www.journals.uchicago.edu/CID/journal/issues/v36n7/30959/30959.text.html.
59. Victoria Stagg Elliott, "Slow start for smallpox vaccine plan," *American Medi-*

cal News, 5 May 2003, n.p., on-line, Internet, 27 January 2004, available from http://www.ama-assn.org/amednews/2003/05/05/hll10505.htm.

60. "Federal Occupational Health Update on Smallpox Immunization Strategies," *Department of Health and Human Services,* 26 December 2002, n.p., on-line, Internet, 27 January 2004, available from http://www.foh.dhhs.gov/Public/Library/smallpox.pdf.

61. Mark G. Kortepeter and Gerald W. Parker, "Potential Biological Weapons Threats," *Emerging Infectious Diseases* 5, no. 5 (July–August 1999), 524.

62. Robert Windem, "U.S. Agency Fears Smallpox Weapon," *MSNBC Interactive News,* 2 February 1999.

63. Alibek, 105–22.

64. William J. Broad and Judith Miller, "Government Report Says 3 Nations Hide Stocks of Smallpox," *New York Times,* 13 June 1999, n.p.; on-line, Internet, 4 February 2000, available from http://search.nytimes.com/daily.

65. "Smallpox as Biological Weapon," n.p.

66. Alibek, 114.

67. Tara O'Toole, "Smallpox: An Attack Scenario," *Emerging Infectious Diseases* 5, no. 5 (July–August 1999), 542–45.

68. "Smallpox as Biological Weapon," n.p.

69. D.A. Henderson, 538.

70. W. Seth Carus, "The Threat of Bioterrorism," *National Defense University Strategic Forum*, no. 127 (September 1997), n.p., on-line, Internet, 18 January 2000, available from http://www.ndu.edu/inss/strforum/forum127.html.

71. Statistics revalidated in W. Seth Carus, "Bioterrorism and Biocrimes: The Illicit Use of Biological Agents in the 20th Century," *Working Paper* (Washington, DC: National Defense University, December 1998) and Jonathan B. Tucker, "Historical Trends Related to Bioterrorism: An Empirical Analysis," *Emerging Infectious Diseases* 5, no. 5 (July–August 1999), 503.

72. W. Seth Carus, "The Threat of Bioterrorism," n.p.

73. Brad Roberts, ed., *Terrorism with Chemical and Biological Weapons: Calibrating the Risks and Responses* (Alexandria, VA: the Chemical and Biological Arms Control Institute, 1997), 66–70. Also, as Dr. David Franz noted in reviewing this manuscript, "Access and the moral constraints are probably the greatest deterrents to the use of smallpox as a terrorist weapon. Because of its highly contagious nature, it would be unnecessary to weaponize it for use. It is likely that, even if the remaining isolates in Atlanta and Novosibrisk are ceremonially destroyed, illicit stocks or synthesis using the tools of molecular biology will make it available as a weapon in the future. The threat cannot be calibrated; however, whether the threat is small or large, the potential impact of reintroduction of this virus to the human population is catastrophic. Prudence demands that we continue research which will help us control its spread and impact, should the unthinkable happen."

74. August Gribbin, n.p.

CHAPTER 7

1. For an overview of BW proliferation trends see *Proliferation: Threat and Response,* 3rd ed. (Washington, DC: Office of the Secretary of Defense, May 2001).

2. This paper distills insights gained over more than a year of research and

dialogue on these questions. Preliminary propositions were developed in the autumn of 1999 and refined and validated in 2000 in a series of interactions with experts on the region—experts based in the United States, Europe, and the Middle East. Formal publications on the basic questions are few and far between, so every effort has been made here to uncover areas of consensus and disagreement among analysts and to reflect these in the broader analysis.

3. See Erhard Geissler and John Ellis van Courtland Moon, *Biological and Toxin Weapons: Research, Development and Use from the Middle Ages to 1945* (Stockholm: Oxford University Press for the Stockholm International Peace Research Institute, 1999).

4. Parties in the region include Bahrain, Egypt, Iraq, Iran, Jordan, Kuwait, Lebanon, Libya, Qatar, Saudi Arabia, Syria, Tunisia, United Arab Emirates, Yemen. Of these states parties, some have signed but not ratified. Nonparties include Algeria, Israel, Oman, and Sudan.

5. Such work has been undertaken in associated project activities by the National Defense University and SAIC. See *Motivations to Acquire and Use Biological Weapons in the Middle East*, Science Applications International Corporation, August 24, 2000 (unclassified). See also Jonathan B. Tucker, "Motivations For and Against Proliferation: The Case of the Middle East," in Raymond A. Zilinskas, ed., *Biological Warfare: Modern Offense and Defense* (Boulder, CO: Lynne Rienner, 1999), 27–52. For country-specific assessments, see Shahram Chubin, *Eliminating Weapons of Mass Destruction: The Persian Gulf Case* (Washington, DC: Henry L. Stimson Center, March 1997); Joshua Sinai, "Libya's Pursuit of Weapons of Mass Destruction," *Nonproliferation Review* (Spring–Summer 1997), 92–9; Dany Shoham, "Chemical and Biological Weapons in Egypt," *Nonproliferation Review* (Spring–Summer 1998), 48–58; Dany Shoham, "Does Saudi Arabia Have or Seek Chemical or Biological Weapons?" *Nonproliferation Review* (Spring–Summer 1999), 122–29; M. Zuhair Diab, "Syria's Chemical and Biological Weapons: Assessing Capabilities and Motivations," Nonproliferation Review (Fall 1997), 104–11; and Al J. Venter, "New-Era Threat: Iraq's Biological Weapons," Middle East Policy, vol. 6, no. 4 (June 1999), 104–17.

6. See W. Seth Carus, *"The Poor Man's Atomic Bomb?" Biological Weapons in the Middle East* (Washington, DC: Washington Institute for Near East Policy, 1989), especially chapter 5, "The Effectiveness and Utility of Biological Warfare." See also Brad Roberts, "Between Complacency and Panic: Calibrating the Biological Warfare Threat," in Stuart Johnson, ed., *The Niche Threat: Deterring the Use of Chemical and Biological Weapons* (Washington, DC: National Defense University, 1995).

7. For purposes of the original survey, preliminary research drew on the following sources: *Strategic Survey* and *Military Balance* (prepared as annual surveys by the International Institute for Strategic Studies in London), the annual *Strategic Assessment* prepared by the Institute for National Strategic Studies at the National Defense University, and various publications of the Center for Strategic and International Studies, the Jaffee Center for Strategic Studies at Tel Aviv University, The Nixon Center, RAND, USCENTCOM, and the Washington Institute for Near East Policy. A strawman taxonomy of potential conflicts over the next decade was then developed and tested over a period of months with individual experts.

8. Ahmed Hashim, "The State, Society, and the Evolution of Warfare in the

Middle East: The Rise of Strategic Deterrence?" *Washington Quarterly* 18, no. 4 (Autumn 1995), 53–72.

9. See Ehud Sprinzak, "On Not Overstating the Problem," and Brian Michael Jenkins, "The WMD Terrorist Threat—Is There a Consensus View?" in Brad Roberts, ed., *Hype or Reality? The "New Terrorism and Mass Casualty Attacks"* (Alexandria, VA: Chemical and Biological Arms Control Institute, 2000).

10. Simon Whitby and Paul Rogers, "Anti-crop Biological Warfare—Implications of the Iraqi and US Programs," *Defense Analysis* 13, no. 3 (1997), 303–18.

11. For a discussion of multiple aspects of the international response to NBC proliferation in the region, see Lawrence Scheinman, "NBC and Missile Proliferation Issues in the Middle East," in Barry Schneider, ed., *Middle East Security Issues In the Shadow of Weapons of Mass Destruction Proliferation* (Maxwell Air Force Base, AL: Air University Press, 1999).

12. Michael Moodie, *Will Deterrence Work?* (Alexandria, VA: Chemical and Biological Arms Control Institute, 1998).

13. For a historical perspective on CBW terrorism in the region, with a review of contemporary issues, see Dany Shoham, "Chemical and Biological Terrorism: An Intensifying Profile of a Non-Conventional Threat" (Tel Aviv: Ariel Center for Policy Research, 1998).

14. See Brad Roberts, *Biological Weapons in Major Theater War*, IDA Document D-2234 (Alexandria, VA: Institute for Defense Analyses, November 1998). See also Roberts, "Terrorism and Asymmetric Conflict," in Roberts, ed., *Hype or Reality,* 147–58.

15. For more on this argument concerning technical challenges, see Karl Lowe, "Analyzing Technical Constraints on Bioterrorism: Are They Still Important?" in Brad Roberts, ed., *Terrorism With Chemical and Biological Weapons: Calibrating Risks and Responses* (Alexandria, VA: Chemical and Biological Arms Control Institute, 1997), 53–64.

16. For more on this argument, see Brian Jenkins, "Understanding the Link Between Motive and Methods," in Roberts, ed., *Terrorism With Chemical and Biological Weapons,* 43–52.

17. Ahmed S. Hashim, "Syria," and Michael Eisenstadt, "Iran," case studies nos. 1 and 2, respectively, in *The Deterrence Series* (Alexandria, VA: Chemical and Biological Arms Control Institute, 1998).

18. From James K. Campbell, "On Not Understanding the Problem," in Roberts, ed., *Hype Or Reality?,* 19.

19. These latter arguments were made with particular force by Ministry of Defence participants in a project-related symposium on BW in the Middle East in London in June 2000.

20. Jonathan B. Tucker, "Lessons from the Case Studies," in Tucker, ed., *Toxic Terror: Assessing Terrorist Use of Chemical and Biological Weapons* (Cambridge, MA: MIT Press, 2000), 249–68.

21. Edward M. Spiers, *Chemical and Biological Weapons: A Study of Proliferation* (London: Macmillan Press, 1994), especially chapter 4; "Rabta: A Case Study in International Action," 65–83.

22. Roberts, *Biological Weapons in Major Theater War.*

23. The term "spasm" is Herman Kahn's and is drawn from his analysis of thresholds in the escalation and de-escalation process. See Kahn, *On Thermonuclear War.*

24. For an exploration of the possible escalation and de-escalation dynamics of a major theater war involving the use of weapons of mass destruction, see Brad Roberts, "Rethinking How Wars Must End: NBC War Termination Issues in the Post-Cold War Era," in Victor Utgoff, ed., *The Coming Crisis: Nuclear Proliferation, U.S. Interests, and World Order* (Cambridge, MA: MIT Press, 2000).

CHAPTER 8

1. Jonathan B. Tucker, "The Future of Biological Warfare," in *The Proliferation of Advanced Weaponry: Technology, Motivations, and Responses*, ed. W. Thomas Wander and Eric H. Arnett (Washington, DC: American Association for the Advancement of Science, 1992), 73.

2. Humphry Crum Ewing et al., *Cruise Missiles: Precision & Countermeasures*, Bailrigg Memorandum 10 (Lancaster, UK: Centre for Defence and International Security Studies, 1995), 60.

3. Department of Defense, *Final Report to Congress on the Conduct of the Persian Gulf Conflict, Vol. I* (Washington, DC: U.S. Government Printing Office, April 1992), 244.

4. These examples of United States use of LACMs were obtained from numerous on-line news sources.

5. Susanne M. Schafer, "12/17 Cruise Missiles Reduce Iraqi Military Sites to Rubble," *Nando Times News*, 18 December 1998, n.p.; on-line, Internet, 8 February 2000, available from http://www.business-server.com/newsroom/ntn/world/121898/worldt_26518_S8_body.html.

6. Kori Schake, "Rogue States and Proliferation: How Serious Is the Threat?" in *Strategic Assessment 1999: Priorities for a Turbulent World*, ed. Hans Binnendijk et al. (Washington, DC: U.S. Government Printing Office, June 1999), 220. The U.S.-identified rogue nations of BW proliferation concern and believed to be sponsors of terrorism are Iran, Iraq, Libya, North Korea, and Syria. There is no single, universally accepted definition of a rogue nation. Rogue states have been defined by the Clinton administration as "recalcitrant and outlaw states that not only choose to remain outside the family [of democracies] but also assault its basic values." Some of the characteristics of rogue nations are that they are aggressively pursuing unconventional means to threaten U.S. and international interests, they do not conform to the norms of international behavior and are not easily persuaded to do so, and they tend to be sponsors of terrorism.

7. Ramesh Thakur, "Arms Control, Disarmament and Non-Proliferation: A Political Perspective," in *Arms Control in the Asia-Pacific Region*, ed. Jeffrey A. Larsen and Thomas D. Miller (Washington, DC: U.S. Government Printing Office, August 1999), 43.

8. "Iran, Other Rogue Regimes Developing Cruise Missiles," May 1999, n.p.; on-line, Internet, 1 February 2000, available from http://www.ourjerusalem.com/documents/febmay99/0412docs.htm.

9. National Intelligence Council, *Foreign Missile Developments and the Ballistic Missile Threat to the United States Through 2015*, September 1999, n.p.; on-line,

Internet, 21 January 2000, available from http://www.usconsulate.org.hk/uscn/others/1999/0909.htm.

10. Richard K. Betts, "The New Threat of Mass Destruction," *Foreign Affairs* 77, no. 1 (January/February 1998), 27.

11. Ibid., 28. See also Eugene Gholz, Daryl G. Press, and Harvey M. Sapolsky, "Come Home America: The Strategy of Restraint in the Face of Temptation," *International Security* 21, no. 4 (Spring 1997), 7.

12. Betts, 28.

13. Ibid., 28–29.

14. Robin Ranger and David Wiencek, *The Devil's Brews II: Weapons of Mass Destruction and International Security*, Bailrigg Memorandum 17 (Lancaster, UK: Centre for Defence and International Security Studies, 1997), 16.

15. David G. Wiencek, *Dangerous Arsenals: Missile Threats In and From Asia*, Bailrigg Memorandum 22 (Lancaster, UK: Centre for Defence and International Security Studies, 1997), 8.

16. Ranger and Wiencek, 17. See also Stephen I. Schwartz, *Atomic Audit: The Costs and Consequences of U.S. Nuclear Weapons Since 1940*, Brookings Institution, 1998, n.p.; on-line, Internet, 11 May 2000, available from http://www.brook.edu/FP/PROJECTS/NUCWCOST. After four years of intensive research investigating what the United States spent on nuclear weapons, Schwartz concludes that the United States spent at least 29 percent of its national defense budget on nuclear weapons. This larger percentage, however, includes not only the costs for the nuclear warheads and strategic delivery systems but also the costs associated with targeting, controlling nuclear weapons, defending against the Soviet Union's nuclear arsenal, dismantling nuclear weapons, nuclear waste management and environmental remediation, and so on.

17. Efraim Karsh, "Rational Ruthlessness: Non-Conventional and Missile Warfare in the Iran-Iraq War," in *Non-Conventional-Weapons Proliferation in the Middle East*, ed. Efraim Karsh, Martin S. Navias, and Philip Sabin (New York: Oxford University Press, 1993), 36–42.

18. Leonard S. Spector, "Nuclear Proliferation in the Middle East: The Next Chapter Begins," in *Non-Conventional-Weapons Proliferation in the Middle East*, ed. Efraim Karsh, Martin S. Navias, and Philip Sabin (New York: Oxford University Press, 1993), 143.

19. Ranger and Wiencek, 9 and 18.

20. Betts, 31.

21. Dennis M. Gormley and K. Scott McMahon, "Counterforce: The Neglected Pillar of Theater Missile Defense," n.p.; on-line, Internet, 29 September 1999, available from http://www.cdiss.org/colsep1.htm.

22. Committee on Armed Services, House of Representatives, *Countering the Chemical and Biological Weapons Threat in the Post-Soviet World*, Special Inquiry into the Chemical and Biological Threat, Report to the Congress (Washington, DC: U.S. Government Printing Office, 23 February 1993), 4.

23. Willis Stanley and Keith Payne, "Chapter II. Missile Proliferation: Threat and U.S. Response," *Comparative Strategy* 16, no. 2 (1997), 135.

24. Dennis Gormley and Richard Speier, "Cruise Missile Proliferation: Threat, Policy, and Defenses," presentation to the Carnegie Endowment for International Peace Proliferation Roundtable, 9 October 1998, n.p.; on-line, Internet, 21 September 1999, available from http://www.ceip.org/programs/npp/cruise4.htm.

25. Betts, 32.

26. Edward M. Eitzen, "Use of Biological Weapons," in *Medical Aspects of Chemical and Biological Warfare*, eds. Frederick R. Sidell, Ernest T. Takafuji, and David R. Franz (Washington, DC: Office of The Surgeon General at TMM Publications, 1997), 446.

27. U.S. Congress, Office of Technology Assessment, *Proliferation of Weapons of Mass Destruction: Assessing the Risks*, OTA-ISC-559 (Washington, DC: U.S. Government Printing Office, August 1993), 54.

28. World Health Organization Group of Consultants, *Health Aspects of Chemical and Biological Weapons* (Geneva, Switzerland: World Health Organization, 1970), 98–99.

29. Lester C. Caudle, "The Biological Warfare Threat," in *Medical Aspects of Chemical and Biological Warfare*, eds. Frederick R. Sidell, Ernest T. Takafuji, and David R. Franz (Washington, DC: Office of The Surgeon General at TMM Publications, 1997), 437–50.

30. Biological agents are either replicating agents, bacteria or viruses, or non-replicating materials, toxins or physiologically active proteins or peptides that can be produced by living organisms. The replicating nature and extreme infectivity at low doses of pathogens such as *Bacillus anthracis* (organism that causes anthrax) and *Yersinia pestis* (organism that causes plague) are what make them weight-for-weight more deadly than CW nerve agents. Additionally, toxins such as the staphylococcal enterotoxins and botulinum toxins are extraordinarily toxic—1,000- to 10,000-fold more toxic than classic nerve agents. For further information, see *The Biological & Chemical Warfare Threat* (Washington, DC: U.S. Government Printing Office, 1999), 1–23; Frederick R. Sidell and David R. Franz, "Overview: Defense Against the Effects of Chemical and Biological Warfare Agents," in *Medical Aspects of Chemical and Biological Warfare*, eds. Frederick R. Sidell, Ernest T. Takafuj, and David R. Franz (Washington, DC: Office of The Surgeon General at TMM Publications, 1997), 1–7; and Eitzen, 437–50.

31. Caudle, 458. See also Lord Lyell, "Chemical and Biological Weapons: The Poor Man's Bomb," 4 October 1996, n.p.; on-line, Internet, 11 May 2000, available from http://www.pgs.ca/pages/cw/cw980327.htm. The author of this article states that "a more specific assessment suggests that the development of biological weapons would cost less than $100,000, require five biologists, and take just a few weeks using equipment that is readily available."

32. *The Biological & Chemical Warfare Threat*, 1.

33. Jonathan B. Tucker, "The Future of Biological Warfare," in *The Proliferation of Advanced Weaponry: Technology, Motivations, and Responses*, ed. W. Thomas Wander and Eric H. Arnett (Washington, DC: American Association for the Advancement of Science, 1992), 67.

34. W. Seth Carus, *Bioterrorism and Biocrimes: The Illicit Use of Biological Agents in the 20th Century* (Washington, DC: Center for Counterproliferation Research, National Defense University, August 1998 [March 1999 revision]), 25.

35. Carus, 24.

36. Tucker, 67.

37. Carus, 25.

38. Ibid., 26.

39. Milton Leitenberg, "Deadly Unknowns about Iraq's Biological Weapons Program," 9 February 2000, n.p; on-line, Internet, 14 February 2000, available from http://www.isis-online.org/publications/iraq/leitenberg.html.

40. Center for Nonproliferation Studies, Monterey Institute of International Studies, "Chemical and Biological Weapons Possession and Programs: Past and Present," n.p.; on-line, Internet, 14 February 2000, available from http://www.cns.miis.edu/research/cbw/possess.htm.

41. Arnold Beichman, "Arsenal of Germs in Iran?" *Washington (DC) Times*, 26 January 1999.

42. Paula DeSutter, "Deterring Iranian NBC Use," *National Defense University Strategic Forum*, no. 110 (April 1997), 1.

43. Beichman.

44. Tony Capaccio, "CIA: Iran Holding Limited Stocks of Biological Weapons," *Defense Week* 17, no. 32 (5 August 1996), 15.

45. Barbara Crossette, "Iraq Suspected of Secret Germ War Effort," *The New York Times On the Web*, 8 February 2000, n.p.; on-line, Internet, 10 February 2000, available from http://www10.nytimes.com/library/world/mideast/020800iraq-inspect.html.

46. Milton Leitenberg, "Prescription for Disaster," *Washington (DC) Post*, 10 February 2000, A23; on-line, Internet, 14 February 2000, available from http://www.washingtonpost.com/wp-srv/WPlate/2000-02/10/1151-021000-idx.html. See also Leitenberg, "Deadly Unknowns about Iraq's Biological Weapons Program."

47. Edward M. Eitzen and Ernest T. Takafuji, "Historical Overview of Biological Warfare," in *Medical Aspects of Chemical and Biological Warfare*, eds. Frederick R. Sidell, Ernest T. Takafuji, and David R. Franz (Washington, DC: Office of The Surgeon General at TMM Publications, 1997), 421–22.

48. Arms Control and Disarmament Agency, *Adherence to and Compliance with Arms Control Agreements: 1997 Annual Report to Congress*, n.p.; on-line, Internet, 14 February 2000, available from http://dosfan.lib.uic.edu/acda/reports/annual/chpt7.htm.

49. Center for Nonproliferation Studies, Monterey Institute of International Studies, "Chemical and Biological Weapons Possession and Programs: Past and Present."

50. Carus, 32.

51. Center for Nonproliferation Studies, Monterey Institute of International Studies, "Chemical and Biological Weapons Possession and Programs: Past and Present."

52. "Japan Concerned Over N. Korea Biochemical Warheads," 14 September 1999, n.p.; on-line, Internet, 12 January 2000, available from http://nucnews.net/nucnews/1999nn/9909nn/990914nn.htm.

53. The Ministry of National Defense, Republic of Korea, *Defense White Paper 1998* (Korea Institute for Defense Analysis, 1999), 65.

54. Michael Eisenstadt, "Syria's Strategic Weapons," *Jane's Intelligence Review* 5, no. 4 (April 1993), 168–69.

55. *A Study On Exploring U.S. Missile Defense Requirements in 2010: What Are the Policy and Technology Challenges?* April 1997, n.p.; on-line, Internet, 6 October

1999, available from http://fas.org/spp/starwars/advocate/ifpa/report696_ch4_syr.htm. See also Center for Nonproliferation Studies, Monterey Institute of International Studies, "Chemical and Biological Weapons Possession and Programs: Past and Present" and Eisenstadt, 169.

56. *A Study On Exploring U.S. Missile Defense Requirements in 2010: What Are the Policy and Technology Challenges?*

57. U.S. Congress, Office of Technology Assessment, *Proliferation of Weapons of Mass Destruction: Assessing the Risks*, OTA-ISC-559 (Washington, DC: U.S. Government Printing Office, August 1993), 3.

58. In Joint Pub 1-02, *Department of Defense Dictionary of Military and Associated Terms*, 23 March 1994 (amended through 15 April 1998), a cruise missile is defined as a "guided missile, the major portion of whose flight path to its target is conducted at approximately constant velocity; depends on the dynamic reaction of air for lift and upon propulsion forces to balance drag." A guided missile is "an unmanned vehicle moving above the surface of the Earth whose trajectory or flight path is capable of being altered by an external or internal mechanism."

59. The range of cruise missiles is stated throughout the literature in a variety of units: kilometers (km), miles (mi) and nautical miles (nmi). The conversion between these units is 1 km = 0.621 mi = 0.54 nmi.

60. National Air Intelligence Center, *Ballistic and Cruise Missile Threat*, NAIC-1031-0985-99 (Dayton, OH: Wright-Patterson Air Force Base, April 1999), 6.

61. Centre for Defence and International Security Studies, "Cruise Missile Capabilities: An Assessment," n.p.; on-line, Internet, 1 February 2000, available from http://www.cdiss.com/tabanaly.htm.

62. W. Seth Carus, *Cruise Missile Proliferation in the 1990s* (Washington, DC: Center for Strategic and International Studies), 15.

63. Ibid.

64. Marshall Brain, "How Cruise Missiles Work," n.p.; on-line, Internet, 21 September 1999, available from http://www.howstuffworks.com/cruise.htm.

65. Humphry Crum Ewing et al., *Cruise Missiles: Precision & Countermeasure*, Bailrigg Memorandum 10 (Lancaster, UK: Centre for Defence and International Security Studies, 1995), 49 and 51. Inertial Navigation systems (INS) use gyroscopes and accelerometers to detect changes in speed and direction of the LACM, which can then be used to compute changes in relative positions. Although an INS guidance system has the advantage of being jam-proof, the gyroscopes have inherent inaccuracies, which result in increasing positional errors (called drift) with increasing LACM flight time. As an example, the U.S. TLAM INS drifts by 900 meters per hour. At the TLAM's cruising speed of 800 km per hour, an uncorrected INS would result in a 1.8 km positional error for striking a target at a range of 1,600 km. Thus, to strike targets at long range, the LACM's INS must be supplemented with other guidance systems, such as GPS or TERCOM. TERCOM corrects any INS by taking periodic fixes on the terrain features (must be areas of distinctive topography) over which the LACM is flying. To accomplish this, the TERCOM system uses an on-board computer, in which maps of the relevant terrain, obtained from high-resolution satellite images, are stored, along with a radar altimeter. The computer correlates data received from altimeter readings with elevation data from the stored maps. The system then calculates the corrections needed to put the LACM back on course and provides this information to the missile's autopilot.

66. DSMAC is a two-dimensional, map-matching technique that employs an onboard sensor to obtain a sequence of images of the ground directly below the missile. The images are compared to reference data stored in the missile's navigational computer, and position changes are made as needed prior to final target acquisition. DSMAC is a complex technology that significantly improves the terminal accuracy of the cruise missile.

67. The MTCR was created in 1987 by the G-7 governments of Canada, France, Italy, Japan, the United Kingdom, the United States, and West Germany. It is an informal, voluntary export control arrangement with guidelines prohibiting the sale or transfer of certain categories of ballistic and cruise missiles and their related technologies. The regime grew out of the mutual fears of the G-7 nations that rogue states would acquire offensive missiles for use as WMD delivery platforms. The current membership includes thirty-two countries.

68. K. Scott McMahon and Dennis M. Gormley, *Controlling the Spread of Land-Attack Cruise Missiles*, The AISC Papers, no. 7 (Marina del Rey, CA: The American Institute for Strategic Cooperation [AISC], January 1995), 22.

69. DGPS is a method of correcting GPS that allows a weapon system to obtain extremely high positional accuracies. The concept of DGPS is as follows: A receiver is placed at a presurveyed location whose position has been determined very accurately. Both the GPS receiver at the known location and the DGPS receiver on the weapon system acquire the same set of GPS signals from the same set of satellites. The errors in the GPS signals are determined by comparing the surveyed site's known position to the position determined using the GPS signals. Correction terms are then calculated and transmitted to the weapon system DGPS receiver allowing elimination of most of the errors of the GPS signals. The DGPS technique can yield weapon system positional accuracies of 1 to 5 m.

70. McMahon and Gormley, 21.

71. "IKONOS Satellite Launches into Space," n.p.; on-line, Internet, 1 October 1999, available from http://www.spaceimage.com/newsroom/releases/1999/inorbit.htm. The U.S. firm, Space Imaging, successfully launched its IKONOS satellite on 24 September 1999. This is the first commercial imaging satellite of its kind, simultaneously collecting 1-m resolution panchromatic and 4-m resolution multispectral images. Space Imaging is now selling and distributing imagery. Many other commercial imaging satellites, both U.S. and foreign, providing 1-m resolution imagery are scheduled for launch in 2000, 2001, 2002, and so on. See also McMahon and Gormley, 24.

72. McMahon and Gormley, 25.

73. Dennis Gormley and Richard Speier, "Cruise Missile Proliferation: Threat, Policy, and Defenses," presentation to the Carnegie Endowment for International Peace Proliferation Roundtable, 9 October 1998, n.p.; on-line, Internet, 21 September 1999, available from http://www.ceip.org/programs/npp/cruise4.htm.

74. Dennis M. Gormley, "Hedging Against the Cruise-Missile Threat," *Survival*, Spring 1998, 92–111; on-line, Internet, 21 September 1999, available from http://www.ceip.org/programs/npp/gormley%20survival.htm.

75. National Intelligence Council, *Foreign Missile Developments and the Ballistic Missile Threat to the United States Through 2015*.

76. Ewing, 50.

77. Carus, 22.

78. David A. Fulghum, "Stealth, Cheap Technology Complicate Defense Schemes," *Aviation Week & Space Technology* 147, no. 2 (14 July 1997), 47.

79. Ibid.

80. Bryan Bender, "Cruise Control," *Jane's Defence Weekly* 30, no. 3 (22 July 1998), 21.

81. Dennis M. Gormley, "Remarks from a Panel on the Missile Proliferation Threat at the Conference on Nuclear Non-Proliferation: Enhancing the Tools of the Trade," 9–10 June 1997, Washington, DC, n.p.; on-line, Internet, 29 September 1999, available from http://www.ceip.org/programs/npp/np9715gohtm. See also K. Scott McMahon and Dennis M. Gormley, *Controlling the Spread of Land-Attack Cruise Missiles*, The AISC Papers, no. 7 (Marina del Rey, CA: The American Institute for Strategic Cooperation [AISC], January 1995), 14–18; Amy Truesdell, "Cruise Missiles: The Discriminating Weapon of Choice?," *Jane's Intelligence Review*, February 1997, 87–90; and Carus, 69 and 83.

82. Gormley and Speier.

83. Carus, 25.

84. *Militarily Critical Technologies List (MCTL) Part II: Weapons of Mass Destruction Technologies, Section I—Means of Delivery Technology*, September 1998, II-1–2; on-line, Internet, 10 September 1999, available from http://www.fas.org/irp/threat/mctl98-2/p2sec01.pdf.

85. K. Scott McMahon and Dennis M. Gormley, *Controlling the Spread of Land-Attack Cruise Missiles*, The AISC Papers, no. 7 (Marina del Rey, CA: The American Institute for Strategic Cooperation [AISC], January 1995), 1.

86. National Air Intelligence Center, *Ballistic and Cruise Missile Threat*, NAIC-1031-0985-99 (Dayton, OH: Wright-Patterson Air Force Base, April 1999), 19.

87. Robert Wall, "Cruise Missile Threat Grows," *Aviation Week & Space Technology* 149, no. 4 (27 July 1998), 24.

88. Ibid.

89. The Arms Control Association, "The Missile Technology Control Regime," July 1999, n.p.; on-line, Internet, 21 January 2000, available from http://www.armscontrol.org/FACTS/mtcr.html. The MTCR was created in April 1987 to restrict the proliferation of missiles and related technology. It is the only multilateral missile nonproliferation regime and is neither an international agreement nor a treaty. The MTCR is a voluntary arrangement among countries (currently thirty-two) that share a common interest in arresting missile proliferation. The regime consists of a common export control policy (the Guidelines) applied to a shared list of controlled items (the Annex), which each MTCR member implements in accordance with its national legislation. The purpose of the regime is to limit the spread of missiles and unmanned air vehicles/delivery systems capable of carrying a 500-kilogram payload at least 300 kilometers. The MTCR Annex of controlled items is divided into two sections (Category I and Category II) and includes military and dual-use equipment and technology relevant to missile development, production, and operation.

Category I

According to the MTCR Guidelines, exports of Category I items are subject to a strong presumption of denial and are rarely licensed for export. Category I items include complete missile systems (ballistic missiles, space launch vehicles, and sounding rockets) and unmanned air-vehicle systems (including cruise-missile systems, target drones, and reconnaissance drones) capable of delivering at least a 500-kg payload to a range of at least 300 km, as well as the specially designed production facilities for these systems. Also included are certain complete subsystems such as rocket engines or stages; reentry vehicles; guidance sets; thrust vector controls; and warhead safing, arming, fuzing and firing mechanisms. Transfers of production facilities for Category I items are flatly prohibited.

Category II

The MTCR Guidelines permit licensing of Category II (dual-use) items as long as they are not destined for end-use in the development of a missile of MTCR range/payload capability. Category II items cover a wide range of parts, components and subsystems such as propellants, structure materials, test equipment and facilities and flight instruments. These items may be exported at the discretion of the MTCR Partner Government, on a case by case basis, for acceptable end uses. They may also be exported under government-to-government assurances, which provide that they not be used on a missile system capable of delivering a 500-kg payload to a range of at least 300 km.

90. K. Scott McMahon, "Cruise Missile Proliferation: Threat, Policy, and Defenses," presentation to the American Institute of Engineers Conference on Missile Defense, 5 March 1999.

91. Ibid.

92. Dennis M. Gormley, "Hedging Against the Cruise-Missile Threat," *Survival*, Spring 1998, 92–111; on-line, Internet, 21 September 1999, available from http://www.ceip.org/programs/npp/gormley%20survival.htm.

93. Mr. K. Scott McMahon, Assistant Program Manager for Defense Policy, Pacific-Sierra Research Corporation, Arlington, VA, telephone conversations and email exchanges with author, 23 September 1999, 1 October 1999, and 8 October 1999.

94. Dennis Gormley and Richard Speier, "Cruise Missile Proliferation: Threat, Policy, and Defenses," presentation to the Carnegie Endowment for International Peace Proliferation Roundtable, 9 October 1998, n.p.; on-line, Internet, 21 September 1999, available from http://www.ceip.org/programs/npp/cruise4.htm. See also Jean-Paul Philippe, "Matra to Develop APTGD Missile: A New 'Stealth' Cruise missile for France," *Military Technology* 19, no. 2 (February 1995), 60–2.

95. Gormley.

96. Ibid.

97. Richard D. Fisher, Appendix to "How America's Friends Are Building China's Military Power," *The Heritage Foundation Backgrounder*, no. 1146, 5 November 1997, n.p.; on-line, Internet, 2 February 2000, available from http://www.heritage.org/library/categories/natsec/bg1146/appendix.html.

98. Ibid.

99. Richard D. Fisher, Jr., "China Increases Its Missile Forces While Opposing U.S. Missile Defense," *The Heritage Foundation Backgrounder*, no. 1268, 7 April 1999, n.p.; on-line, Internet, 12 January 2000, available from http://www.heritage.org/library/backgrounder/bg1268es.html.

100. "Current Missile News," n.p., on-line, Internet, 10 September 1999, available from http://www.cdiss.com/99aug19_b.htm.

101. Seymour Johnson, "China Seeks Technology for Next-Generation Missiles," *Foreign Affairs News*, 3 October 1999, n.p.; on-line, Internet, 3 October 1999, available from http://208.138.42.193/forum/a37f7495d3eac.htm. See also Richard D. Fisher, Appendix to "How America's Friends Are Building China's Military Power."

102. Richard D. Fisher, Jr., "China Increases Its Missile Forces While Opposing U.S. Missile Defense."

103. David A. Fulghum, "Cruise Missile Threat Spurs Pentagon Research," *Aviation Week & Space Technology* 147, no. 2 (14 July 1997), 44.

104. Humphry Crum Ewing et al., *Cruise Missiles: Precision & Countermeasures*, Bailrigg Memorandum 10 (Lancaster, UK: Centre for Defence and International Security Studies, 1995), 37.

105. Amy Truesdell, "Cruise Missiles: The Discriminating Weapon of Choice?" *Jane's Intelligence Review*, February 1997, 89.

106. Ibid., 90.

107. Ibid.

108. Donald Rumsfeld, et al., "The Growing Ballistic Missile Threat: How Much, How Soon, and How Dangerous?" *The Heritage Foundation Heritage Lectures*, no. 632, 1 February 1999, n.p.; on-line, Internet, 2 February 2000, available from http://www.heritage.org/library/lecture/h1632.html.

109. Ibid.

110. *A Study On Exploring U.S. Missile Defense Requirements in 2010: What Are the Policy and Technology Challenges?* April 1997, n.p.; on-line, Internet, 6 October 1999, available from http://fas.org/spp/starwars/advocate/ifpa/report696_ch4_iran.htm.

111. Ibid. and McMahon, telephone conversations.

112. *A Study On Exploring U.S. Missile Defense Requirements in 2010: What Are the Policy and Technology Challenges?*

113. Ewing, 35 and 40.

114. McMahon, telephone conversations.

115. Michael Eisenstadt, "Syria's Strategic Weapons," *Jane's Intelligence Review* 5, no. 4 (April 1993), 172.

116. Gormley and Speier.

117. McMahon, telephone conversations.

118. Ibid.

119. Robert Wall, "Smarter TBMs on Horizon," *Aviation Week & Space Technology*, 30 August 1999, 31.

120. National Intelligence Council, *Foreign Missile Developments and the Ballistic Missile Threat to the United States Through 2015.*

121. Judith Miller, "U.S. Intelligence: Flying Blind in a Dangerous World," *New York Times*, 6 February 2000, n.p.; on-line, Internet, 7 February 2000.

CHAPTER 9

1. Stephen M. Block, "Living Nightmares: Biological Threats Enabled by Molecular Biology," in *The New Terror: Facing the Threat of Biological and Chemical*

Weapons, eds. Sidney Drell, Abraham D. Sofaer, and George D. Wilson (Stanford, CA: Hoover Institution Press, 1999), 58; see also, Robert G. Webster, William J. Bean, Owen T. Gorman, Thomas M. Chambers, and Yoshihiro Kawaoka, "Evolution and Ecology of Influenza A Viruses," *Microbiological Reviews*, March 1992, 152–179.

2. Genetic engineering is a type of molecular biotechnology that uses laboratory techniques to isolate, manipulate, transfer, recombine, and allow expression of genes (DNA segments) between different organisms. In biological warfare or bioterrorism, adversaries might use genetically engineered agents that included both modified existing microbes and possibly novel synthetic life forms created to render them more effective as biological weapons than found in naturally occurring organisms.

3. Tom Mangold and Jeff Goldberg, *Plague Wars* (New York: St. Martin's Press, 1999), 92.

4. Ken Alibek with Stephen Handelman, *Biohazard* (New York: Random House, 1999), 43; see also, Lester C. Caudle III, "The Biological Warfare Threat," in *Textbook of Military Medicine: Medical Aspects of Chemical and Biological Warfare*, eds. Frederick R. Sidell, Ernest T. Takafuji, and David R. Franz (Washington, DC: Office of the Surgeon General, U.S. Army, 1997), 454. Biopreparat constituted only half of the Soviet BW program. See Alibek's *Biohazard*.

5. Jonathan B. Tucker, *Toxic Terror: Assessing Terrorist Use of Chemical and Biological Weapons* (Cambridge, MA: MIT Press, 2000), 4–5; and Jim A. Davis, "The Anthrax Terror," *Aerospace Power Journal* 14, no. 4 (Winter 2000), 17.

6. Mangold and Goldberg, 182.

7. Ibid., 91–105; and Caudle, 453–54.

8. Mangold and Goldberg, 93–95.

9. Caudle, 454. Bacterial cells frequently contain extrachromosomal (located outside the cell nucleus), autonomously replicating DNA molecules known as plasmids. Some plasmids carry DNA sequences that can produce antibiotic resistance, virulence, or infectivity. Plasmids can move between bacteria.

10. Mangold and Goldberg, 94–95, 164; Col. John Alexander, *Future War: Non-Lethal Weapons in the Twenty-First Century* (New York: St. Martin's Press, 1999), 191.

11. Mangold and Goldberg, 93–97.

12. Ibid., 91–99.

13. Ibid., 163–65.

14. Alexander, 192; Mangold and Goldberg, 158–63.

15. Ibid., 164.

16. Block, 55–56.

17. Mangold and Goldberg, 177–95; Alibek, ix–xi.

18. Mangold and Goldberg, 178–79, 182; Alibek, 3–304.

19. Alibek, 40–42, 155–56; Alexander, 191. Immediately after the 1972 Biological Weapons Convention treaty, President Brezhnev initiated the largest biological weapons program in history.

20. Mangold and Goldberg, 186.

21. Ibid., 180, 187–88.

22. Ibid.

23. Ibid., 179.
24. Ibid., 180.
25. Block, 49–50.
26. Mangold and Goldberg, 181.
27. Alibek, 160–61, 163–67, 272.
28. Ibid., 259; and Mangold and Goldberg, 181.
29. Alibek, 258–61; Mangold and Goldberg, 181.
30. Alibek, 273–75.
31. Judith Miller, Stephen Engelberg, and William Broad, *Germs: Biological Weapons and America's Secret War* (New York: Simon and Schuster, 2001), 300–304.
32. Block, 50–51, Alibek, 69–86.
33. *Plague War*, Frontline, PBS Home Video, Public Broadcasting Service, FROL-1706, 1998, 60 minutes.
34. A.P. Pomerantsev, N.A. Staritsin, Yu V. Mockov, and L.I. Marinin, "Expression of Cereolysine AB Genes in *Bacillus anthracis* Vaccine Strain Ensures Protection Against Experimental Hemolytic Anthrax Infection," *Vaccine* 15, no. 17/18 (1997), 1846–50.
35. Miller, Engelberg, and Broad, 218–20.
36. Judith Miller, Stephen Engelberg, and William J. Broad, "U.S. Germ Warfare Research Pushes Treaty Limits," *New York Times*, 4 September 2001, A1, A6.
37. Laurie Garrett, *The Coming Plague* (New York: Penguin Books, 1994), 10.
38. Peter R. Lavoy, Scott D. Sagan, and James J. Wirtz, *Planning the Unthinkable: How New Powers Will Use Nuclear, Biological, and Chemical Weapons* (Ithaca, NY: Cornell University Press, 2000), 5.
39. Malcolm R. Dando, *The New Biological Weapons: Threat Proliferation, and Control* (Boulder, CO: Lynne Rienner Publishers, 2001), 11.
40. Mangold and Goldberg, 182.
41. Ibid., 110, 159–61, 176.
42. Ibid., 183.
43. Ibid., 98.
44. Tucker, 5.
45. *Association of Military Surgeons of the United States Newsletter*, 9, 2 (Summer 2001), 4.
46. Mangold and Goldberg, 181; Alibek, xi.
47. Block, 41–45.
48. Lavoy et al., 4–5.
49. Mangold and Goldberg, 373.
50. Peter L. Hays, Vincent J. Jodoin, Alan R. Van Tassel, *Countering the Proliferation and Use of Weapons of Mass Destruction* (New York: The McGraw-Hill Companies, Inc., 1998), 9; Zilinskas estimates that it may only take five years for scientists working for "proliferant governments or subnational groups" to develop biological weapons from the new biotechnologies. R.A. Zilinskas ed. *Biological Warfare: Modern Offense and Defense* (Boulder, CO: Lynne Rienner, 2000).
51. Tucker, 9.
52. Ibid., 8–9. Lavoy et al., 232, 257.
53. Raymond A. Zilinskas, *Biological Warfare: Modern Offense and Defense* (Boulder, CO: Lynne Rienner Publishers, 2000), 2–3.

54. Laurie Garrett, The Coming Plague: *Newly Emerging Diseases in a World of Balance* (New York: Penguin Books, 1994), 53.

55. Andrew F. Krepinevich, "Cavalry to Computer: The Pattern of Military Revolutions," *The National Interest* no. 37 (Fall 1994), 30–42.

56. Moisés Naím, "Reinventing War," *Foreign Policy*, November/December 2001, 37.

57. Claire M. Fraser and Malcolm R. Dando, "Genomics and Future Biological Weapons: The Need for Preventive Action by the Biomedical Community," online, Internet, 22 October 2001, by Nature Publishing Group available from http// genetics.nature.com.

58. Even crop duster aircraft and mosquito sprayer equipment are potential delivery mechanisms for bioterrorism.

59. Block, 60.

60. Ian O. Lesser, et al., *Countering the New Terrorism* (Santa Monica, CA: RAND, 1999), 7–38. Although the total number of terrorist events worldwide has declined in the 1990s, the percentage of terrorist events resulting in fatalities (and total numbers of fatalities) increased; Ehud Sprinzak, "The Lone Gunman," *Foreign Policy*, November/December 2001, 72–73. According to Sprinzak, today's "megalomaniacal hyperterrorists" are innovators and developers. They incessantly look for original ways to surprise and devastate the enemy. They think big, seeking to go beyond "conventional" terrorism and, unlike most terrorists, could be willing to use weapons of mass destruction. If the intent of terrorists is to inflict mass casualties, then biological agents are likely to be used.

61. Richard Preston, *The Hot Zone* (New York: Anchor Books/Doubleday, 1994). Tom Clancy's *Executive Orders* and Michael Critchton's *The Andromeda Strain* were other popular books on pathogens.

62. Alexander, 215; PDD-62 contained major initiatives to combat international terrorism. PDD-63 addressed protection of the nation's critical infrastructure from both physical and cyber attacks.

63. *Preventing Emerging Infectious Diseases: A Strategy for the 21st Century* (Atlanta: U.S. Department of Health and Human Services, Centers for Disease Control and Prevention, reprinted August 2000), vii.

64. Garrett, 6; Block, 59. New infectious diseases are thought to emerge due to situations where humans now live in close proximity to animals.

65. William J. Broad, "Genome Offers 'Fingerprint' for Anthrax: Analysis of Bacterium Could Help Investigators," *New York Times*, 28 November 2001, B-1–B-8.

66. Block, 45. The minimum lethal dose for inhalational anthrax (reported to be 5,000 to 10,000 spores) is high compared to some other biological agents.

67. Fraser and Dando, 2.

68. Block, 46–47.

69. Drell, 355.

70. Ibid., 355; Sheryl Gay Stolberg with Melody Peterson, "U.S. Orders Vast Supply of Vaccine for Smallpox," *New York Times*, 29 November 2001, B-8.

71. Alibek, 258–61; Block, 49. The FSU's biological warfare program was massive, totaling over 18 complexes and 60,000 workers. Considering that this dwarfed the worldwide commitment to the Human Genome Project, there is significant concern about what the FSU bioscientists were able to accomplish. Despite President

Yeltsin's order to close the Russian BW program, biological warfare research is thought to continue in the FSU.

72. Block, 51.

73. Caudle, 63–64.

74. Personal conversation with Bill Patrick, 6 September 2001.

75. Asymmetric warfare is the use of less technological, less expensive, and/or more unconventional weapons, tactics and strategies. Historically, this has taken the form of guerilla warfare, but today includes cyber war and the use of weapons of mass destruction.

76. Zilinskas, 1–2.

77. Katherine McIntire Peters, "Behind in the Biowar," *Government Executive*, December 2001, 28.

78. Ibid., 28. The potential to inflict damage on the enemy is obvious. Less clear is how to protect friendly troops from disease while spreading it among the enemy.

79. *The Worldwide Biological Warfare Weapons Threat*, 2001, 1.

80. Zilinskas, 6.

81. David Franz quoted by Peters in "Behind in the Biowar," 30.

82. Fraser and Dando, 2.

83. Dando, 58.

84. Donald Rumsfeld, *Report of the Quadrennial Defense Review* (Washington, DC: Department of Defense, September 2001), 7.

85. Block, 39–40.

86. Ibid., 51–70.

87. Ibid., 52–56.

88. Ibid., 56–60.

89. International Human Genome Sequencing Consortium, "Initial Sequencing and Analysis of the Human Genome," *Nature*, Vol. 409, 15 February 2001, 860–921 (http://www.tigr.org/tdb/mdb/mdbcomplete.html); see also, David Baltimore, "Our Genome Unveiled," *Nature*, Vol. 409, 15 February 2001, 814–16.

90. International Human Genome Sequencing Consortium, 860–921.

91. Rachel Nowak, "Disaster in the Making," *New Scientist*, 13 January 2001, 4–5.

92. Fraser and Dando, 3.

93. Clyde A. Hutchison, et al., "Global Transposon Mutagenesis and a Minimal Mycoplasma Genome," *Science*, Vol. 286, 10 December 1999, 2165–69.

94. A minimal genome can be defined as the smallest set of genes that allows for replication of the organism in a particular environment.

95. Philip Cohen, "A Terrifying Power," *New Scientist*, 30 January 1999, 10.

96. Carina Dennis, "The Bugs of War," *Nature*, 17 May 2001, 232–235.

97. Block, 60–63.

98. Zilinskas, 13. The bacteria *E. coli* have been genetically engineered to produce commercial quantities of valuable complex proteins, including insulin, human growth hormone, interferon, hepatitis B surface antigens, and angiotensin.

99. Bernard Moss, "Genetically Engineered Poxviruses for Recombinant Gene Expression, Vaccination, and Safety," *Proceedings of the National Academy of Sciences of the United States of America*, 1996, Vol. 93, 11341–48, as abstracted in the *Journal of the American Medical Association*, 6 August 1997, Vol. 278, No. 5, 350.

100. Block, 60.

101. Ibid., 62.

102. Ronald J. Jackson, et al., "Expression of Mouse Interleukin-4 by a Recombinant Ectromelia Virus Suppresses Cytolytic Lymphocyte Responses and Overcomes Genetic Resistance to Mousepox," *Journal of Virology*, February 2001, 1205–10.

103. Nowak, 4–5; see also, Stanley L. Robbins, Ramzi S. Cotran, and Vinay Kumar, *Pathologic Basis of Disease*, 3rd ed. (Philadelphia: W.B. Saunders Company, 1984), 158. The immune response compromises all the phenomena that result from the specific interaction of cells of the immune system with antigens (foreign material). Entrance of an antigen into the body can have two possible outcomes: (1) a humoral immune response, involving the synthesis and release of antibody molecules within the blood and extracellular fluids; or (2) cell-mediated immunity, manifested by production of "sensitized" lymphocytes capable of interacting with antigens such as bacterial toxins and cause neutralization of the toxin, or they can coat the antigenic surfaces of microorganisms and render them susceptible to lysis by complement or to phagocytosis by macrophages. In the second type of reaction, the sensitized cells are responsible for such actions as rejection of foreign tissue grafts and resistance against many intracellular microbes (i.e., viruses, fungi, and some bacteria).

104. Dennis, 232–35.

105. Jose B. Cibelli, Robert P. Lanza and Michael D. West, with Carol Ezzell, "The First Human Cloned Embryo," *Scientific American*, January 2002.

106. Gina Kolata with Andrew Pollack, "A Breakthrough on Cloning? Perhaps, or Perhaps Not Yet," *New York Times*, 27 November 2001, A1–12.

107. Cibelli, x.

108. Gina Kolata, "Company Says It Produced Embryo Clones," *New York Times*, 26 November 2001, A–14.

109. Sharon Begley, "Brave New Monkey," *Newsweek*, 22 January 2001, 50–52.

110. Block, 63–65.

111. Garrett, 226–33.

112. Block, 65–68.

113. Zilinskas, 18.

114. Block, 68–71.

115. Fraser and Dando, 2.

116. Block, 51.

117. Dando, 41.

118. Fraser and Dando, 3.

119. Block, 47–48; Dando, 125–29.

120. Dennis, 232–35.

121. Fraser and Dando, 4; see also Dando, 127. Polymorphisms are differences in a specific gene. Single nucleotide polymorphisms (SNP) arise from the change of just one base pair in the DNA sequence. SNPs are markers that may lead to the genetic basis of many diseases. Theoretically, an SNP or sets of SNPs may provide new targets for new drugs, toxins, or bioregulators.

122. Peters, 30.

123. Mildred K. Cho, David Magnus, Arthur L. Caplan, Daniel McGee, and the Ethics of Genomics Group, "Ethical Considerations in Synthesizing a Minimal Genome," *Science*, Vol. 286, 10 December 1999, 2087–90.

124. Zilinskas, 13–15.

125. Fraser and Dando, 3.
126. Rick Weiss, "A Terrorist's Fragile Footprint," *Washington (DC) Post*, 29 November 2001, 1.
127. Broad, B1–8.
128. Fraser and Dando, 3.
129. Robins, 158. See footnote 102 for definitions of humoral and cell-mediated immunity.
130. Zilinskas, 21.
131. Dennis, 232–35.
132. Fraser and Dando, 3.
133. William A. Haseltine, "Beyond Chicken Soup," *Scientific American*, November 2001, 56–63.
134. Peters, 30.
135. Dennis, 232–35.
136. Dando, 11.
137. Block, 71.
138. Zilinskas, 5–6.
139. Alexander, 119–121, 196.
140. Block, 42.
141. Alexander, 190.
142. LTC George W. Christopher, LTC Theodore J. Cieslak, MAJ Julie Pavlin, and COL Edward M. Eitzen, "Biological Warfare: A Historical Perspective," *Journal of the American Medical Association* 278, no. 5 (6 August 1997), 412–17.
143. Alexander, 192.
144. Jeffery K. Smart, "History of Chemical and Biological Warfare: An American Perspective," in *Textbook of Military Medicine: Medical Aspects of Chemical and Biological Warfare*, eds. Frederick R. Sidell, Ernest T. Takafuji, and David R. Franz (Washington, DC: Office of the Surgeon General, U.S. Army, 1997), 73.
145. Drell, 358.
146. Jeffery D. Simon, "Biological Terrorism: Preparing to Meet the Threat," *Journal of the American Medical Association* 278, no. 5 (6 August 1997), 428–30.
147. Amy Smithson, et al., *Ataxia: The Chemical and Biological Terrorism Threat and the U.S. Response, October 2000*, as quoted by Peters in "Behind in the Biowar," 33.
148. Elizabeth Becker and Tim Weiner, "New Office to Become a White House Agency," *New York Times*, 28 September 2001.
149. Zilinskas, 128.
150. Alexander, 116.
151. Sir William Stewart as quoted by Patricia Reaney, "Animal Disease Is Reminder of Bioterrorism Danger," in Reuters news report, 3 September 2001.

CHAPTER 10

1. "Remarks by the President to Students and Faculty at National Defense University," 1 May 2001; on-line, Internet, 11 September 2001, available from http://www.whitehouse.gov/news/releases/2001/05/20010501-10.html.
2. Wohlstetter, Roberta, *Pearl Harbor: Warning and Decision* (Stanford, CA: Stanford University Press, 1962), vii.

3. Anthony H. Cordesman, *Trends in US Military Forces and Defense Spending: Peace Dividend or Underfunding*? Center for Strategic and International Studies, 26 July 1999, 4; on-line, Internet, 11 September 2001, available from http://www.csis.org/mideast/reports/peacedividendorunderfunding.pdf.

4. James E. Gibson, *Dr. Bodo Otto and the Medical Background of the American Revolution* (Baltimore: George Banta Publishing Company, 1937), 88–89; Jonathan B. Tucker, *Scourge: The Once and Future Threat of Smallpox* (New York: Atlantic Monthly Press, 2001), 18–22.

5. Sheldon H. Harris, *Factories of Death: Japanese Biological Warfare, 1932–45, and the American Cover-up* (New York: Routledge, 1994), 74–76.

6. Ken Alibek with Stephen Handelman, *Biohazard* (New York: Random House, 1999), 29–31.

7. Frederick R. Sidell, Ernest T. Takafuji, and David R. Franz, eds., *Textbook of Military Medicine: Medical Aspects of Chemical and Biological Warfare* (Washington, DC: Office of the Surgeon General, U.S. Army, 1997), 656.

8. W. Seth Carus, *Bioterrorism and Biocrimes: The Illicit Use of Biological Agents in the 20th Century*, rev. ed. (Washington, DC: National Defense University, Center for Counterproliferation Research, 1998), 58; Jessica Stern, *The Ultimate Terrorists* (Cambridge, MA: Harvard University Press, 1999), 63; Dean A. Wilkening, "BCW in Attack Scenarios," in *The New Terror: Facing the Threat of Biological and Chemical Weapons* (Stanford, CA: Hoover Institution Press, 1999), 91–93.

9. W. Seth Carus, "The Rajneeshees (1984)." in *Toxic Terror: Assessing Terrorist Use of Chemical and Biological Weapons*, ed. Jonathan B. Tucker (Cambridge, MA: MIT Press, 2000), 115–37.

10. David E. Kaplan, "Terrorism's next wave: Nerve gas and germs are the new weapons of choice," *U.S. News Online*, 17 November 1997, available from http://www.infowar.com/CLASS_3/class3_112897b.html-ssi.

11. Dr. Tara O'Toole, presentation given at "Medical and Public Health Aspects of Bioterrorism," Johns Hopkins University, Baltimore, MD, 25 June 2001.

12. Amazon.com Web site; on-line, Internet, 4 Feb 2002, available from http://www.amazon.com/exec/obidos/ASIN/0970148534/qid=1012831204/sr=2-3/ref=sr_2_11_3/103-7688308-1145469.

13. Dr. Tara O'Toole, presentation given at "Medical and Public Health Aspects of Bioterrorism," Johns Hopkins University, Baltimore, MD, 25 June 2001; Michael T. Osterholm and John Schwartz. *Living Terrors: What America Needs to Know to Survive the Coming Bioterrorist Catastrophe* (New York: Random House, 2000), 37–39; Judith Miller, Stephen Engelberg, William Broad, *Germs: Biological Weapons and America's Secret War* (New York: Simon and Schuster, 2001), 316.

14. Wilkening, 91–93; and David E. Kaplan and Andrew Marshall, *The Cult at the End of the World* (New York: Crown Publishers, 1996), 1–283.

15. Stern, 81–33.

16. Simon Reeve, *The New Jackals: Ramzi Yousef, Osama bin Laden and the Future of Terrorism* (Boston: Northeastern University Press, 1999), 24.

17. Phillips, James, "After World Trade Center Bombing, U.S. Needs Stronger Anti-Terrorism Policy," *The Heritage Foundation Backgrounder, Update #240*, 22 February 1995; on-line, Internet, 12 September 2001, available from http://www.heritage.org/library/categories/natsec/bgu240.html.

18. "Sentenced To Die—Online Newshour with Jim Lehrer," PBS, 13 June 1997;

on-line, Internet, 12 September 2001, available from http://www.pbs.org/newshour/bb/law/june97/mcveigh_6-13.html.

19. "Deadly Explosion—Online Newshour with Jim Lehrer," PBS, 19 April 1995; on-line, Internet, 12 September 2001, available from http://www.pbs.org/newshour/bb/law/mcveigh/oklatv_4-19-95.html.

20. "September 11, 2001 Victims," American Liberty Partnership, 2 February 2002 update; on-line, Internet, 5 February 2002, available from http://www.september11victims.com/september11victims.

21. John Pike, FAS Military Analysis Network. Subject: Administrative Support Unit Southwest Asia (ASU SWA) Manama, Bahrain; on-line, Internet, 12 September 2001, available from http://www.fas.org/man/dod-101/fac/port/manama.htm.

22. "World Population," PBS; on-line, Internet, 12 September 2001, available from http://www.pbs.org/kqed/population_bomb/hope/worldp.html.

23. "Responding to the Threat of Agroterrorism: Specific Recommendation for the United States Department of Agriculture," BCSIA Discussion Paper 2000-29, ESDP Discussion Paper 2000-04 (Cambridge, MA: John F. Kennedy School of Government, Harvard University, October 2000), 12.

24. Mark Wheelis, *Agricultural Biowarfare & Bioterrorism: An Analytical Framework & Recommendations for the Fifth BTWC Review Conference*; on-line, Internet, 2 February 2002, available from http://www.fas.org/bwc/agr/agwhole.htm.

25. "The (hidden) epidemic of foot-and-mouth disease." News & Highlights—Food and Agriculture Organization of the United Nations; on-line, Internet, 12 September 2001, available from http://www.dallasnews.com/national/0627nat4agroterror.htm.

26. Steve Goldstein/Knight Ridder Newspapers, "U.S. officials awakening to threat of agroterror," *The Dallas Morning News*, 27 June 1999; on-line, Internet, 12 September 2001, available from http://www.dallasnews.com/national/0627nat4agroterror.htm.

27. Ibid.

28. Ibid.

29. "Chemical and Biological Weapons: Possession and Programs Past and Present," Center For Nonproliferation Studies—Chemical and Biological Weapons Resource Page; on-line, Internet, 12 September 2001, available from http://cns.miis.edu/research/cbw/possess.htm.

30. Rex R. Kiziah, *Assessment of the Emerging Biocruise Threat*, Future Warfare Series, no. 6 (Maxwell AFB, AL: USAF Counterproliferation Center, 2000).

Index

About the Contributors

COLONEL MICHAEL J. AINSCOUGH, USAF, MD, MPH, is the Air Force Surgeon General Chair to Air University at Maxwell AFB, Alabama. Previous assignments include tours as Chief of Aerospace Medicine at the 343d Medical Group, Eielson AFB, Alaska; Chief of Operations Branch, Hyperbaric Medicine Division, Armstrong Laboratory, Brooks AFB, Texas; Chief, Aeromedical Evacuation Branch, Professional Services Directorate, Office of the Air Mobility Command Surgeon; Chief, Clinical Aeromedical Evacuation for the Global Patient Movement Requirements Center of USTRANSCOM at Scott AFB, Illinois and 92d Aeromedical-Dental Squadron Commander at Fairchild AFB, Washington. He earned his Bachelor's degree from the St. Louis College of Pharmacy and his Doctorate of Medicine from the Southern Illinois University School of Medicine. He completed a USAF Residency in Aerospace Medicine and a Fellowship in Hyperbaric Medicine at Brooks AFB, Texas. He also completed a Masters in Public Health degree at the University of Texas. He is a diplomat of the American Board of Preventive Medicine in Aerospace Medicine and is a Chief Flight Surgeon with 1,100 total flying hours in over twenty types of military aircraft.

BARBARA F. BULLOCK is an acquisition program manager at the Standard Systems Group, Maxwell AFB-Gunter Annex, Alabama. A June 2001 graduate of the Air Command and Staff College, she entered federal service in July 1974 as a computer programmer after earning a Bachelor of Science degree in mathematics from Alabama A&M University. Her career encompasses over twenty-seven years of experience facilitating the acquisition, development, testing, deployment, and sustainment of Air Force base-level automated systems. She holds acquisition professional development program Level II ratings in program management and communications-computers.

In her current assignment as the Deputy Program Manager for the Case Execution Management Information System (CEMIS), she works to develop a replacement management information system for the ordering and shipping of U.S. defense articles and services to foreign countries.

COLONEL JIM A. DAVIS, USAF, DVM, DrPH, DACVPM, FAAD is the Deputy Director of the USAF Counterproliferation Center. He is the co-editor of and contributing author to *The War Next Time: Countering Rogue States and Terrorists Armed with Chemical and Biological Weapons* (USAF Counterproliferation Center, 2003) and has contributed a number of other professional articles to journals on the WMD threat. Colonel Davis has several academic degrees including a Doctorate of Veterinary Medicine from Texas A&M and a Doctorate of Public Health from the University of Texas. Previously, Colonel Davis was the AF Surgeon General's Chair to Air University where he also served on the faculty of Air War College. Before coming to Air University, he was the Commander, 48th Aerospace Medicine Squadron at RAF Lakenheath, UK, which was the largest Aerospace Medicine Squadron in USAFE. He managed flight medicine, optometry, preventive medicine, health promotion, public health, industrial hygiene, and bioenvironmental engineering. He provided support to USAFE fighters, European Tanker Task Force, and MOOTW in Europe, Africa, and the Middle East. He also served as UK Medical Intelligence Officer and USAFE Consultant for Public Health. Colonel Davis had various other Air Force assignments as well as four years in the U.S. Army Veterinary Corps. He was in private veterinary medical practice for six years. His areas of special interest include CBW, bioterrorism, and occupational epidemiology. He is board certified with the American College of Veterinary Preventive Medicine.

COLONEL RICHARD A. HERSACK, USAF, MC, CFS, is the Command Surgeon, Air Force Reserve Command, Robbins AFB, Georgia, and was previously the Air Force Surgeon General Chair to Air University. He earned his Bachelor's degree in Chemistry from Colorado College in 1979 and his Doctorate of Medicine from St. Louis University School of Medicine in 1983. After completing his surgical internship, Colonel Hersack served for six years as a squadron medical element flight surgeon assigned to tactical fighter squadrons at Torrejon AB, Spain and Shaw AFB, SC. He completed his residency in anesthesiology at Wilford Hall Medical Center in 1993 and is certified by the American Board of Anesthesiologists. He remained at Wilford Hall as a staff anesthesiologist serving in a variety of positions, including the Author B. Tarrow Chairman of Anesthesia. He attended the Air War College, graduating from the in-residence program in 2000. Colonel Hersack helped develop the Critical Care Air Transport Teams and the Mobile Field Surgical Teams and has participated in several operational deployments to Europe, Africa, and Central America. His awards and honors include the Malcolm C. Grow Award as the USAF Flight Surgeon of the Year for 1985, the Society of Air Force Clinical Surgeons Surgeon General's Award for Outstanding Research in Anesthesia, and Distinguished Graduate of the Anesthesia Residency Program at Wilford Hall. A chief flight surgeon, Colonel Hersack has logged over 750 total flying hours, including 337 hours in F-16 aircraft, and holds a private pilot's certificate.

DR. ANNA JOHNSON-WINEGAR (BA, Hood College; MS, PhD, Catholic University of America) is the deputy assistant to the Secretary of Defense, Chemical/Biological Defense. She serves as the single focal point within OSD for the oversight, coordination, and integration of the chemical/biological defense, counterproliferation support, chemical demilitarization, and Assembled Weapons Assessment (ACWA) programs. Prior assignments include Director, Environmental and Life Sciences in the Office of the Director of Defense Research and Engineering (DDR&E); and Director, Medical Chemical and Biological Research Programs at the U.S. Army Medical Research Institute of Infectious Diseases. Dr. Johnson-Winegar has published numerous technical manuscripts and authored/co-authored several book chapters. She represents the Mid-Atlantic Division, National Board of Directors of the American Cancer Society. In 1998, she received the Women in Science and Engineering Lifetime Achievement Award.

LIEUTENANT COLONEL REX R. KIZIAH, USAF (BS, USAF Academy; PhD, The University of Texas at Austin), is currently the Chief, Combat Support and Counterair Division in the Air Staff's Directorate of Global Power Programs. Previous assignments include serving as the Air Force Research Laboratory Commander's representative to the National Reconnaissance Office; Deputy Program Manager of the Office of the Secretary of Defense Counterproliferation Support Program; Special Assistant for Research and Technology for the Assistant to the Secretary of Defense for Nuclear, Chemical, and Biological Defense Programs; Associate Professor of Physics at the USAF Academy; and Section Chief and Neutral Particle Beam Research Officer at the Air Force Weapons Laboratory. He is a graduate of Squadron Officer School, Air Command and Staff College, Defense Systems Management College, and the Air War College.

LIEUTENANT COLONEL BRENDA J. McELENEY, USAF, is the Commander, 374th Medical Operations Squadron and Chief Nurse Executive, 374th Medical Group, Yokota Air Base, Japan. As commander, she manages an emergency room, 14 specialty clinics, and a 15-bed hospital; commands more than 200 people; and delivers quality medical care to more than 11,000 eligible beneficiaries in the Tokyo, Japan, area. As Chief Nurse Executive, she creates and evaluates nursing policies and programs for over 170 active-duty, reserve, and civilian nursing personnel. She interacts with Pacific Air

Forces Major Command and other military services on nursing service matters to ensure the highest caliber of policies and people. LTC McEleney has held various positions in medical-surgical nursing, technical training, and executive leadership. She served as nurse manager, squadron commander, and deputy division chief on the Air Force Surgeon General's staff prior to assuming her current position. LTC McEleney has jointly authored an article, "An Oral History of the Joint Nursing Experience at Landstuhl Regional Medical Center," in *Military Medicine*. She is a Distinguished Graduate of the School of Aerospace Medicine Flight Nurse Course and is board certified in nursing administration advanced.

MAJOR MICHAEL E. PETERSON, USAF, is a USAF aviator assigned to Headquarters Air Combat Command, Battle Management Operations Division, Langley AFB, Virginia. He graduated from the United States Air Force Academy in 1987 with a Bachelor of Science degree, and the Ohio State University in 1995 with a Master of Arts degree in Military History. He earned his navigator wings in 1988 and has had flying assignments in both U.S. and NATO E-3 AWACS squadrons. Major Peterson also served a tour at the U.S. Air Force Academy as an assistant professor and course director in the Military Arts and Sciences Department. He is a 2001 graduate of the Air Command and Staff College, Maxwell AFB, Alabama.

DR. BRAD ROBERTS (PhD, Erasmus University, The Netherlands) is a member of the research staff at the Institute for Defense Studies and Analyses in Alexandria, Virginia. He joined IDA in 1995, having previously served as editor of *The Washington Quarterly* and research fellow at the Center for Strategic and International Studies. Dr. Roberts is an adjunct professor at George Washington University, chairman of the Research Advisory Board of the Chemical and Biological Arms Control Institute, a member of the Threat Reduction Advisory Committee of DTRA, a consultant to Los Alamos National Laboratory, and a member of the executive board of the U.S. Committee of the Council for Security Cooperation in the Asia Pacific. A specialist on strategy and policy questions associated with nuclear, biological, and chemical weapons, he has written widely on counterproliferation, nonproliferation, defense threat reduction, and counterterrorism.

DR. BARRY R. SCHNEIDER is the Director of the USAF Counterproliferation Center at Maxwell AFB and a Professor of International Relations at the Air War College. Dr. Schneider specializes in NBC counterproliferation and nonproliferation issues. He is the author of *Future War and Counterproliferation: U.S. Military Responses to NBC Proliferation Threats* (Praeger, 1999) and contributor to and co-editor of *The War Next Time: Countering Rogue States and Terrorists Armed with Chemical and Biological Weapons* (USAF Counterproliferation Center, 2003), *Know Thy*

Enemy: Profiles of Adversary Leaders and Their Strategic Cultures (USAF Counterproliferation Center, 2002), *Middle East Security Issues: In the Shadow of Weapons of Mass Destruction Proliferation* (USAF Counterproliferation Center, 1999), *Pulling Back from the Nuclear Brink: Reducing and Countering Nuclear Threats* (Frank Cass Ltd., 1998), *Battlefield of the Future: 21st Century Warfare Issues* (Air University Press, 1998), *Missiles for the Nineties: ICBMs and Strategic Policy* (Westview, 1984), and *Current Issues in U.S. Defense Policy* (Praeger, 1976). He has served as a Foreign Affairs Officer and Public Affairs Officer at the U.S. Arms Control and Disarmament Agency, as a Congressional staffer on arms control and defense issues, and was a Senior Defense Analyst at The Harris Group and the National Institute for Public Policy. He has taught at the Air War College since 1993. As a faculty member, he teaches courses such as International Rivals: Leader Profiles and Strategic Cultures of States and Groups of Concern, Counterproliferation Issues, and CBW Issues for the USAF. He has taught at six other colleges and universities, and has a PhD in Political Science from Columbia University.